Bureaucratic Culture in Early Colonial India

This book looks at how the fledgling British East India Company state of the 1760s developed into the mature Anglo-Indian empire of the 19th century. It investigates the bureaucratic culture of early Company administrators, primarily at the district level, and the influence of that culture on the nature and scope of colonial government in India. Drawing on a host of archival material and secondary sources, James Lees details the power relationship between local officials and their superiors at Fort William in Calcutta, and examines the wider implications of that relationship for Indian society.

The book brings to the fore the manner in which the Company's roots in India were established despite its limited military resources and lack of governmental experience. It underlines how the early colonial polity was shaped by European administrators' attitudes towards personal and corporate reputation, financial gain, and military governance.

A thoughtful intervention in understanding the impact of the Company's government on Indian society, this volume will be of interest to researchers working within South Asian studies, British studies, administrative history, military history, and the history of colonialism.

James Lees is a Research Advisor at Karlstad University in Sweden. He holds an MA and a PhD in Imperial and South Asian History from King's College London. Dr Lees's research has examined power relations and bureaucratic culture among the European civil servants of the East India Company state in the 18th and 19th century, with a particular focus on the use of armed force in a colonial context. He has worked in research administration and policy roles at universities and funding bodies, and taught at universities in the UK and Asia.

War and Society in South Asia

Series Editors: Douglas M. Peers, Professor of History and Dean of Arts, University of Waterloo, Canada; Kaushik Roy, Guru Nanak Chair Professor, Department of History, Jadavpur University, Kolkata, West Bengal, India and Global Fellow, Peace Research Institute Oslo (PRIO), Norway; and Gavin Rand, Principal Lecturer in History, University of Greenwich, London, UK

The War and Society in South Asia series integrates and interrogates social, cultural and military histories of South Asia. The series explores social and cultural histories of South Asia's military institutions, as well as the impacts of conflict and the military on South Asian societies, polities and economies. The series reflects the varied and rich histories that connect warfare and society in South Asia from the early modern period through the colonial era to the present. By situating the histories of war and society in wider contexts, the series seeks to encourage greater understanding of the multidimensional roles played by warfare, soldiers and military institutions in South Asia's history.

BOOKS IN THIS SERIES:

Culture, Conflict and the Military in Colonial South Asia
Edited by Kaushik Roy and Gavin Rand

Bureaucratic Culture in Early Colonial India
District Officials, Armed Forces, and Personal Interest under the East India Company, 1760–1830
James Lees

For a full list of titles in this series, please visit: www.routledge.com/War-and-Society-in-South-Asia/book-series/WSSA

Bureaucratic Culture in Early Colonial India

District Officials, Armed Forces, and Personal Interest under the East India Company, 1760–1830

James Lees

Routledge
Taylor & Francis Group
LONDON AND NEW YORK

First published 2020 by Routledge

2 Park Square, Milton Park, Abingdon, Oxon, OX14 4RN
605 Third Avenue, New York, NY 10017

Routledge is an imprint of the Taylor & Francis Group, an informa business

First issued in paperback 2020

British Library Cataloguing-in-Publication Data
A catalogue record for this book is available from the British Library

Library of Congress Cataloging-in-Publication Data
A catalog record for this book has been requested

ISBN: 978-1-138-61549-6 (hbk)
ISBN: 978-0-367-78593-2 (pbk)

Typeset in Sabon
by Apex CoVantage, LLC

Contents

Maps

Acknowledgements

This book has emerged from a number of years of research and writing on the European district officials of the East India Company state, and the relationship between armed force and bureaucratic culture. As with all historians writing books, it would not have been possible without the help and goodwill of other people, and I have accumulated a great many debts of gratitude along the way.

King's College London, the Royal Historical Society and the University of London provided me with several generous research grants and subsidies. In particular, I wish to acknowledge the support of the Scouloudi Foundation, in association with the Institute of Historical Research, whose award funded significant archival work for this book at the British Library.

I am also indebted to the participants in various seminars and conferences at the universities of Cambridge, Dhaka, Greenwich, and Liverpool, the Institute of Historical Research, King's College London, Trinity College Dublin, and Nanyang Technological University, Singapore, for their comments, which have helped shape this book.

I have benefitted immensely from the help of many people, but I wish expressly to thank Professor Sharif uddin Ahmed, Dr Jack Harrington, Professor Andrew Porter and Dr Jon Wilson. I owe a particular debt to Professor P. J. Marshall for his advice and guidance.

I would also like to thank Professor Douglas Peers, Dr Gavin Rand and Dr Kaushik Roy for inviting me to submit a manuscript to their series, as well as the staff at Routledge India, Mr Aakash Chakrabarty and Ms Brinda Sen for their efficiency and patient help.

All historians owe much to the work of archive staff, and I am especially grateful to those at the British Library's Asian and African Studies Reading Room and the Gloucestershire Archives. I would also like to single out Mr Ali Akbar for his assistance in helping me to navigate the collections of the National Archives of Bangladesh in Dhaka.

A great deal of archival work would not be possible without understanding friends who are willing to provide bed and board during research trips, so I must end by thanking Sonya Bhonsle, Andrew Christie, Iona Christie, Natalia Martinez and Oliver Parish for their unstinting hospitality and support.

James Lees
Karlstad, Sweden. August 2018

Abbreviations

Add MSS	Additional Manuscripts
BDR	Bengal District Records
BL	British Library
BRC	Bengal Revenue Consultations
Eur MSS	European Manuscripts
GA	Gloucestershire Archives
IOR	India Office Records
NAB	National Archives of Bangladesh

Glossary

Amin Mughal revenue official
Anna Low denomination coin
Barqandaz Indian mercenary with firearm (lit. 'lightning thrower')
Batta Field allowance in the Indian army
Bheel Marsh
Bigha One-third of an acre
Chakma A people of the Chittagong Hill Tracts
Chela *Sannyasi* follower
Dakait Bandit
Daroga Indian police constable
Dhing Peasant rebellion
Diwan Indian revenue official
Diwani The right to benefit from revenue
Dusadh Indian watchman (also an untouchable caste)
Faqir Muslim mendicant
Gomasta Indian commercial agent
Jagir Rent-free land grant
Jemadar Indian commissioned officer rank corresponding to second lieutenant
Jhum Slash-and-burn cultivation practice
Jumma A people of the Chittagong Hill Tracts (who practice *jhum*)
Kachari Collector's office
Kotwal Indian police officer
Kuki A people of the Chittagong Hill Tracts
Lakh 100,000 rupees
Lakheraj Rent-free land
Magh Bengali term for the Rakhine people of Arakan
Mahtaut Tax extorted by Mughal revenue officials for their personal benefit
Maund Measure of weight equivalent to 80 lbs

Mofussil Countryside
Mohunt *Sannyasi* leader
Naik Indian NCO rank corresponding to corporal
Nawab Ruler of a state
Nazr Ceremonial gifts signifying submission
Nishans Banners signifying independence
Paik Indian police constable
Parwana Government warrant
Pindari Maratha irregular horseman
Raiyat Indian peasant farmer
Rohilla Pashtun community in north-central India
Sanad Land grant
Sannyasi Hindu mendicant
Sezawal Indian revenue official
Sihbandi (sebundy) Indian irregular infantryman employed on revenue service
Sipahi (sepoy) Indian regular infantryman
Sowar Indian regular cavalryman
Subah Mughal province
Subahdar Mughal provincial governor
Subedar (also subahdar) Indian commissioned officer rank corresponding to captain
Thanadar Police chief of a *thanah*
Thanah Permanent military station
Wadahdar Indian revenue official
Wazir Chief minister of a ruler
Zamindar Landlord
Zamindari Landlord's estate

Notes on spelling and usage

Modern spelling conventions have been followed throughout for Indian terms, place names and personal names, except where this seems anachronistic (e.g. 'Kolkata' rather than 'Calcutta'), where the precise modern equivalent is uncertain, or where words have entered into standard English usage (e.g. 'sepoy' rather than 'sipahi'). In quotations from original material, capitalisation and punctuation have generally been reproduced.

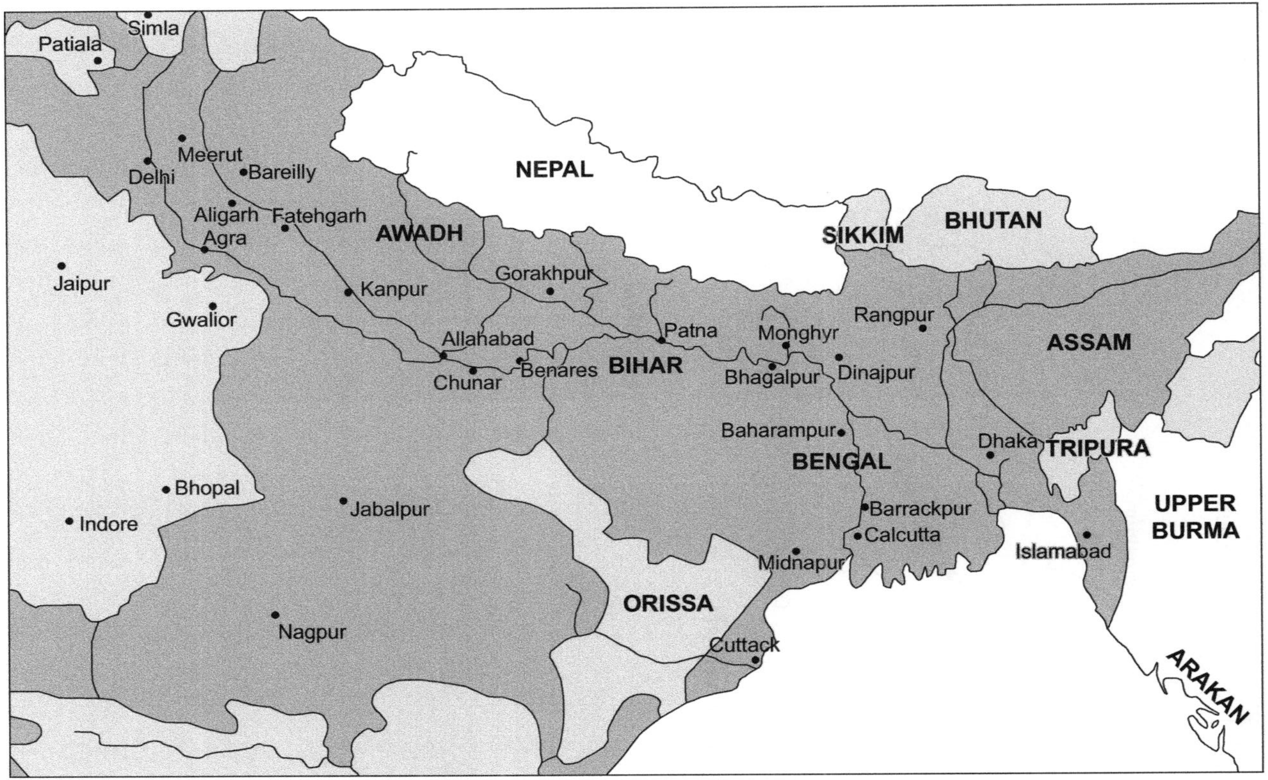

Map 0.1 North-eastern India at the turn of the 19th century

Source: Derivative of British_india.png by Kmusser. Wikimedia Commons

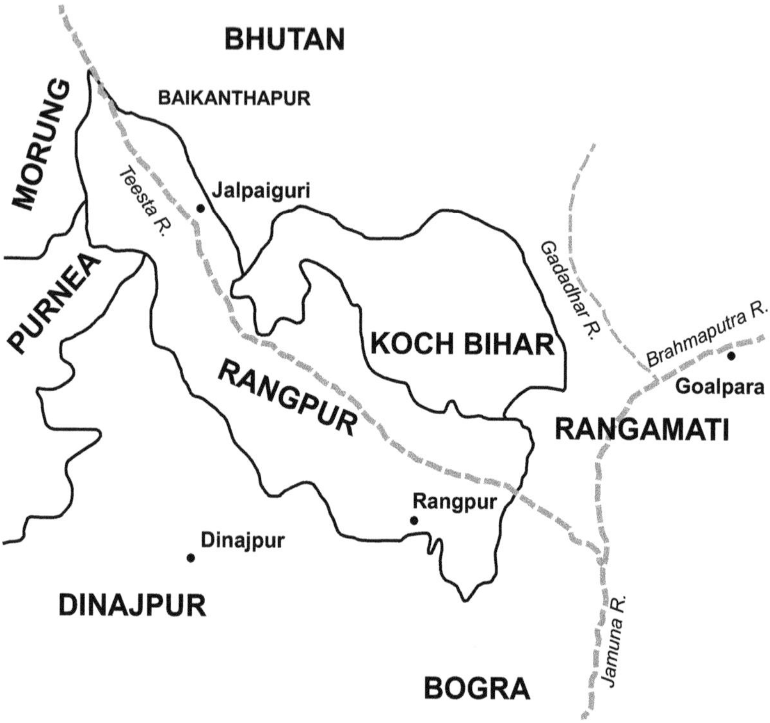

Map 0.2 Rangpur district, northern Bengal (c. 1800)

Source: Derived from an actual survey of the Provinces of Bengal, Bahar & c. by Major James Rennell Esq. Engineer to the Honourable the East India Company. Published by permission of the Court of Directors from a drawing in their possession by A. Dury. Wikimedia Commons

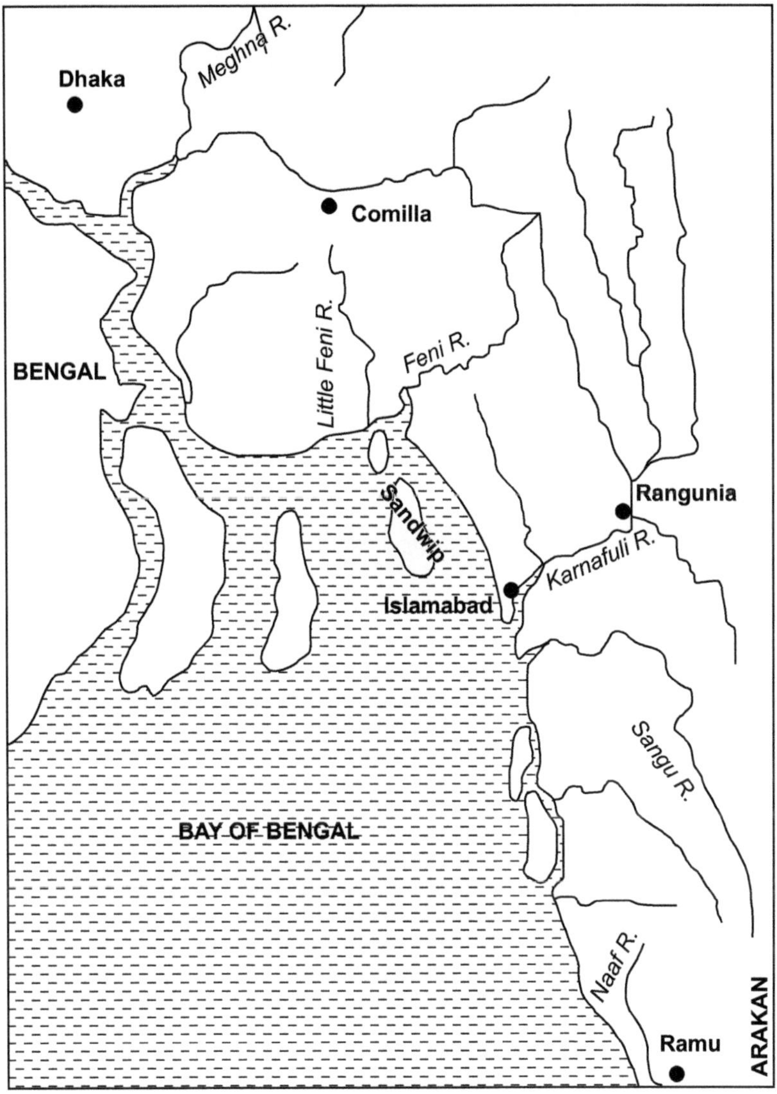

Map 0.3 Chittagong district, eastern Bengal (c. 1800)

Source: Derived from 'Relief and Rivers in South-Eastern Bangladesh' in W. van Schendel (ed.), *Francis Buchanan in Southeast Bengal (1798): His Journey to Chittagong, the Chittagong Hill Tracts, Noakhali and Comilla*, Dhaka: University Press, 1992, p. xxxvii. Reproduced with permission from the original publisher.

Introduction

This book is concerned with how the fledgling British East India Company state of the mid-18th century developed into the mature Anglo-Indian empire of the 1820s and how that development was shaped by colonial administrators' attitudes towards personal and corporate prestige, financial gain and military resources. Specifically, it investigates the bureaucratic culture of Company servants, primarily at the district level, and the influence of that culture on the character and scope of colonial government.

This book considers the nature of that government through an examination of the rival motives of personal and corporate interest which informed the conduct of the Company's district officials. It details the power relationship between these local officials and their superiors at Fort William in Calcutta, the seat of Company power in India. Further, given the limited military support available to early district officials and the absence at that time of any accumulated body of Anglo-Indian governmental knowledge to guide their actions, this book will question the extent to which European administrators were able to impose the Company's authority on local society and even whether this was a priority.

In examining the bureaucratic culture of the early colonial state, and its relationship with the Company's armed forces, this book draws on the experiences of Company servants in Madras and Bombay, but it focuses primarily on personnel in Bengal. The Mughal emperor's grant of the *diwani* (the right to collect the province's revenues) to the Company in 1765 is taken as the starting point for this study since it marked the culmination of a process which would decisively shift the balance of the Company's activities from trade to rule. The Company had been involved in colonial governance, to a limited extent, at the other two presidencies for more than a century, but the grant of Bengal's diwani signalled the beginning of imperial activities on a hugely increased scale.[1] Bengal immediately became the Company's most significant territory, requiring direct governance (unlike Madras) over a vast province (unlike Bombay). This makes it by far the richest source of material for examining the workings of the Company's colonial bureaucracy.

The Madras and Bombay presidencies had both been within the Company's ambit since the 17th century, yet neither stood comparison with Bengal as a bridgehead for empire, or as a source of illicit income for European officials (a key concern for many). Bombay's territory was tiny – consisting only of the towns of Surat and Bankot, and the island of Salsette, all hedged in by powerful Maratha states – with a correspondingly negligible revenue base. Madras was a far larger – and potentially richer – territory, but here the Company was forced to operate through a client ruler (the *nawab* of the Carnatic) who struggled to maintain the integrity of his state in the face of internal disaffection and external threats from local powers. Madras possessed no stable, centralised bureaucracy through which the Company could impose its authority directly. Of the three presidencies, Bengal not only had the largest territory, the greatest potential revenue yield and the best developed trading links; it also had the most substantial pre-colonial bureaucratic infrastructure. This administrative skeleton enabled the Company's European servants to insinuate themselves into government at the district level in a way that was not possible for them elsewhere in India, where the structures of power were more decentralised. It opened up the most lucrative opportunities for personal enrichment, a motivation which frequently militated against the corporate objectives of the Company as a colonial power. As one contemporary put it, 'I find the principle most people go to India upon is, every man for himself'.[2]

The 'empire of opinion'

In 1826, the Anglo-Indian soldier and administrator Sir John Malcolm, reflecting on the British position in India, concluded that, although it had been in existence for some 50 years, Britain's Indian empire was perpetually teetering on the brink of disaster; the colonial state was being held together by a staggeringly audacious, and fragile, piece of political theatre. A tiny cadre of Company servants was attempting to impose government on an inconceivably huge and diverse Indian population – one which had little reason to love the Company or any other centralising authority – aided by only very few European troops and a comparatively small body of Indian military and civilian personnel. Its existence, according to Malcolm, was enabled 'solely by opinion' – that is, by the opinion of Indian society that the Company's government was capable of overcoming armed resistance to its authority.[3] Indian public opinion, Malcolm believed, could only be influenced in this way by a concerted effort on the part of Company officials to act as a single, cohesive body, ensuring that their daily conduct projected a uniform image of their rule as backed by irresistible military strength applied with justice. It was vital, Malcolm argued, that the Indian population's 'dread of our arms' was buttressed by 'confidence in our truth' and 'reliance on our [good] faith'.[4] This combination threatened annihilation for individuals who dared to resist the Company's authority, while, simultaneously, it sought to remove any perception of unjust government, which might serve as a trigger for resistance by stirring up resentment against the Company's administration.

Throughout his career, Malcolm published nine major works on imperial and Asian topics, in addition to many articles, pamphlets and even poetry. His writings, informed by a long Indian career which incorporated high-level military, diplomatic and administrative responsibilities, held tremendous sway with his contemporaries, as well as with future generations of imperial administrators.[5] Even those who rejected his arguments were compelled to acknowledge his expertise on matters of Indian governance. The philosopher and historian James Mill, who disagreed with Malcolm's belief in the necessity of governing India through indigenous institutions, referred extensively to Malcolm's *Sketch of the Political History of India* (1811) when composing his own *History of British India* (1817).[6] Nor was Malcolm a lone voice in the 1820s. Although, in addition to Mill, many others among Malcolm's contemporaries prioritised 'Anglicising' and 'modernising' Indian institutions, a highly influential rival school of thought existed for which Malcolm was a key advocate. This 'Empire of Opinion' school took as its first priority the military security of the Company state, and among its adherents, it numbered such luminaries of the East India Company as Mountstuart Elphinstone, Charles Metcalfe and Thomas Munro. It sought to govern British India according to widely accepted indigenous practices, thereby minimising Indian discontent with Company rule and cultivating the 'good opinion' of Indians. Above all, it lobbied to prioritise the role of the Indian Army in supporting a colonial government whose 'first consideration . . . must always be its own safety'.[7] Malcolm's most recent biographer, Jack Harrington, has argued that this soldier-administrator was a 'complete ideologue of British India between the conquest of Bengal in 1757 and the Indian uprising in 1857'.[8] Certainly, his influence on contemporary Anglo-Indian political thought was immense, lasting well after his death in 1833, and it informed thinking not just among Company servants, but in the broader political sphere also.

Yet, in 1826, Malcolm was writing more than half a century after the inception of British rule in India. The Company state was now in its prime, with a professional civil service and a vastly larger military establishment than that which the first British governor of Bengal, Lord Clive, could have called on 50 years earlier. Furthermore, the influence of Britain's European rivals in the subcontinent had been all but snuffed out, and those local powers which could have seriously threatened the security of British India – Mysore and the Maratha Confederacy – had been subjugated by the late 1810s. Even then, with all these advantages, Malcolm still stressed the fragility of the British position in India, which he considered to be 'always in a state of danger' from both external and internal threats.[9] It could only be safeguarded, he argued, by the highly stage-managed display of military power and a comprehensive strategy of governance implemented at all levels of the Company's service. A key consideration of this book will be to identify the origins of 'Empire of Opinion' thinking in the relative insecurity of the Company's earlier governmental experiences.

Vulnerable though the British India of the 1820s appears in Malcolm's estimation, the Company state of the earlier period was even less secure. Eric Hobsbawm has made a general observation on the condition of early modern states which encapsulates much of the experience of the 18th-century colonial administrator:

> No state, before the railways, and the telegraphs . . . could know what happened in its remoter corners or move its agents rapidly to take action. Hardly any state before the nineteenth century could pretend to control its borders, or tried to, or had clearly demarcated frontier-lines. No state before the nineteenth century had the ability to maintain an effective rural police force acting as a direct agent of the central government and covering its entire territory.[10]

Not only was it menaced by powerful rivals, but, until the early 19th century, the Company state consisted of a fragile network of isolated and under-resourced district officials whose capacity to react quickly, vigorously and effectively to the multitude of threats facing them is doubtful. This was not a modern Weberian administration with the ability to mobilise a comprehensive mechanism of physical coercion to crush resistance; the armed forces immediately available to the Company's district officials in the opening decades of British rule were usually scanty and of inferior quality, and they frequently struggled to overcome semi-militarised local groups.

In addition to the lack of reliable armed force at the immediate disposal of the district authorities, a significant hindrance to the government's penetration of local society lay in the fact that the business of colonial administration was still relatively new to the Company's servants. It had taken the Mughal government nearly 150 years to develop fully its mechanisms of coercion and to gain a working administrative purchase on Bengal's rural hinterland.[11] Although these organisational networks still existed to varying degrees in the 1760s, they could not be fully exploited by the British because there simply had not been enough time for homogenous, India-specific doctrines of rule to evolve and proliferate throughout the Company's bureaucracy. In his examination of the Company's residency system between 1764 and 1854, Michael Fisher has argued that 'Gradually a body of understanding developed within the Company's political line as a composite of Residents' empirically derived knowledge about indirect control over various aspects of Indian states'.[12] As this book will show, the accumulation of such a composite of professional knowledge was also only a very gradual process among those charged with the internal government of British India. In the early Company state, responses to anti-government resistance in a district were more likely to be dictated by an official's personal inclinations than by an institutionally approved code of conduct, held uniformly throughout the service. The collector of the late 18th century did not enjoy the guidance of decades of accumulated Anglo-Indian governmental wisdom, nor did the limited resources at his disposal encourage any very active imposition of governmental authority over local society. Additional obstructions to effective government lay not just in the almost total ignorance of many Company servants with regard to Indian customs and languages, but also in the factionalism which pervaded the Company's service throughout this period, particularly under the governor-generalship of Warren Hastings. The discord extended from the supreme council in Calcutta, which, Hastings declared, met 'to dispute and part[ed] without doing anything else', to the district administrations, where the 'consequences of this divided state are equally bad' and where any mistake on a local official's part would be leapt on by ever-vigilant colleagues, eager for professional advancement.[13] This, then, together with an even chance of death by disease, constituted the working environment of the district official in early colonial Bengal.[14]

There were, however, very great enticements to counterbalance the dangers and discomforts. Men were drawn to the Company's service primarily by the 'perquisites and unofficial profits attached to offices and above all from trading'.[15] Competition for these posts, with their tremendous potential for accumulating wealth, was intense, and the civil service became so overstaffed by the 1780s that many were forced to accept either unemployment in India or a return to Europe on a modest pension.[16] Accordingly, once in a profitable post, Company servants would tenaciously defend their place in the professional hierarchy and became very sensitive about their reputation with their employers; incurring the wrath of their superiors might lead to their replacement by one of the eager competitors who were always waiting in the wings.

This book will argue that the desire for professional advancement, or even simply the retention of an existing post, strongly coloured the relationship between the local authorities and the central government at Fort William in Calcutta, to the extent that district officials often concealed or misrepresented major events in their territory so as to portray themselves and their abilities more favourably. This was to have appreciable consequences for the quality and scope of the knowledge which the colonial government could utilise in its operation.

In the later 18th century, Indian governance was only just beginning to move away from the pre-colonial 'model of familiar relations between ruler and ruled' towards an impersonal modern bureaucracy.[17] Indians closely monitored the fortunes of government, 'spread rumours and hatched plots to the detriment of local officials'[18] and could disseminate information about these individuals through 'dense social networks of communication'.[19] In such an environment, self-interested behaviour on the part of the Company's civil servants could have a considerable impact on its governmental authority and, consequently, its ability to secure the vital territorial revenues.

These problems, although recognisable in the later Anglo-Indian experience, were much more acute before the mechanisms of the Company state began to be regularised during the first quarter of the 19th century. This raises questions about the nature of the government imposed on Indians in the earlier period, the aims and limitations of 18th-century colonial rule and the processes behind the evolution of the Company state as it was transformed from being a competitor among other Indian polities into the subcontinental hegemon.

Sources, structure and aims of the book

The core source material for this book is the private and public correspondence of the Company's district officials, both with their superiors and among themselves. For public correspondence, the volumes of district records edited by W. K. Firminger and Sirajul Islam have provided much invaluable material. These works are, of course, necessarily selective. To supplement and cross-check the accuracy of this published material, as well to widen the source base of the book, the British Library's India Office Records have been consulted extensively, particularly the Bengal Revenue Consultations (P), as have the original district letter books which are held at the National Archives of Bangladesh in Dhaka. Useful sources for private correspondence have been identified in the British Library's Additional and European Manuscripts, together with the Ducarel family papers held in the Gloucestershire Archives. The papers of various governors-general have also been consulted in establishing the governmental assumptions at the head of the Company's service, both in edited and manuscript form, in addition to a variety of contemporary published works. The bulk of the military information used in this book is taken directly from the Bengal Military Consultations (P), the Bengal Annual Military Statements (L/MIL) and the Board of Control Records (F).

The book's opening chapter contextualises the professional experience of the Company's officials in the later 18th century and provides the historiographical background to the study. It examines the capacity of Indian rural society to resist the encroachment of government and details the military and financial resources available to officials. It also looks at the deeply partisan culture which existed within the Company's bureaucratic hierarchy.

The second chapter examines the conflict between personal and professional interest at the head of the Company's service from 1773 until the early 1800s, and its perceived influence on Indian reactions to colonial rule. It draws principally on the writings of Warren Hastings and Lord Cornwallis to illustrate the shift from an extreme reliance on personal reputation as an instrument of government, to its gradual replacement by an impersonal bureaucracy as the century closed. It ends by questioning the extent to which this change of ethos at the centre managed to reach the peripheries of the state and identifies the military resources available to district officials as crucial to its adoption.

The third chapter is concerned with the armed forces of the Company state and their influence on the nature of the district-level government. It details the composition of the Company's regular army and the strategic purpose behind its deployment. It goes on to examine the forces which were available to district officials and investigates the paramilitaries of various descriptions who were employed to help exert a measure of control over the Company's territory, providing an administrative history of this neglected arm of the colonial state.

Having shown that the Company's service was racked by internecine conflict and that district officials were frequently isolated and under-resourced, the fourth and fifth chapters illustrate the consequences of these factors for the Company's local government through case studies of two districts in Bengal (Rangpur and Chittagong) from the 1760s to the early 1800s. They demonstrate how the problems of governing an antagonistic and keenly observant population with only limited military resources affected the nature of the Company's local government, restricting the scope of what district administrators could achieve, or were even prepared to attempt, in terms of imposing the government's authority. They also illustrate how the conflict between professional responsibility and personal interest in the context of the Company's highly competitive service shaped both the relationship between the central and local authorities, and the experience of early colonial governance at a district level.

The rationale behind the selection of these two districts is that they were both home to disruptive internal groups and were also positioned on the borders of expansionist local powers (Nepal and Burma). The population throughout the entirety of the Company's territory in this period was quite capable of low-level resistance to governmental authority, but the combination of external and internal pressures on the scale exhibited in Rangpur and Chittagong heightened the responses of local officials in a way which is less apparent in districts farther removed from the frontier regions. This is not to say that the conclusions which may be drawn from this book about the conduct of district officials are applicable only to a small proportion stationed on the frontier: for the Company, much of Bengal in this period was considered to be on a frontier. Only a very few of Bengal's districts were abutted on all sides by Company territory, and case studies on even these more insulated areas reveal significant armed resistance being exerted against the Company's collectors across the province; witness, for instance, John R. McLane's study of Burdwan in this period, or, indeed, Hunter's *Annals of Rural Bengal*.[20] It is merely the scale of violence which is different. The conduct of frontier district officials is amplified in the records, because, regardless of an individual collector's self-interested attempts at concealment or misrepresentation, the events in which they were embroiled were usually too large to be hidden indefinitely. The principles underlying that conduct remained the same for officials throughout the province, but they are more easily observed under conditions of stress, in the face of mass uprisings and invasions by hostile neighbours, than in the pursuit of smaller scale, although still deeply troublesome, bands of *dakaits* (bandits) and *sannyasis* (armed Hindu mendicants).

The final chapter provides a survey of the mature Company state between 1818 and c. 1830, looking at how the Anglo-Indian political ideologies current at that time had been informed by the experience of the previous 50 years of government. Specifically, it examines changes in thinking with regard to the priorities of colonial rule, particularly the role played by the military, following the establishment of a British hegemony.

Together, these six chapters tease out the broad issues surrounding personal reputation, corporate prestige and military rule. They chart the conflict between centrally conceived policies and the personal interests of local officials in a range of ways, ultimately presenting a more complex and nuanced view of governmental practices in the early Company state than has hitherto been seen.

Notes

1 P. J. Stern, *The Company-State: Corporate Sovereignty and the Early Modern Foundations of the British Empire in India*, Oxford: Oxford University Press, 2011, pp. 6–7.
2 G. Scott to C. Townsend, 30 November 1761, Public Records Office (now the National Archives), WO 1/319, p. 263. Quoted in P. J. Marshall, *The Making and Unmaking of Empires: Britain, India, and America, c. 1750–1783*, Oxford: Oxford University Press, 2005, p. 132.
3 J. Malcolm, *The Political History of India from 1784 to 1823*, Vol. 1, London: John Murray, 1826, p. 146.
4 *Ibid.*, p. 144.
5 In addition to his military career, culminating in service during the third Anglo-Mysore war, Malcolm also undertook diplomatic missions to Persia and Mysore, was the Company's resident at Gwalior (1803–04) and, finally, was made governor of Bombay (1827–30).
6 J. H. L. Harrington, *Sir John Malcolm and the Creation of British India*, Basingstoke: Palgrave Macmillan, 2010, p. 39.
7 J. Malcolm, quoted in *Interesting Extracts from the Minutes of Evidence Taken before the Committee of the Whole House to Whom It Was Referred to Consider of the Affairs of the East India Company*, London: House of Commons, 1814, p. 3, cit. Harrington, *Sir John Malcolm*, p. 50.
8 Harrington, *Sir John Malcolm*, p. 13.
9 Malcolm, *Political History*, I, p. 76.
10 E. Hobsbawm, *Bandits*, 2nd ed., London: Abacus, 2007, pp. 15–16.
11 M. Alam and S. Subrahmanyam (eds.), *The Mughal State, 1526–1750*, 3rd ed., New Delhi: Oxford University Press, 2003, p. 42.
12 M. H. Fisher, *Indirect Rule in India: Residents and the Residency System, 1764–1854*, New Delhi: Oxford University Press, 1991, p. 432.

13 'A Summary Abstract of Mr Hastings' Government and Present Situation (1781)', in H. H. Dodwell (ed.), *Warren Hastings' Letters to Sir John Macpherson*, London: Faber & Gwyer, 1927, p. 73.
14 For example, 44 percent of those who joined the civil service in Bengal between 1767 and 1775 died in office during the same period. P. J. Marshall, *East Indian Fortunes: The British in Bengal in the Eighteenth Century*, Oxford: Oxford University Press, 1976, p. 218.
15 *Ibid.*, p. 18.
16 *Ibid.*, p. 15.
17 J. E. Wilson, *The Domination of Strangers: Modern Governance in Eastern India, 1780–1835*, Basingstoke: Palgrave Macmillan, 2008, p. 1.
18 C. A. Bayly, *Origins of Nationality in South Asia: Patriotism and Ethical Government in the Making of Modern India*, New Delhi: Oxford University Press, 1998, p. 66.
19 C. A. Bayly, *Empire and Information: Intelligence Gathering and Social Communication in India, 1780–1870*, Cambridge: Cambridge University Press, 1996, p. 204.
20 J. R. McLane, *Land and Local Kingship in Eighteenth-Century Bengal*, Cambridge: Cambridge University Press, 1993, pp. 125–305; W. W. Hunter, *Annals of Rural Bengal*, London: Smith, Elder & Co., 1868.

1 The Company state after 1765

Structures of the colonial state

Although several of Bengal's districts had been ceded to the Company from as early as 1760, the assumption of the diwani in 1765, following the Company's defeat of the Mughal emperor and his allies at the battle of Buxar in the previous year, gave it access to what was, potentially, a source of wealth on a hugely increased scale. Robert Clive, upon signing the treaty of Allahabad which formalised the arrangement, estimated that the lucrative territorial revenues of some 30 additional districts would yield approximately £1,650,900 sterling annually, a vast sum in contemporary terms.[1]

Initially, the functions of the state were to be shared in a 'dual government' between the Company and the Mughal *nizamat* (civil ministry). The Company would be responsible for the administration of the revenues and civil justice; the nizamat would be charged with overseeing criminal justice and policing, which was vital in maintaining the social stability required to generate a healthy revenue yield. Under this partnership, the pre-colonial Mughal police network remained in place, with the *faujdars* (district police commissioners) maintaining forces of up to 1,500 men. These officers were intended to operate in conjunction with local *zamindars* (rural magnates) to keep the peace, but, as will be discussed in later chapters, the ineffectiveness of this system soon obliged the Company to assume the police duties of the nizamat also.[2]

In the years immediately following 1765, the Company's existing mercantile bureaucracy – by no means ideally suited to the imposition of government – was grafted onto the remnants of the Mughal state system in Bengal.[3] Initially, it was decided to operate as far as possible through existing Mughal structures and to employ only Indian *diwans* (revenue officials) in supervising the collections, both because of the additional expense of using Europeans, and because of the widespread ignorance among the Company's European servants, not only of Indian languages but also of the various systems of assessment which were in use across the province. However, widespread discontent among the Company's European servants about the alleged misappropriation of funds by these Indian middlemen (and, doubtless, their own lack of access to such opportunities) meant that this system of 'double government' by a central European administration and a local Indian one was to be short-lived.[4]

Those districts which had been ceded to the Company prior to 1765 had continued to be supervised directly by Europeans. These individuals, sensing an opportunity for personal profit if all the province's districts were to be thrown open to them, 'trumpeted their ability to uncover the deceits of Indian intermediaries'.[5] In this way, the credibility of double government was wholly undermined, and in 1769, it was decided that European officials would be sent to administer the diwani districts directly.

With the exception of a brief hiatus in the 1770s – when the more cost-effective Indian diwans were reintroduced – the key official of local government became the European collector. This civil servant held supreme executive authority within the district, control of its armed forces and, with occasional intervals, supreme judicial power.[6] In some districts, judicial functions were shared with a magistrate, both to ease the collector's workload and to prevent supreme executive and judicial authority residing in one person.[7] However, the districts of Bhagalpur, Chitra, Chittagong and Rangpur were made exceptions to this, owing to their vulnerable frontier locations, which rendered a fully unified local authority especially desirable.[8]

The prime function of the district as a component of the Company's military-fiscal state was the extraction of agrarian revenue, which was periodically remitted to Calcutta or directly to other districts where it was judged to be needed. Collectors were charged with encouraging the *raiyats* (peasant cultivators) to bring waste areas 'under the plough' and to take 'all such measures as they deemed necessary for the promotion of agriculture and the protection of peasants, either against the ravages of nature or the oppression of landholders'.[9] In this way, the rural economy would be developed and the Company's profits secured. The problems of revenue assessment on the lands of Bengal's zamindars are well documented, and it is sufficient to say that, following the appointment of Warren Hastings as the first governor-general of Bengal under the 1773 Regulating Act, the colonial government continued to experiment with various systems of assessment until some measure of stability was achieved with Lord Cornwallis's Permanent Settlement of Bengal in 1793. Under all these systems, broadly speaking, once the levels of taxation had been calculated the zamindars would collect the revenue from their tenants and make payment at the collector's office (*kachari*) at the district's administrative headquarters. Zamindars in outlying areas of the district would pay their taxes at regional kacharis, which would then transfer money to the district's treasury.

However, as was indicated earlier, Clive's initial assessment of the revenues which could be expected from the newly acquired diwani districts was hopelessly optimistic. By 1772, the Company's bonded debt at Calcutta stood at over 10 million rupees, some £1.4 million at later 18th-century rates.[10] The original appreciation of precisely how much agrarian revenue could be wrung from Bengal was grossly unrealistic, and it was rendered even less feasible by the appalling famine which hit the province in 1769–70. Following a weak monsoon in 1768, and a complete failure in 1769, there were no reserve stocks of grain to fall back on, and the crucial winter rice crop was severely curtailed.[11] Modern studies of the famine have tended to question the traditional view, which puts the figure for those who died in the famine at one-third of the population of Bengal, but even so, it was a catastrophe unprecedented in the recent history of the region.[12] Communities, especially rural communities, were fractured, if not destroyed, and the government's efforts at relieving the crisis were largely ineffectual. Indeed, the main concern remained achieving a reduction in the Company's debt: 'Few remissions of revenue were allowed to relieve the burden of taxation', and the state's revenue-collecting machinery was cranked up several notches in the vain attempt to extract every *anna* from the shattered countryside.[13] Unsurprisingly, many of the survivors, deprived of their land, dislocated from their communities and discontented with the Company, circulated throughout the province, seeking an alternative living and an outlet for their energies. The presence of these itinerant groups would inform the district administrator's experience of government in Bengal for decades to come.

Cultures of violence in northern India

A marked characteristic of north Indian society in the late 18th and early 19th century, and one which profoundly influenced the forms of the Company's government, both by challenging its sovereign authority and by providing the means through which that authority could be maintained, was the proliferation of weapons and martial skills among the Indian population. The highly militarised nature of north Indian rural culture during this period, and the subsequent capacity of the populace for undertaking violent action among themselves and against external authority, is well established within the historiography. Dirk Kolff has shown that Hindustan was home to a significant military labour market composed of peasant cultivators who used *naukari* (military service) as a supplementary source of income.[14] Zamindars engaged many of them as armed retainers, and there was much employment to be found as police constables under the local faujdar, as caravan guards for merchants, or even, in many cases, as dakaits.[15] As Kolff has argued of society in Hindustan during this period, 'Identities . . . were plural', and so many 'soldiers' had an agrarian income, and many 'peasants' had some familiarity with arms.[16] Consequently, the Company was able to tap into this pool of military manpower in north India to recruit sepoys for its Bengal Army.[17]

The Bengal Army was drawn from these external groups because the indigenous population of Bengal was thought to be feeble and unwarlike; there was a widespread belief in the Company's service that 'Bengalis were unfit to be soldiers'.[18] However, while the martial culture of Bengal may not have been as pronounced as that of the regions farther west, the province was, as this book will argue, home to significant numbers of people who were well able to take up arms and thwart the governmental efforts of the Company's early local officials. This was particularly the case after the great famine of 1769–70 had swelled the ranks of the militant dispossessed.

Despite widespread rural recruitment for the Company's army during this period, the early British administrators were unable either to employ or to eradicate fully these potentially disruptive elements from north India.[19] In 1812, a British parliamentary committee found that the problem of banditry in India was more severe than it had been 40 years previously.[20] Kolff argues that it was not until the late 1810s that the colonial authorities were able to demilitarise north Indian society to any significant extent.[21] Ranajit Guha goes further in observing that 'agrarian disturbances in many forms and on scales ranging from local riots to war-like campaigns spread over many districts were endemic throughout the first three-quarters of British rule until the very end of the 19th century'.[22]

If, as was certainly the case for at least the first 50 years of Company rule, the government could not impose a comprehensive 'central monopoly, or something nearly approaching it, on the use of arms', then it is doubtful whether attempts only partially to demilitarise rural society were desirable.[23] The major polities in India from the

15th-century Lodi dynasty to the Company state were underpinned by territorial revenue. Attempts to curtail martial capacity among the rural population could, therefore, have a significant, negative impact on the state's realisation of its revenue by imperilling the cultivator's survival in a turbulent social environment. As a secondary consideration, it would also deny cultivators a martial source of income which could be ploughed into their eminently taxable agrarian activities; 'weapons were as indispensable as ploughs in peasant society'.[24] In such a context, where the government could not safeguard its subjects from unauthorised violence, any significant demilitarisation of the peasant cultivators would make them easy prey to bandits and raiding parties from neighbouring territories and would, therefore, damage the revenue base which formed the economic foundation of the state. In essence, until the Company was able to exert some measure of military hegemony across northern India after the late 1810s, it was necessary for Fort William to strike a balance between allowing the peasants to defend themselves (and the state's financial interests) from raiders and preventing them from taking up arms against the government in dangerous numbers.

The militarised nature of the population was not demonstrated simply through the presence of seasonal rural mercenaries: the physical landscape also provided ample proof of its inhabitants' martial concerns. Writing on the belligerent nature of Indian society during the early years of the Company state, G. J. Bryant has remarked,

> Operational forts in 18th-century India existed in far greater profusion and variety than in Europe . . . every lesser chieftain felt a need for his own armed force and some kind of fort with a garrison to display his power and to use as a refuge against external enemies, imperial tax collectors, and internal unrest or bandits.[25]

This abundance of static fortifications, although applicable to north India in general, is not representative of conditions in 18th-century Bengal. The province's predominantly low-lying terrain was not conducive to the prolific construction of fortresses seen in other parts of the subcontinent, and while some villages might be protected by thickly planted thorn hedges, the violence of a discontented Bengali raiyat, a recalcitrant zamindar, or a dakait chief was more likely to adopt a different form. As the later chapters of this book will show, rather than seeking refuge in a conventional stronghold, in Bengal, those who wished to resist the encroachment of the local authorities, to protect themselves from stronger neighbours or to take up the life of a bandit or a mendicant sannyasi would in the first instance usually decamp to some hilly or heavily forested liminal zone, beyond the easy reach of whatever agency threatened them and then, moving from place to place, would conduct a guerrilla campaign to achieve their ends, be they defensive or offensive. Mobility lay at the heart of the Bengali strategy; stronger enemies could be eluded, weaker ones could be surrounded and cut off.

There was, then, the potential for significant armed resistance to the Company's government at every level of north Indian rural society, and it did not require the leadership of a major zamindar to release that potential. This was true even outside the great military recruitment zones of Hindustan. The widespread occurrence and mercurial nature of violent resistance in neighbouring Bengal during the final decades of the 18th and early years of the 19th century were to make imposing government there an extremely difficult enterprise for the Company's administrators. The Company state in the 18th century was, to borrow Anand Yang's term, a 'Limited Raj', constrained by the practical need to operate through Indian collaborators.[26] However, as this book seeks to demonstrate, it was also limited by the unwillingness of its under-resourced district officials to risk their professional standing by engaging any more than they could avoid with a violent and disorderly local society. By attempting, with limited forces, to counter all armed threats in his district, a collector might badly damage his reputation for administrative competence by courting a defeat. Much as the Company insinuated itself into the administrative skeleton of the old Mughal regime, the colonial state was still essentially a newborn polity, particularly in terms of its European governmental personnel. It was administered on an ad hoc basis by a loose conglomeration of individuals whose amateurism and personal ambition, combined with a paralysing lack of resources, often smothered even the notion of professional responsibility and acted against the penetration of Indian society by any monolithic corporate mechanism.[27]

Insecurity and its impact on colonial government

From the grant of the diwani, across the whole span of British rule in India, the defining characteristic of the colonial administration was its militarism. As a foreign body grafted onto Indian society, the belief that the government's fragile existence was guaranteed primarily by its armed forces was never far from the surface of the Anglo-Indian consciousness.

The exercise of colonial rule was complicated by the relative slightness of the British military establishment in India. Much has been made of the fact that the Company's Indian Army grew rapidly after the early 1770s and that, by the turn of the 19th century, it was one of the largest standing armies in the world.[28] However, the Company's armed forces, of which the vast majority were indigenously recruited infantrymen, known as 'sepoys' (*sipahis*), never amounted to more than a tiny fraction of the population over which they were intended to maintain governmental authority. Nor could the loyalty of this 'great military apparatus' ever be taken entirely for granted; as P. J. Marshall has observed, 'Both the European soldiers and the sepoys were mercenaries who could not tolerate anything other than the strictest and most punctual observance of what they considered to be due to them'.[29]

Furthermore, the Company's army was intended by its political masters in London and Calcutta to fight the armed forces of other Indian powers. During this early period, its function as an instrument of regular warfare took almost complete precedence over its potential as a police force for countering unrest within Company territory; it was considered too valuable a resource to be squandered in the routine patrolling of outlying districts. Indeed, the weight of Anglo-Indian military opinion actively opposed such measures; the employment of regular troops in these 'provincial duties' was 'pregnant with Evils of a most serious nature'.[30] Regular soldiers, whose training and maintenance represented a significant investment of time and money, would be killed, either by disease or violence, in countering relatively trivial low-level resistance. Additionally, it was feared that the nature of the service, with the regiments dispersed in small, independent parties to meet these countless, minor threats, would be detrimental to the discipline of those who survived. Therefore, the burden of enforcing governmental authority at the district level was usually delegated to the small numbers of locally raised paramilitaries,[31] which were placed at the disposal of the district collector.[32]

These forces were employed in guarding district treasuries and kacharis, escorting revenue convoys and undertaking operations against dakaits, sannyasis and *faqirs* (armed Muslim mendicants), or any other groups which disrupted the production and collection of revenue. Given the highly militarised nature of Bengal's rural population during the late 18th and early 19th century, these policing duties were a serious undertaking. Yet the forces assigned by Fort William to police this militant society sometimes consisted of only a company or two of low-quality paramilitary sepoys to a district – at best, a strength on paper of 200 men – and not every district was allotted even this meagre force: less fortunate collectors often had to make do with small bands of armed peasants.[33] Such an establishment did little to encourage the active imposition of government by the district officials of the early Company state.

As has been seen, the Anglo-Indian concern with how a necessarily militarised form of rule was to be maintained with comparatively slender military resources was given its most cogent airing by the Company's 'hawkish soldier-diplomat' Sir John Malcolm in the 1820s.[34] In Malcolm's view, it was vital to rule by the 'established' tenets of Oriental Despotism, to which, it was thought, Indian society was accustomed. Malcolm and his adherents feared that a shift away from the overtly coercive Mughal pattern of government would present an appearance of weakness, encouraging widespread resistance, and thereby exposing the Company's relative military frailty.[35] Writing shortly before Malcolm's arrival in India in 1783, the MP and historian Edward Gibbon had summarised an earlier period of Asian empires with the observation that 'Fear is the first principle of a despotic government'.[36] Clearly, this was a maxim which Malcolm, and many of his contemporaries, had thoroughly absorbed.

The existence of an Indian public opinion was widely recognised by the British from the late 18th century onwards.[37] For Malcolm, influenced by Scottish Enlightenment notions of the relationship between public opinion and government, it underpinned the basic assumption of colonial rule: that this was an 'Empire of Opinion' based chiefly on the Indian population's acceptance of an idea of British superiority. Given the fundamentally coercive basis of the Company's government, military considerations, specifically the reputation attached to its armed forces, were clearly to the fore. The Company's military prestige was considered central to imposing its will on the population; the safeguard of its rule was the overawing display of military power. Malcolm saw the Company's impressive record in warfare on the subcontinent – an almost unbroken series of successful campaigns from the middle of the 18th century onwards – as central to forming an Indian opinion of British invincibility. It was the force of this history which underpinned the government's authority; as he observed, 'It is only by continually reverting to the past that we can hope for success in the future'.[38] The awe, with which the British believed the army was viewed by Indian society, was based upon the public's belief in its capacity to put down armed resistance, and this, in turn, was reliant upon the manner in which armed force was employed by individuals within the government framework, whether they were military officers in the field, or administrators making decisions at Calcutta or in district centres.

The ability of early Company officials, particularly those isolated in far-flung districts, to maintain the government's reputation within

Indian society in the manner later prescribed by Malcolm was dependent largely upon the armed forces immediately available to them; as was widely acknowledged, 'the Company's arms [could not] be everywhere'.[39] In this period, not every district could have access to a body of troops sufficient to enable a collector to counter unrest with confidence; the norm was a scarcely adequate force, and its employment was fraught with risk. There were evident dangers in using 'what was potentially powerful, but which might turn out not to be the swift, surgical strike that restored order and demonstrated British power'.[40]

There was no automatic technological or, in many cases, organisational, British dominance in warfare before the early 19th century, and, even later, it was by no means guaranteed in contests with Indian powers. As P. J. Marshall has observed, 'The future Duke of Wellington's victory at Assaye in 1803 was no more an easy triumph for superior Western technology and organisation than had been Francisco de Almeida's at Diu in 1509'.[41] Such was the early Anglo-Indian experience of regular warfare, and, as this book will demonstrate, a similar pattern is present in the processes of irregular 'pacification' and internal military policing. The Company developed a range of methods to consolidate its territorial gains, most of which were centred, either directly or indirectly, on its armed forces. Perhaps surprisingly, neither the policing strategies nor the irregular paramilitary groups employed by the Company in this pacification process have received significant attention, and this is an area which later chapters will address.

The Company's troops were engaged in numerous, low-level pacification campaigns throughout its territory from the mid-18th century onwards. Aside from being agents of physical coercion, they also played a crucial secondary role in encouraging acquiescence to Company rule by acting as a source of indigenous political legitimacy for the colonial regime. The army was used as a means of 'bridging the gap between the conqueror and the conquered',[42] and this was to be achieved by 'the expropriation of symbols and the building of alliances with Indian elites'.[43] As mentioned earlier, the Company favoured the recruitment of high caste Hindus for its regular Bengal Army; co-opting this elite group was intended to promote tolerance for the Company's regime among their familial and social networks, and with the wider Indian public.[44] However, the Company's armed forces were not composed solely of regular regiments of sepoys, and the experience of the many Indian paramilitaries employed by the Company could also influence the way in which the colonial authorities were perceived by Indian society.

There are two crucial points here which underpin the concerns of this book. Firstly, regardless of the terms used, in the period under examination, north India was home to a considerable number of people with a high degree of martial skill, higher than was, for example, the norm in contemporary England. This facilitated military recruitment for the Company, but it was also a cause of violent social instability. While previous studies have focussed principally on Hindustan, this book will demonstrate that Bengali society was also capable of violent resistance to colonial rule, albeit on a reduced scale. The second important point is that perceptions of the Company's armed force underpinned its government both directly, by overawing potential opponents, and indirectly, by providing a source of 'honourable employment' which allowed sections of Indian society to be co-opted.

This availability of armed force shaped the operation of the Company state, as did the geo-political context in which it existed. The dominant model throughout 18th-century India was 'military fiscal', a state form in which a centrally controlled armed force conquered and consolidated territory, the revenues of which were then largely consumed in maintaining that armed force. Military-fiscal state systems have been identified in India both prior to, and in parallel with, the early Company regime, challenging the notion that the British colonial state marked a complete break with previous Indian polities. As Burton Stein has argued, 'Thrusting centralisation was the signature of regimes of 18th-century India, and everywhere this was dictated by military requirements'.[45]

Yet this does not present a wholly accurate picture of the 18th-century Company state. Certainly, as will be seen, serious efforts were being made by senior Company officials towards the centralisation of power throughout the later 18th century, but it would take decades, well into the period during which Malcolm was writing his *Political History*, before their effects would be fully felt. Until this point, the relationship between the central and local agencies of the Company's government resembled more a loose confederation, albeit within a single, overarching political framework. Until relatively late in the colonial state's development – beyond the turn of the 19th century – the relationship between these two components of government remained loose, with Fort William able to exert only limited control over district officials.

The picture of the Company state which emerges is one of a colonial administration reliant on the judicious application of military force and perpetually conscious of the need to impress Indians with its capacity to compel obedience through the physical coercion of dissidents. C. A. Bayly has argued that, from the 18th century, 'public opinion . . . was not the preserve of modern or western polities'.[46] In India, it was expressed through a 'vigorous sphere of public debate'[47] and 'was led by respectable men who could draw limits to the actions of government and seek to impose their standards of belief and practice on the populace'.[48] This is not to suggest the presence of any embryonic Indian nationalist movement acting against colonial rule; 'India' in this period was no more than a geographical expression. That said, many groups within Indian society pursued agendas, if not nationalist ones, and they were 'acutely aware of parties and crises in the British domestic political system'. Evidence of this awareness is suggested by the increase in 'subversive' activity during the Hastings trial and when the Company's charter was being revised by Parliament, and, naturally, Indian public opinion was even more conscious of the factionalism present among the Company's servants in India.[49] The Indian public closely monitored the colonial government, and news of the local successes or failures of its representatives was swiftly disseminated throughout the subcontinent.[50]

Those historians who have been explicitly concerned with assumptions among Anglo-Indian colonial administrators regarding public opinion and military rule have tended to focus on the 19th century, and on senior Company servants. Most have taken Malcolm's ideas, or at least those of the period in which he was writing, as their starting point, and the assumptions of the previous generation of local Company officials remain largely uninvestigated. In a *longue durée* survey of the Anglo-Indian 'official mind', D. G. Boyce has argued, after Malcolm, that the maintenance of what he terms the Company's 'moral authority' through its military prestige was a fundamental tenet of rule from its inception as a governmental entity up until the 20th century. The Company's army, spread across the subcontinent in cantonments and garrisons, was a highly visible symbol of British power, and anything which tarnished the reputation of that army, either in terms of conduct or appearance, would have a detrimental effect on the prestige of the Company's regime. The key to maintaining the authority that buttressed the government's prestige lay in the actions of its military leaders and their judgement about the correct application of force. Drawing upon examples of British military interaction with the civilian population, Boyce argues that the perceived need on the part of the British for this moral authority over the Indian population was the animating spirit behind their military government.

> It was not mere force that counted, but the authority behind it; force implied authority, and authority was strengthened and given

> credibility by force – by the fact that force represented the British state in India in all its might and majesty.[51]

Reflecting Malcolm's trinity of 'dread of our arms', 'confidence in our truth' and 'reliance on our faith', Boyce argues that the threat of force alone was not enough. That force needed to be 'carefully and responsibly exercised' to form the basis of a government.[52] 'Swift, decisive [military] action was the only response to rebellion', argues Boyce, an idea that was 'embedded in British thinking'.[53] The Indian administration rested ultimately on force, and just as 'physical force was necessary to inform moral force', a lack of moral force, a public error on the part of the colonial establishment, could expose the limitations of physical coercion of the populace as a strategy of rule.[54] This argument is perhaps useful in explaining a particular aspect of the Anglo-Indian mindset over 182 years of British rule in India, but, as the later chapters of this book will show, it is not representative of the predominant attitudes in the late 18th and early 19th century, particularly on the fringes of the Company's territory. While senior, central officials in this period may have talked of 'swift, decisive action', and sometimes even taken it, it was certainly not the automatic response of many district officials of the early Company state, at least not until the armed forces available to them grew from the 1810s onwards. Boyce's model does not reflect the assumptions and priorities of the previous generation of officials, who were operating before the establishment of a British hegemony on the subcontinent, when the Company's military dominance was less certain, its civil service less homogenous, and its state mechanisms less hallowed by the passage of time than was to be the case by the 1820s.

The work which deals most fully with the concept of prestige as a component of military rule by an Anglo-Indian minority is that of Douglas Peers, who examines it between 1819 and 1835.[55] To explain the primacy of armed force in Anglo-Indian political thinking he has coined the term 'Anglo-Indian militarism', a theory of statehood which sought to consolidate British rule by constructing an overtly military mode of colonial government as a consequence of a 'garrison state' mentality. Drawing on Malcolm, Peers argues that the Company's precarious position as the foreign overlord of an immense population led to a perpetual atmosphere of near hysteria among officials. The Indian bureaucracy was much concerned with external military threats and ensuing civil disaffection, and this prompted a pattern of government in which constant watchfulness and preparation for war became overriding. Military success had to be guaranteed because anything that cast doubt on the Company's military reputation would be a potentially fatal mistake 'in an empire of opinion where opinion was read as being the fear and respect generated by British arms'.[56]

A subordinate, yet still crucial, consideration in this theory of Anglo-Indian militarism follows on from Stein's observations on the military-fiscal colonial state. Peers argues that the enormous expense of maintaining an army to enforce the Company's paramountcy was one of the main driving forces behind British territorial expansion in India, particularly since the relative importance of territorial revenue over commerce became more marked during this period. Armed conquest was the Company's principal means of gaining revenue-bearing territory, and the relative civil stability enforced by the army helped to safeguard the flow of revenue into the Company's treasury. However, the army itself was a huge financial burden, and while it helped secure the generation of territorial revenue, it also consumed a massive share. In essence, the Company's profit consisted of whatever portion of the revenue survived the extraordinary expense of maintaining a standing army.

For Peers, the regular army was the keystone of the Company state. It was 'a gendarmerie of last resort', which would 'monitor local society and if needs be stamp out any signs of resistance'.[57] Echoing Malcolm, he emphasises the importance which was placed on 'making the army appear as omnipotent as possible. It had to impress both conquered peoples and neighbouring states of its readiness to act quickly, vigorously and effectively'.[58] Furthermore, this view was widespread among Anglo-Indians: 'While there were many differences of opinion . . . they were mitigated by the presence of certain underlying assumptions, of which the pressing need to guarantee security was the foremost'.[59] Little work has been undertaken which explicitly deals with these concerns for the 50 years leading up to the period covered by Peers, so this book aims to complement his ideas, showing that his model of the Company's regular army as central to the military-fiscal state is not directly applicable to the earlier period, particularly as regards its role as a military police force, monitoring the internal society of British India. A major concern will be to nuance the idea of 'the military' in this context by revealing the various strategies employed by the Company to control its military overheads, through the use of paramilitary substitutes, while continuing to extract the optimum level of territorial revenue.

Recent, scholarly works on the early Company state, particularly those of Jon Wilson and Robert Travers, have also examined the characteristics of the colonial government, although in different ways. Travers looks back to the 18th century and is interested in the British discovery (or invention) of an ancient Indian/Mughal constitution which could be deployed to underpin the Company's rule. Wilson draws on and amplifies these ideas in identifying the emergence of 'a form of governance in early nineteenth century colonial Bengal [which was] characterised by the way it treated its subjects as strangers' and is keen to chart the development of the Company's regime as it moved from a pre-colonial system of 'familiar interaction between ruler and ruled' towards a modern impersonal bureaucracy.[60]

This book departs from the existing historiography of prestige and Anglo-Indian military rule by examining the inception of such ideas, specifically in the late 18th and early 19th century and in a peripheral context. It aims to complement the work of Fisher, which looks at networks of Company servants away from the centre of government, of Wilson in understanding the changes occurring within the colonial administration in Bengal from the late 18th century and, crucially, of Marshall in explaining the conduct of Company servants. In *East Indian Fortunes*, Marshall has shown that the major concern of 18th-century Britons in the Company's service lay in trying 'to ensure that the most lucrative opportunities for personal enrichment were confined to them'.[61] While a sense of public duty may have existed, it was not that of the 19th century. The nature of the Company's early bureaucracy was too fluid and unstable; it did not give the kind of guarantee of preferment for good service which 19th-century officials could expect, and it bred a defensive, self-centred attitude. The following chapters seek to gauge the impact of this primacy of personal interest among its servants on the operation of government in the early Company state.

Notes

1 R. Travers, *Ideology and Empire in 18th-Century India: The British in Bengal*, Cambridge: Cambridge University Press, 2007, p. 73.
2 However, in 18th century Bengal, 'the number of Faujdars being very small, the Zamindari was the true local unit of police administration in the countryside'. B. Chatterji, 'The Darogah and the Countryside: The Imposition of Police Control in Bengal and Its Impact (1793–1837)', *Indian Economic and Social History Review*, 1981, 18 (1): 22.
3 P. J. Marshall, *Bengal: The British Bridgehead: Eastern India 1740–1828*, Cambridge: Cambridge University Press, 1987, p. 100.
4 *Ibid.*, p. 100.
5 Travers, *Ideology and Empire*, p. 76.
6 The district's detachment of revenue troops was usually commanded by a subaltern seconded from the Company's army, but he was subordinate to the civil authority of the collector. That said, particularly in this early

period and at a local level, the lines between civil and military authority in British India were often blurred: army officers fulfilled civil functions and collectors commanded forces in the field, as Rangpur's collector D. H. McDowall did against against a large force of sannyasis in the Morung Forest in 1789 (See W. W. Hunter, *Imperial Gazetteer of India, Vol. XI, Páli to Ratiá*, 2nd ed., London: Trubner & Co., 1886, p. 492). For a fuller account of this kind of 'Anglo-Indian militarism', see D. M. Peers, 'Between Mars and Mammon: The East India Company and Efforts to Reform Its Army, 1796–1832', *Historical Journal*, 1990, 33 (2): 385–401.

7 In 1787, the Revenue Department decreed, 'The union of the Revenue and Judicial authority throughout the provinces with the exception only of the Cities of Moorshedabad, Dacca and Patna'. J. Dunstan to D. H. McDowall, 18 April 1787, NAB, Rangpur District Records (Letters Received), A12.1/23, p. 36.

8 B. B. Misra, *The Central Administration of the East India Company, 1773–1834*, Manchester: Manchester University Press, 1959, p. 154.

9 *Ibid*., p. 127.

10 W. Hastings to R. Becher, 19 September 1776, BL Add MSS 29,128, f. 10 r, cit. Travers, *Ideology and Empire*, p. 102.

11 This was largely confined to Bengal's northern and western districts. Chittagong, to the east, produced enough surplus rice for 2,000 maunds (some 55 tonnes) of it to be sent to relieve the starving in Calcutta. See S. Islam (ed.), *Bangladesh District Records: Chittagong, 1760–1787*, Dhaka: University Press, 1978, p. 313.

12 Rajat Datta, for example, considers the consensus figure of 10 million dead to be somewhat high. See R. Datta, *Society, Economy and the Market: Commercialization in Rural Bengal, c. 1760–1800*, New Delhi: Manohar, 2000, p. 240.

13 Travers, *Ideology and Empire*, p. 72.

14 D. H. A. Kolff, *Naukar, Rajput and Sepoy: The Ethnohistory of the Military Labour Market in Hindustan, 1450–1850*, Cambridge: Cambridge University Press, 1990.

15 Strictly speaking the word 'dakait' refers to a hereditary bandit, but in the vernacular of the Company administrator it was also used as a blanket term to cover any indigenous armed group without an overt allegiance engaged in resistance to the Company's administration. Thus the label was variously applied to discontented cultivators during Rangpur's 1783 peasant rebellion, to religious mendicants and unemployed mercenaries and to the Chakma rebels of Chittagong, as well as to both hereditary and opportunist bandits.

16 Kolff, *Naukar, Rajput and Sepoy*, p. 185.

17 *Ibid*., p. 180.

18 *Ibid*.

19 S. Alavi, *The Sepoys and the Company: Tradition and Transition in Northern India, 1770–1830*, New Delhi: Oxford University Press, 1995.

20 F. D. Ascoli, *Early Revenue History of Bengal and the Fifth Report of 1812*, Oxford: Clarendon Press, 1917, pp. 245–246, cit. G. J. Bryant, 'Pacification in the Early British Raj', *Journal of Imperial and Commonwealth History*, 1985, 14 (1): 9.

21 Kolff, *Naukar, Rajput and Sepoy*, p. 7.

22 R. Guha, *Elementary Aspects of Peasant Insurgency in Colonial India*, Durham, NC: Duke University Press, 1999, p. 1.
23 Kolff, *Naukar, Rajput and Sepoy*, p. 9.
24 *Ibid*., p. 16.
25 G. J. Bryant, 'Asymmetric Warfare: The British Experience in 18th-Century India', *Journal of Military History*, 2004, 68 (2): 460.
26 A. A. Yang, *The Limited Raj: Agrarian Relations in Colonial India, Saran District, 1793–1920*, Berkeley: University of California Press, 1989, p. 226.
27 By 'amateurism' I mean that the conduct of these men was not informed by a broader professional code, since in 18th-century India (and Britain), such a notion was not common. As Roy Porter has argued, 'Professional pride of the kind later prominent in the Victorian civil service code of "duty" meant little'. R. Porter, *English Society in the 18th Century*, London: Penguin, 1982, p. 75.
28 In 1772, the Company's Indian Army (the combined armed forces of the Bengal, Bombay and Madras presidencies) numbered some 55,000 men; by 1805, it was 150,000 strong. 'Ninth Report of the Secret Committee of 1773', in *Reports from Committees of the House of Commons*, 12 vols. (1803–1806), Vol. 4, pp. 506–507. Also, R. Callahan, *The East India Company and Army Reform, 1783–98*, Cambridge, MA: Harvard University Press, 1972, p. 6.
29 Marshall, *Bengal: The British Bridgehead*, p. 95.
30 Governor-general's minute, 29 June 1795, IOR, F/4/8/709.
31 Although it was more normal for paramilitary troops to be used in the districts during this period, the regular army did periodically take over their duties, once in 1773 and again, in small numbers, between 1785 and 1795. Governor-general's minute, 2 October 1783, IOR, F/4/8/709, and extract of letter from governor-general, 31 January 1785, IOR, F/4/8/709.
32 Between 1760 and 1787, the official charged with governing several of Bengal's districts was actually the Company's commercial 'chief of the factory'. Following Lord Cornwallis's reconstruction of Bengal's district administration in April 1787, the senior official at each district became the 'collector'. Misra, *Central Administration*, p. 128, 154–156.
33 In the later 18th century, Bengal was divided into more than 30 districts, yet in 1777, there were only 35 companies of militia (some 4,294 men) available for provincial duties. Again, in 1785, there were a mere nine district sepoy units, nominally based at Bhogalpur, Burdwan, Calcutta, Dhaka, Dinajpur, Murshidabad, Patna, Rangpur and Tripura. Less than half of these units were the equivalent of a single battalion (Calcutta, Murshidabad, Patna and Dhaka), while one, Dinajpur, was only about two-thirds of a battalion's strength; the remaining four units contained under 240 sepoys, with Rangpur's allowance being just 160, and rather fewer for Tripura. Bengal Military Consultations, 22 January to 31 December 1777, proceedings of the governor-general and council, 21 August 1777, IOR, P/18/44, 109 and 162. Also, the sebundy returns for 1785 in Bengal Military (incomplete) and Civil Statement, 1784–85, IOR, L/MIL/8/1, pp. 75–77.
34 Harrington, *Sir John Malcolm*, p. 2.
35 Marshall, *Making and Unmaking of Empires*, p. 201.
36 E. Gibbon, *The History of the Decline and Fall of the Roman Empire*, London: Westley and Davis, 1837, p. 1177.

37 Bayly, *Origins of Nationality in South Asia*, p. 66.
38 Malcolm, *Political History*, I, p. 7.
39 D. G. Boyce, 'From Assaye to the *Assaye*: Reflections on British Government, Force, and Moral Authority in India', *Journal of Military History*, 1999, 63 (3): 647.
40 *Ibid*., p. 644.
41 P. J. Marshall, 'Western Arms in Maritime Asia in the Early Phases of Expansion', *Modern Asian Studies*, 1980, 14 (1): 28.
42 Peers, 'The East India Company and Efforts to Reform Its Army', p. 388.
43 D. M. Peers, *Between Mars and Mammon: Colonial Armies and the Garrison State in Early Nineteenth Century India, 1819–1835*, London: I. B. Tauris, 1995, p. 12.
44 See Alavi, *The Sepoys and the Company*.
45 B. Stein, 'State Formation and Economy Reconsidered: Part One', *Modern Asian Studies*, 1985, 19 (3): 392.
46 Bayly, *Empire and Information*, p. 181.
47 Bayly, *Origins of Nationality in South Asia*, p. 64.
48 Bayly, *Empire and Information*, p. 204.
49 *Ibid*., p. 59.
50 Bayly, *Empire and Information*, p. 204.
51 Boyce, 'From Assaye to the *Assaye*', p. 647.
52 *Ibid*., p. 649.
53 *Ibid*., p. 651.
54 *Ibid*., p. 668.
55 Peers, *Between Mars and Mammon*.
56 *Ibid*., p. 151.
57 *Ibid*., p. 11.
58 *Ibid*., p. 62.
59 *Ibid*., p. 7.
60 Wilson, *Domination of Strangers*, p. 183.
61 Marshall, *East Indian Fortunes*, p. 11.

2 'The essence of the state itself'
Reputation and the Company's government

Reputations and their sources

The governmental priorities and practices of the Company's servants varied considerably depending on their position within its professional hierarchy, the location and duties of their postings, and the period in which they operated. This chapter seeks to complement the later district case studies, which examine the concerns of the Company's officials on the fringes of the state, by charting the development of thinking at the head of the colonial administration about Indian society's perceptions of Company rule during the final quarter of the 18th century. Its preoccupations are therefore with the central, rather than the local government. The principal foci of this chapter will be the terms as governor-general of Warren Hastings (1773–85) and Lord Charles Cornwallis (1786–93). An analysis of their conduct and correspondence reveals the difficulties encountered in projecting a positive public image for the early colonial regime, deemed by both men to be crucial in offsetting its material shortcomings and demonstrates the gradual change in attitudes of its most senior servants during this important period of consolidation for the Company state.

In his review of British rule in India, the 1826 *Political History*, Sir John Malcolm wrote,

> It may appear difficult to fix the nature or extent of the exertions which a state would be warranted in making upon any occasion to maintain its reputation and character; because these are qualities of which the precise value can never be ascertained; but the history of every nation of the globe sufficiently proves that they have always been most cherished by states which were rising, or in the zenith of their power; and neglected by those only which were on their decline, or on the eve of dissolution.[1]

Indeed, such was the importance that Malcolm attached to this nebulous concept that he went so far as to write, 'We can contemplate no danger so great as the smallest diminution of the reputation upon which the British Empire in the East is founded'.[2] As one Company officer put it, shortly after the publication of the *Political History*, 'Our strength is in the high opinion the natives entertain of the European character; weaken that opinion and you undermine the foundation of our power'.[3] Historians have struggled to unpack the assumptions which lay behind the use of terms such as 'reputation', 'prestige' and 'character' in this context, but it is indisputable that concepts of reputation, interpreted and applied in various ways, were of vital concern to Company servants. However, while the primacy of presenting a positive corporate image of the Company – or, indeed, 'the British' – in India appears to have been broadly accepted by the 1820s, such a concern did not seriously diminish the culture of personal interest within the Company's local administration in the earlier period, nor was it always a key concern even in higher reaches of government at that time.

The problem of defining or categorising thinking about reputation among Company officials during this period lies in the fact that it was a quality which could be attached to a range of sources and interpreted in a variety of ways; the dividing line between individual and institutional reputations was frequently blurred. There were concerns with the perception of European or British identity, with the reputation attached to certain government offices, with corporate reputation and with personal reputations which impressed themselves on Indian society and which were acquired through an individual's conduct, rather than being primarily informed by either a national stereotype or the status accorded to a specific role within the colonial administration. It was, of course, also possible – indeed likely – that individuals would be driven by concern about reputation in several of these areas simultaneously, with the emphasis shifting back and forth over time.

Although reputation was a characteristic which could be used by those in authority to serve their political ends, it was not simply a professional tool. Reputation could also be intensely personal, rooted in the concern of individuals about their self-worth and 'honour'. The government's reputation was based to a great extent on the conduct of the people who composed it, but duty towards this greater corporate reputation often failed to override an individual's personal inclinations.

These different 'reputations' – racial, national, governmental and personal – often overlapped and were not easily separable; the dividing lines between them were, at best, distorted. Malcolm's discussion of the 'Empire of Opinion' in the *Political History* demonstrates this confusion by positing a 'reputation', which is a medley of national, military, and cultural influences:

> There can be no doubt that that empire is held solely by opinion; or, in other words, by that respect and awe with which the comparative superiority of our knowledge, justice, and system of rule, have inspired the inhabitants of our own territories; and that confidence in our truth, reliance on our faith, and dread of our arms, which is impressed on every nation in India.[4]

Malcolm, writing in the 1820s, although drawing upon a wealth of Indian experience stretching back to his first commission in the Madras Army in 1783, was concerned with broad concepts of national character, bolstered first and foremost by the 'dread' of British arms within Indian society. His description of the Empire of Opinion lacks any substantial reference to the importance of personal reputation – although his appraisal of the various governors-general, especially Cornwallis, began to move towards this – but ultimately he was more concerned with their attitude towards a 'forward policy' than with making a genuine exposition of their personal standing in Indian society. For Malcolm, the individual reputations of colonial officials were subsumed by the reputation of a monolithic governmental mechanism, but however true this may have been of ruling in the 1820s, it was not characteristic of the early Company state.

The sociologist Bernd Wegener has argued that an individual's prestige or reputation 'is evaluated morally along several dimensions: membership in a kinship unit, personal qualities, achievements, possessions, authority, and power'.[5] In the context of the Company's government it is not too hard to identify those constituents of reputation which were considered most important to its standing in Indian society: a favourable public opinion of its military power and of the authority arising from a unified executive; in short, of the government's capacity to overcome indigenous resistance.[6] As James C. Scott has emphasised, 'Prestige is something that others confer, not something that can be universally acquired', and in many ways, the first concern of the colonial government throughout the period of British rule in India lay in convincing key groups within Indian society that the colonial state was firmly established and well able to resist the vicissitudes of subcontinental politics.[7] Central to this was the theatrical display of power, manipulating Indian public opinion into believing that the colonial government was virtually omnipotent and omniscient. The skill with which this was carried out by the Company is underlined by a comment attributed to Haider Ali, the ruler of Mysore, who is reported to have remarked, 'I am not alarmed at what I see of the forces and resources of the Company, but at what is unseen'.[8]

A great deal of the colonial government's prestige was, then, based on a series of successful bluffs, and this was an ongoing process. Scott has observed that 'domination, once established, does not persist on its own momentum . . . it generates considerable friction and can only be sustained by continuous efforts at reinforcement, maintenance, and adjustment'.[9] Key groups within the Indian population had to be constantly reminded of the solidity of the colonial edifice. The instruments for this work – the military and civil arms of the colonial state – and the accumulation of knowledge among Anglo-Indian officials about how they should be wielded for maximum effect, only developed gradually from the late 18th century onwards. These first steps towards the establishment of a functional colonial state and a mechanism through which it could be governed were groping, hesitant and often deeply flawed.

When applied to a government, the concept of reputation can be seen not only as the public opinion of the current individuals within the administration but also of that administration's previous actions and, in a wider sense, of the actions of its predecessors. In this way, 'government' might well stand for 'nation' in Edmund Burke's definition of that entity as 'an idea of continuity, which extends in time, as well as in numbers, and in space' and which forms a bond between 'those who are living, those who are dead, and those who are yet to be born'.[10] Each successive British administration in India had to operate in an environment where public notions of the relationship between ruler and ruled had been shaped by the public actions of its predecessors, at the centre, and on the fringes of government.

Both Hastings and Cornwallis believed strongly in the symbolic importance of the governor-general as the figurehead of the Company state; for them, the visible conduct of that office-holder profoundly influenced Indian perceptions of the administration as a whole. Those perceptions were informed not just by their own personal qualities; they were also heavily influenced by the conduct of their predecessors, stretching back beyond Clive and well into the Mughal era. Indian public opinion was both vigorous and well-informed, and Indian society was accustomed to dealing with powerful, authoritative individuals, whether they were Mughal *subahdars* or British governors-general.[11] Assumptions existed about 'right conduct' on the part of the government, and Indians were 'perceptive observers of rivalries within the East India Company's councils, which they understood how to exploit'.[12]

Warren Hastings and personal prestige in government

Nowhere is the idea of the symbolic importance of the governor-general more explicitly articulated than in Hastings's reflections on the revolt of Chait Singh, the raja of Benares. Chait Singh, who held his *zamindari* (estate) through the Company, was expected to pay a large subsidy, levied by Fort William to cover the cost of the war with France and to provide for the maintenance of the two battalions of Company sepoys which were quartered in his territory near Ramnagur. In 1779, he failed to fulfil his obligations and allowed the sepoys' pay to fall heavily into arrears, prompting mass desertions from the two battalions.[13] He was then asked, under the terms of his agreement with Fort William, to provide a body of 5,000 cavalry for the Company's use. This demand not being met, the number stipulated was reduced to 2,000, then 1,500 and, finally, 1,000; Chait Singh offered 250 horsemen, but provided none.[14] In 1781, Hastings decided that it was time to move against the raja, suspecting that he 'was collecting, or had prepared, every provision for open revolt [and was] waiting only for a proper season to declare it'.[15] Accordingly, in August of that year, Hastings proceeded to Benares, accompanied by a small body of infantry, intending to awe the raja into obedience. However, having placed Chait Singh under arrest, the two companies of grenadier sepoys forming the governor-general's bodyguard were overwhelmed by some 2,000 of the raja's adherents, who set him free, and Hastings found himself in immediate personal danger from a hostile population, with only the handful of sepoys who had escaped the massacre remaining for his protection.[16] Later, he was moved to consider the consequences which would have attended his violent death at that time:

> Let it not be supposed that I attribute too much consequence to my own person when I suppose the fate of the British Empire in India connected with it. Mean as its substance may be, its accidental properties were equivalent to those which, like the magical characters of a Talisman in Arabian mythology, formed the essence of the state itself; representation, title, and the estimate of public opinion.[17]

Even though he was unharmed, the news that the governor-general was detained by force at Benares and that, in effect, the head of the Company state had been, both literally and figuratively, cut off, resulted in widespread disturbances. No sooner had Benares rebelled than the 'contagion' spread to Faizabad and Gorakhpur in Awadh, with relatives of the *nawab-wazir*[18] publicly supporting Chait Singh's cause.[19] Furthermore, disaffection spread throughout the Company's own territories, particularly Bihar, where some zamindars openly entertained armed levies in the hope of adding to their wealth and influence during the political upheaval which was predicted as a result of Hastings's tenuous position.[20] In the north-eastern districts, external groups quickly moved to take advantage of the situation. On the Nepal-Rangpur border, an armed group 'dared to seize by force some villages to which they had a claim and had some time before supplicated the attention of our government to', an event which will be detailed in the later Rangpur district case study, demonstrating the link between central reputation and local events.[21] Such was the symbolic importance of the governor-general that whatever befell that individual was held by various Indian groups to be 'decisive of the national fate'.[22] It was believed that the 'body politic' was disordered and that the government could not co-ordinate its response to opposition without the guidance of an authoritative figure at its head. As P. J. Marshall has commented, 'Native acceptance of British domination suddenly appeared to be fragile, hanging on the thread of a single life'.[23] This was most certainly the official opinion at Fort William, with a declaration being made immediately after the event that 'we will never sheathe the sword till Justice is done to the Honor of the Company and that of all England attached in the person of their Governor General'.[24]

For certain elements within Indian society, then, the person of the governor-general was symbolic of the government as a whole. Consequently, the personal authority of the office-holder underpinned that of the Company's regime, and, if it were imperilled, the effect would spread outwards from the centre to the extremities of government. However, the stabilising influence of this authority was threatened not only by Indian agencies but also by cliques within the Anglo-Indian community itself. Dissent was a serious problem throughout this period, and Hastings's administration was fraught with internal opposition to his authority. This opposition came chiefly from two-quarters. Firstly, there was the intense competition for ascendancy between the British Supreme Court and the governor-general and council which raged throughout the 1770s:

> The Love of Power in the Gentlemen of the Law is too notorious to be disputed, and Rome never saw a Pope that contended more vigorously for Supremacy than the Chief Justice hath done at Calcutta.[25]

The Regulating Act of 1773 had created the mechanism of the governor-general and council, but, by imperfectly defining the governor-general's powers, it generated what Nasser Hussain has termed 'a foundational schism in the conceptualization of authority'.[26] It established, in court and council, 'two distinct sources of authority in the colony and two distinct sources of law'.[27] The court strove to establish a paramount position within this framework, making determined efforts to extend its jurisdiction over the Company's district collectors and to block the executive powers of the government. The friction between the executive and the judiciary reached its height over the case of the raja of Kasijora during 1779–80. The raja, a Company revenue farmer, was summonsed to appear before the court for non-payment of private debts, but he was advised by the council, who feared that his removal would set a damaging precedent, not to attend.[28] Furthermore, the court's sheriffs, detailed to sequester the raja's estate, were forcibly prevented from executing the court's decision by Company troops dispatched at the council's order.[29] In consequence, the judges charged Hastings and his colleagues with high treason, accompanied by 'all the personal Consequences attendant on such a Crime'.[30] The threat of prosecution nearly forced Hastings into acts 'of the most dangerous Resistance, such as would have thrown our whole constitution into Convulsions, or exposed our Government to Contempt and poverty'.[31] He later wrote,

> You may judge of the Influence which this Contention produced on our Minds when I tell you that to avoid the dreadful Consequences which would ensue on every Writ issued against our Servants charged with Criminal Acts in the Execution of our Orders I seriously, though not formally, proposed that in the Event of Such Excesses We should abandon Calcutta and carry the Seat of Government to some other place which we could circumscribe by a Line of our own, and keep the Devil of the Law without: And every other Member of the Board approved it.[32]

Ultimately, these extreme measures did not prove necessary, since on 12 March 1780, the individual who had brought the case against the raja, one Kashinath, withdrew his charge.[33] Even so, the actions of the judiciary had clearly threatened the stability of the Company's government, and this infighting could not but inflict serious damage on its authority in the eyes of its subjects. As Hastings, who was admittedly rather partisan, observed, 'I saw the Credit of the Government sinking, and even its Revenue hurt by the Suppression of Justice'.[34]

A second source of internal dissent, although it was motivated less by a desire to change the structures of executive control than by personal malice against Hastings as an individual, was perhaps even more damaging both to the efficiency of the administration and to its public image. This was the marked division between the five members of the supreme council, with General John Clavering (commander-in-chief of the Company's military forces), Colonel George Monson and Philip Francis opposing Hastings and Richard Barwell.[35] At that time, the governor-general was simply the first among equals, and the arrival of these new council members in October 1774 created 'the Majority' which would hamper Hastings's every move until 1780, by which time Monson's and Clavering's deaths and Francis's resignation removed this collective opposition. However, it was a powerful factor in Indian politics during the period of its existence and seriously hindered the smooth running of colonial administration:

> As it is impossible that five Men can manage such an exclusive and complicated Government as Bengal unless They cordially and heartily unite in giving every portion of their time and Abilities to this One grand Object, Let the Company tremble for the Consequences when They are told, the former is consumed in debate and the latter exerted in Altercation only, That the Governor and Council meet to dispute and part without doing anything else.[36]

This division at the heart of government was perceived by Hastings to be damaging to its reputation in two ways. Firstly, it impeded the efficiency of the lower levels of the government's administration through the self-interest which factionalism bred among the Company's servants:

> In the Inferiour departments the Consequences of this divided state are equally bad. If the Officers of any One are inclined to Neglect their duty. They are encouraged to it, because their Superiours have not time to attend to their Conduct. On the other hand if they are desirous of gaining the applause of their Superiours. They are discouraged because their endeavours are neglected.[37]

The consequences of this neglect on the conduct of junior officials could be perceived by Indian society and cause a lessening of respect for the Company's administration. Secondly, it damaged the government's authority through the impact which it had on Hastings's personal reputation among the Company's Indian subjects. The recall of his agent Nathaniel Middleton from the residency at Lucknow, at the behest of the Majority, who wished to install their man John Bristow,[38] prompted the governor-general to observe that he was the victim of an indignity which was both 'personal and direct'.[39] It was an act, he believed, with far-reaching implications for the way Indians would view his administration: 'A declaration [was] made to all Industan that my authority was extinct, and that new men and new measures would henceforth prevail'.[40] In the ebb and flow of this struggle, both Middleton and Bristow were each appointed as residents at Lucknow three times in the ten years between 1773 and 1783, which at the very least must have advertised to the nawab-wazir the power struggle within Fort William. This was only one of many slights perpetrated by the Majority; perhaps more serious was their nurturing of Nanda Kumar's charge of peculation against Hastings in 1775, an act which his biographer G. W. Forrest described as one of 'gross impertinence' and which, had it been successfully prosecuted, would have been 'an insult to the Governor-general and the death-blow to his prestige and authority in the eye of every native in Bengal'.[41]

Hastings was particularly sensitive to the effect of personal slights on his ability to govern, and his writings contain frequent allusions to the 'talismanic' properties of his character and the benefits which this conferred on the Company state. He saw this as quite distinct from the authority derived through the official powers of the governor-general, which he deemed to be insufficient alone for effective rule. The belief which informed every aspect of his governor-generalship was that these official powers had to be augmented by a favourable public opinion of Warren Hastings as a man, rather than simply as an office-holder living off the reputations of previous incumbents. Nor was this something which was reserved for private correspondence or informal reflection among his circle of intimates. Upon resigning as governor-general, he openly expressed his belief to the Court of Directors (the Company's London-based executive body) that the positive public appraisal of his personal qualities had been crucial to the success of his administration:

> The length of time in which I had held the first office of the government, although with no efficient powers derived from its constitution, had invested me with many peculiar or personal advantages. My character was known; or . . . the general opinion of it was fixed: the invariable train of success with which all the measures, which were known to be of my own formation, were attended; the apparent magnitude and temerity attributed to some of these, which proved most fortunate in their termination;

> and the wonderful support and gradual elevation which my personal character had derived during a long and progressive series of contingencies.[42]

In essence, Hastings believed that public knowledge and approval of his character enhanced his professional reputation and, consequently, his capacity to deal with both indigenous resistance and fractious Company servants; he had embarked upon his mission to Benares in August 1781 with only a 'Slender Guard' in the belief that his 'personal Influence' would be enough to bring the raja back into the Company's fold.[43] For all Hastings's confidence, though, his period of office was by no means an easy one; regular public attacks were made on his authority, such as those carried out by the Supreme Court, and details of even his more private affairs were quick to reach the ears of the population at large. The scandal of his duel with Philip Francis in August 1780 is a case in point; its causes and consequences shed light on contemporary ideas of reputation and honour, and emphasise the seriousness with which these concepts were regarded in contemporary society.[44] The origin of the duel was ostensibly a disagreement over the conduct of the war with the Marathas, which was being prosecuted at that time. Hastings believed, with some justice, that this opposition arose principally from a desire to exercise private enmity and claimed that Francis's 'sole purpose and wish are to embarrass and defeat every measure which I may undertake, or which may tend even to promote the public interests, if my credit is connected with them'.[45] Hastings proceeded to make a deliberately provocative attack on Francis's public and private conduct, claiming that both were equally 'devoid of truth and honour'.[46] The violence of this episode demonstrates the intermingling of the private and public concerns which characterised the early Company servants. Personal reputation had a profound effect on the way in which individuals interacted with them on a professional, as well as a social basis, and therefore directly affected their ability to perform in government.

Hastings's interpretation of Chait Singh's behaviour in the aftermath of the duel demonstrates a belief that his private affairs had professional consequences which went far beyond simply causing a stir among the Court of Directors and the British community in India. In his narrative of the insurrection at Benares, he claimed, 'It was the prescribed duty of Cheit Sing's Vakeels in Calcutta to furnish him with every little anecdote which bore any relation to the state of our government' and that the raja's actions were 'invariably guided by the reports which were made to him of the state of my influence'.[47] In July 1780, shortly before the fresh disagreement within the council was generally known, Chait Singh had dispatched an envoy to settle the payment of the subsidy demanded by the government with regard to his tenure of Benares. Immediately after the duel, which provided palpable evidence of the government's disunity, his attitude towards the governor-general changed, as Hastings remarked,

> I believe that the deliberate manner in which he made the first payment of the subsidy of that year was dictated by the doubts suggested of the firmness of my authority; and I am morally certain that his subsequent excuses and delays in payment of the residue of the subsidy were caused by the belief that I was no longer able to enforce it; and, possibly, for such was the report, that a few months would close the period of my administration altogether.[48]

Elements within Indian society clearly monitored the fortunes of key players inside the Company's administration, and this barometer of reputation was the mechanism by which they decided their immediate response to the demands of government. In an effort to work through this construct, a crucial element of Hastings's statecraft was personal interaction with Indian rulers. He saw that the government's will needed to be imposed in the first instance not by means of envoys delegated to negotiate treaties, but by his own force of personality, by the fact that an understanding had been reached with Warren Hastings as an individual, rather than with an abstract 'government'. As P.J. Marshall has remarked, 'The major zamindars were left in no doubt that he personally determined their fate'.[49] This philosophy is made clear in a letter written by Hastings to John Macpherson on the line to be pursued with the Maratha leader Mahadaji Sindhia:

> A meeting with Sindia will have another good Effect, at least I think so, by interesting his Inclination in the Observance of any Treaty which may have been concluded with him; for paper Obligations have but little Force of themselves; and I have seldom met with people yet in this part of the World so absolutely ruled by political principles as not to yield occasionally to the Influence of personal Kindness or of personal Dislike.[50]

Lord Cornwallis and corporate bureaucracy

The importance of personal interaction is also apparent in the first administration of Lord Cornwallis, although it manifested itself to a lesser extent and in a different way to that of his predecessor. While

Hastings had seen service as a volunteer under Clive and had fought at Budge Budge and various other engagements, he was essentially a civil servant.[51] By contrast, Cornwallis was first and foremost a soldier. 'He yearned for military glory from childhood' and carried with him a distinguished service record from campaigns in Europe, where he had served under Frederick the Great, and America, where he had been one of the few British generals to emerge from the Revolutionary War with his reputation relatively intact.[52] Writing in *Political History*, Sir John Malcolm saw Cornwallis's social rank, combined with his professional standing, as a profound boost to the prestige of the Company's government as a whole:

> The impression originally made upon the minds of the native princes of India by the rank and character of Lord Cornwallis was confirmed by their observation of his extended powers. Their attention was directed to the supreme authority of the British nation in India with an awe and respect which they had never felt for it before.[53]

It was with an appreciation of the power of Cornwallis's reputation in mind that the home authorities sought to appoint him; his rank and professional record seemed calculated to elicit the respect of the Indian population. Furthermore, Cornwallis had only accepted the post of governor-general in 1786 on the condition that its powers and those of the commander-in-chief would be united in him.[54] This combination of the supreme civil and military offices, a principle that he had followed throughout his professional career, was made all the more necessary by the example of the internal conflicts which had characterised Hastings's administration. Given the power to override his council, Cornwallis never encountered unmanageable opposition from within his own government, nor was his integrity ever seriously questioned. He enjoyed a number of advantages which Hastings had sorely lacked: not only these enhanced official powers but also high social rank (Hastings, by comparison, was descended from impoverished Worcestershire gentry) and an established public reputation which was largely positive. Concern with the public perception of his character was not so marked with Cornwallis as with Hastings (perhaps because it was not so regularly under attack), and his first period of office saw the commencement of those reforms which would enable the Company's state mechanisms to move away from a personality-driven 'model of familiar relations between ruler and ruled' towards an impersonal bureaucracy. However, this change would be a process stretching over decades; towards the end of the 18th century, definite indicators still remained of Cornwallis's awareness of the importance of personal reputation in dealing with Indian society.

This is not to say that he shared Hastings's view on the importance of personal interaction with Indian princes; there would be no relationships of the sort which Hastings had wished to engineer with Sindhia. Cornwallis had a very limited grasp of native languages and, even though the medium of a translator, he was not inclined to deal directly with Indian notables.[55] Rather, his professional pride as a soldier, combined with the appropriation of the powers of the commander-in-chief, guaranteed that he would personally take charge of any major military expeditions which occurred during his period of office, a significant consideration in a state which was primarily sustained by the reputation of its armed forces. It is in these military activities that one must look for evidence of his concern with the impact of his personal prestige on Indian society, not only through his technical competence in warfare but also in the 'noble' character that he displayed in its prosecution. 'The embers of the desire to take the field in person were yet smouldering' when he chose to direct in person the campaigns against Mysore, the chief military events of his administration.[56] His reasons for taking personal command, as stated in a letter of 22 November 1790 to Henry Dundas at the Board of Control, were

> that we have lost time, and our adversary has gained reputation, which are two most valuable things in war. It is vain now to look back; we must only consider how to remedy the evil, and to prevent the ill effects which our delay may occasion in the minds of our allies. It immediately occurred to me that nothing would be so likely to keep up their spirits, and to convince them of our determination to act with vigour, as my taking command of the army.[57]

Again we see the symbolic importance of personal intervention from the governor-general (and commander-in-chief). It was a public pledge, made both to their Maratha allies and Mysorean opponents, that the Company was carrying on the war in earnest. Yet the usefulness of this piece of political theatre was counterbalanced by a corresponding danger. It was a distinct fillip for Company prestige if the head of the government became personally involved in field operations and was publicly acknowledged as succeeding in his aims. If, however, he failed, then the standing of the Company's military government, and therefore its capacity to interact on a dominant basis with its subjects, would be damaged far more seriously than if the command had been delegated to a more junior, and purely military, officer.

Hastings, Cornwallis and the Company's military reputation

As it happened, Cornwallis's 1791 campaign against Tipu Sultan was seriously hampered by supply problems, arising chiefly from the scorched earth policy pursued by the Mysorean commander, by poor weather and by sickness among the Company's troops. It culminated in a public failure. The siege of Seringapatam, Tipu's capital, had to be raised because of the lamentable state of the army. Cornwallis was forced to retreat to Bangalore and, in so doing, to abandon his heavy siege artillery and to destroy military stores that could not be carried off. His troops were exhausted by privation, and the withdrawal was hampered by difficult terrain and the onset of the monsoon.[58] To make matters worse, his retreat was observed by two allied Maratha armies who had come to take part in the investment of Seringapatam. Cornwallis's appraisal of these events to the Court of Directors was unrealistically sanguine:

> Although a number of circumstances combined to counteract my endeavour to shorten the war, yet, whilst the failure has reflected no disgrace upon the British arms, the attempt has, in other respects, produced many solid advantages to the common cause, and without having been attended with any material addition to the expense which we must necessarily have incurred if the army had during the same period remained in a state of inactivity.[59]

Even though the failure was not the result of defeat in open battle, but rather of Tipu's successful denial of necessary supplies, the fact remained that the Company's army had been driven away from the seat of Mysorean power, that the enemy's will had prevailed over Company policy and that Cornwallis was personally associated with that failure. He had not wanted to miss 'so favourable an opportunity . . . to obtain the reputation to our arms which must necessarily result from a victory in the sight of his [Tipu's] capital' and was now surely aware that failure had earned his army a very different reputation from the one he had anticipated.[60]

Cornwallis did not elaborate convincingly on the 'solid advantages' which he felt were gained from this campaign. If he meant to imply that the operations which took place prior to his withdrawal had produced a favourable impression of the Company's military prowess upon Tipu and the Marathas, then set against that was the public spectacle of the governor-general and commander-in-chief in full, and rather disordered, retreat in open view of both the enemy and his lukewarm Maratha allies. One has only to consider the case of Hastings, cut off in Benares 10 years earlier, to realise that the personal failure of a governor-general under arms could have a distinctly destabilising effect on the Company's subjects and elements on the fringes of British India.

The letter to the Court of Directors, written at Bangalore during the retreat, seems to have been an attempt to put a positive spin on a reverse which had reduced the awe with which the Company's government was regarded by Indian society, a reverse intensified by the public failure of the governor-general in person. Although his relative political security meant he was not forced to place as much reliance on it as Hastings, Cornwallis was perfectly aware of the link between his personal reputation and the fortunes of the state. Prior to this, in his dealings with the Sikhs, Cornwallis had insisted that his agent must emphasise his personal sincerity, and in his earlier correspondence with Tipu, this sense of the force of personal intervention,[61] bolstered by his honourable character, is again apparent: he pledged his 'word of honour', which he was, he said, 'incapable of forfeiting', that the Mysorean ruler would not suffer by trusting in his integrity.[62] It is reasonable to suppose that any significant military setback would reduce the standing of an essentially military government with its Indian subjects, but the effect of the 1791 campaign was potentially even more significant because the supreme representative of that government was personally implicated in the débâcle. Cornwallis's letter was disingenuous: he had previously stated that nothing would be so likely to keep the Company's Indian allies on side as his presence in the field, and he could not but be aware of the likely consequences of an ineffective intervention, consequences which in this case were amplified by the military context of the failure, an area which was regarded as his personal forte.

The discussion of Cornwallis's operations introduces the wider element of the Company's military reputation, which played a vital part in constituting public perceptions of its government. Hastings was also aware of the usefulness of the threat of force in achieving political ends, whether they were the satisfactory negotiation of a treaty or the suppression of a rebellion:

> I will throw away the Sword before those who appear unarmed before Us: I will keep it sheathed in the Presence of those who are as yet undecided; and I will hold it with the Alternative of Peace

> or Destruction to those who are armed against Us with Threats of the latter, and rejection of the former.[63]

The government's authority was underpinned by the army, but, as Hastings appreciated, it was to be used only as a last resort. It was unwise to risk a defeat by using force when there were other means of achieving the government's ends, or where there was not an overwhelming likelihood of success. Despite his attempts at justification following the withdrawal from Seringapatam, Cornwallis too was aware of the disastrous consequences of military defeat on the Company's reputation, and thereby its ability to sustain an Oriental Despotic state which was held together by the threat of force. Well before he embarked on the third Anglo-Mysore war, he had declared that the defeat of Colonel William Baillie's corps, comprising some 3,700 European and Indian soldiers, by Haider Ali's Mysorean army at Perambaucum in September 1780 had 'removed some part of that awe in which the natives stood at the name of British troops'.[64]

For threats of force to be effective, they relied heavily on a favourable public perception of the armed forces and on the capacity of the individual or body that wielded them; defeat would reduce the awe in which both were held. Yet, at the same time, attempts to conserve military strength carried their own risks. Hastings remarked that he had

> ever deemed it even more unsafe than dishonourable to sue for peace; and more consistent with the love of peace to be the aggressor, in certain cases, than to see the preparations of intended hostility, and wait for their maturity.[65]

An excess of caution could be just as damaging as a stinging defeat, and the handling of the Company's relatively slender forces required delicate judgement throughout the period.

Public acknowledgement of the government's military independence was indispensable to its operation. Even when in dire straits during Chait Singh's rebellion, Hastings refused the assistance of the nawab-wazir of Awadh on the grounds that he 'did not think it consistent with the dignity of our government to employ a foreign aid for the suppression of a rebellion of its own subjects'.[66] To have accepted aid from Awadh would have been a public proclamation of the government's weakness at a time when the troubles in Benares were already destabilising the Company's rule.

Concern among Company officials with military reputation was aggravated by a system of government which used a comparatively small body of troops to maintain its authority over a vast population. The sense of bluffing, of living under the constant threat of annihilation, with their meagre armed forces swept away by insurgency or invasion, produced an acute sensitivity about military matters among the Anglo-Indian community, which Peers has characterised as the 'garrison state' mentality. The bulk of the Company's army was recruited from Indian society and many British officials believed that, just as the fearsome reputation of that army kept a larger population in check, so, within that body, the small contingent of European troops acted as a counter to the sepoys. Cornwallis, in particular, was a believer in the importance of the European troops displaying a positive public image:

> I think it must be universally admitted that without a large and well-regulated body of Europeans our hold of these valuable dominions must be very insecure. It cannot be expected that even the best of treatment would constantly conciliate the willing obedience of so vast a body of people, differing from ourselves in almost every circumstance of laws, religion, and customs . . . it would not be wise to place great dependence upon their countrymen, who compose the native regiments, to secure their subjection.[67]

Should the native troops waver in their allegiance to the Company, claimed Cornwallis, then 'a respectable body of Europeans would awe them to obedience'.[68] Consequently, any decline in the military reputation of the European troops would disrupt the hierarchy of authority in their relationship with the Indian troops and so endanger the government's position; which, without an obedient native army, was untenable. He believed that 'nothing can be more prejudicial to our interests and safety, than to degrade the character of Europeans, in a country where a handful of them are to hold millions in subjection'. Unfortunately, the Company's European troops were, in Cornwallis's opinion, formed of such 'contemptible trash [that it] makes me shudder'.[69] Writing on the same matter to Henry Dundas in 1787 he exclaimed, 'I did not think Britain could have furnished such a set of wretched objects',[70] and later that year to the Duke of York, 'the Company's Europeans are such miserable wretches that I am ashamed to acknowledge them for countrymen'.[71]

The importance which Cornwallis attached to the reputation of the Company's Europeans was mirrored in his attitude to the army as a whole, as is apparent in his reaction to an incident which occurred in February 1791, while he was campaigning in Mysore. On the approach to Seringapatam a large party of Company sepoys ran wild and began to plunder and burn the villages along the route of their march. Furious, Cornwallis hanged nine of the instigators 'in the most conspicuous situations of as many bazaars'[72] and issued the following general order:

> His Lordship now calls in the most serious manner for the active assistance of every Officer in the army, and particularly those commanding flanking parties, advance and rear guards, to put a stop to these scenes of horror: which, if they should be suffered to continue, must defeat all our hopes of success, and blast the British name with infamy.[73]

When Malcolm placed 'reliance on our faith' alongside 'dread of our arms' as a key constituent of the reputation which sustained Britain's Indian empire, he was not simply paying lip service to an idealised notion of 'British character'. Cornwallis understood that if the government dealt unfairly with the indigenous population, particularly through unjust physical coercion, then it provoked further resistance to its operation. There was no security in simply possessing armed force; its utility lay in the manner of its application and how it was seen to be applied by the population at large. While the careful use of armed force could sustain the Company's rule, the pointless terrorising of villagers by Company troops would 'blast the British name with infamy' and 'defeat all our hopes of success' by turning them against the government. It is notable that Cornwallis not only executed the ringleaders in public but allocated each of them a separate place of execution in different bazaars to maximise the number of people witnessing the punishment. Clearly, the executions were not designed just as a deterrent for the troops; their open locations suggest that they were also intended to promote the Company's reputation for justice in the eyes of the civilian population by publicly disavowing the legitimacy of the plunderers' conduct.

Hastings was also keenly aware of the effect which adverse opinion of the Company's military could have on its capacity to govern. It was not simply a question of armed presence, but of how force was used, or not used, which shaped public perceptions. In 1774, a dispute over a loan made by the nawab-wazir to the leading men of the Rohillas (a Pashtun community centred on Awadh's western borders) escalated into open warfare. The Company, in receipt of a subsidy from Awadh, intervened in the nawab-wazir's favour, and in April of that year, the Rohillas were decisively beaten. Colonel Alexander Champion, the officer commanding the Company's brigade in Awadh, having defeated the Rohillas, then failed to intervene against the nawab-wazir's brutal persecution of the refugees. Champion, whose troops were subsidised by Awadh, felt that he should remain neutral and contented himself with remarking, rather lamely, that he was 'greatly afraid that the vizier's behaviour . . . will render our connection with him reproachful to us and tend to lessen the reputation of our justice which had heretofore prevailed in these countries'.[74] Hastings's reply conveyed his anger at this course of inaction:

> It never could have been suspected by the Board that their orders to you would have tied up your hands from protecting the miserable, stopped your ears to the cries of the widowed and fatherless, or shut your eyes against the wanton display of oppression and cruelty. I am totally at a loss to distinguish wherein their orders have laid you under any greater restraint than your predecessors.[75]

It seemed to Hastings that the Company, and therefore he personally might be considered culpable in this affair, and he was to be proved right since unwarranted aggression against the Rohillas was the first of the 22 'Articles of Charge' which Edmund Burke brought against Hastings at the opening of his impeachment in 1786.[76] The governor-general's emotive language was more than just an indicator of his distress at the massacre of the Rohillas, and his condemnation of the situation was as much a criticism of Champion's inaction as it was of the nawab-wazir's oppression. For Hastings, Champion's failure to stop the persecution, or indeed to intervene in any way, had damaged the Company's reputation on a number of levels. Military force was not used when, in Hastings's opinion, both justice and policy demanded that it should have been. The Company's troops had been mere spectators of the carnage, which, to exacerbate matters, had been orchestrated by a ruler closely associated with the Company, and this reflected disgrace upon the government in the eyes of its Indian subjects. Hastings instructed Middleton, the resident at the court of Awadh, to inform the nawab-wazir 'that the English manners are abhorrent of every species of inhumanity and oppression and require, and enjoin the gentlest treatment of a vanquished enemy'.[77] His further instructions to Middleton on the line to be taken with the nawab-wazir show his concern with limiting the damage which had been done to the Company's standing with its Indian subjects:

> You may inform him directly that you have my orders to insist upon a proper treatment of the family of Hafiz Rahmat; since in

> our alliance with him our national character is involved in every act which subjects his own to reproach, that I shall publicly exculpate the Government from the imputation of assenting to such a procedure, and shall reserve it as an objection to any future engagements with him.[78]

Indian belief, as later Anglo-Indians saw it, in the 'humane' virtues of the government, complemented by its seeming military might, was the safeguard of the Company state against insurrection. This vital prestige was considered by the Anglo-Indian community to be constantly under threat. Hastings and Cornwallis appear to have been as sensitive about it during their periods of office as Malcolm was when he wrote the *Political History*, and for the same reasons, the government's reputation for the just and forceful action which sustained it was perpetually challenged by new events. The need to emphasise the dual nature of this reputation, the threat of force tempered by justice, can be seen in Hastings's circular, issued in the immediate aftermath of Chait Singh's rebellion, which proclaimed that 'the English renowned over the Earth for their good Faith, have upon that Principle towards their Friends, as well as from their Bravery against their Enemies become the most powerful Nation in the universe'.[79]

Indigenous political legitimacy versus 'the dignity of the British government'[80]

There was then concern that the government should be seen as both morally just and militarily strong in order to avoid the provocation of Indian discontent through what Thomas Macaulay would later describe as 'the most frightful of all spectacles, the strength of civilisation without its mercy'.[81] Perceptions of harsh government, it was thought, would lead Indians to revolt, as they would come to believe that 'the evils of submission are obviously greater than those of resistance'.[82] In addition to the public tempering of force with justice, Hastings believed that the Company's rule could be made more palatable to Indian society if Company administrators were seen to operate through a Mughal framework, to lend legitimacy to the Company's administration, even after the Mughal emperor, the Company's nominal overlord, became a puppet of the Marathas following the fall of Delhi in 1771. That is not to say that he believed that the Company was genuinely subject to the Emperor's sovereignty: 'They received nothing from him, but a presumptuous gift of what was not his to give, but what they had already acquired by their own power'.[83] Indeed, for Hastings, the Company's association with the Emperor was 'an unshaken alliance with a pageant of our own creation'.[84] Rather, Hastings believed that the Company benefitted by its apparent position within the Mughal hierarchy, subject to an indigenous authority which, for a great part of the population, had been hallowed by the passage of time. His appreciation of the importance of the association with Mughal authority was indicated on a number of occasions, notably when he rode in procession with the Mughal princes at Lucknow in 1784.[85] This political fiction was maintained by the British until as late as 1848, and in the earlier period, even the governor-general Richard Wellesley, Lord Mornington (1798–1805), who was not the strongest advocate of Orientalist modes of rule, warned his aides to show respect to the Emperor as 'almost every class of people . . . continue to acknowledge his nominal authority'.[86]

On the other hand, for Cornwallis, the notion of Company servants, particularly Britons, publicly expressing their subservience to an Indian ruler was neither 'politic or necessary'.[87] A particularly contentious issue was the 'humiliating ceremonial' of presenting *nazrs*, or gifts symbolising submission, to Indian royalty by British officials.[88] Cornwallis's belief in the dangers of such personal deference is apparent in a letter from 1789 written to Charles Malet:

> I therefore highly approve of your having declined, previous to your communicating with Captain Kennaway, to present a nuzzer with your own hands to the Peshwa, and I must likewise desire that you will never, even through the medium of one of your servants, agree to place yourself in so degrading a situation, as it will tend to lessen the dignity of the British Government in the eyes of the other Powers of this country.[89]

This indicates that more so than Hastings, or at least more explicitly so, Cornwallis felt that British independence and Indian belief in the unbending character of Britons, was central to the Company's power. Both his anxiety about the feeble state of the Company's European recruits and his determination to stamp out the practice of offering nazrs demonstrate a conviction that Indian society should not be presented with a degraded example of the Briton. The conduct of the most senior of his colleagues was not safe from his scrutiny in this regard, with Cornwallis excoriating Sir John Macpherson, the acting governor-general immediately after Hastings, for 'basely degrading the national character by . . . quibbles and lies . . . his Government was a system of the dirtiest jobbing'.[90] The struggle to preserve the reputation of British nationals and so maintain what he saw as Indian respect for British rule, was a running theme in Cornwallis's first administration. In addition to the examples already given, he opposed plans in 1790 to transfer the Company's governmental functions directly to the Crown, leaving only the commercial activities under its control. This arose from his fear that the Company's employees 'would be soon looked upon as an inferior class of people' to those employed by the British government and, he observed, 'The contempt with which they would be treated would not pass unobserved by the natives, and would preclude the possibility of their being of essential use'.[91] So strongly held were Cornwallis's convictions about the example set by Britons, and other Europeans, in colonial society that, when the Bishop of Salisbury asked for permission to send missionaries to the courts of native princes, he replied,

> I believe there are but few instances of Europeans having acquired an influence at the courts of the native princes, without converting it to the most interested purposes; and the natives, with a strong propensity to intrigue, are so little capable of distinguishing the real objects of Government, and the different gradations of rank amongst us, that . . . they would infallibly treat them as persons of great importance, and endeavour by the most alluring offers, to engage their support against the influence or power of the Company's Residents or Collectors, in the districts to which they might be appointed.[92]

Cornwallis's fear that even Anglican envoys would convert their influence 'to the most interested purposes' underlines his acute sensitivity about Indian perceptions of British character and its impact on the Company's capacity to impose rule. He would not risk Europeans, even those chosen by a bishop, to be residents at princely courts if they were not under direct government control, lest they became the playthings of the princes, who could use them to enhance their status with both their rivals and their subjects at the Company's expense.

Conclusions

Operating within an alert and well-informed Indian public sphere, the Company's reputation was shaped by the conduct of individuals associated with British rule and that association was believed to encompass not only those who were its direct employees but also indigenous elites whose relationship with the Company implied shared values (such as the nawab-wazir of Awadh), and individuals whose actions were thought to reflect on the government simply by virtue of their being Europeans in India, whether they were traders, mercenaries or missionaries. As they were part of this hierarchy, both Hastings and Cornwallis saw their personal conduct, magnified by their tenure of the supreme office, as crucial in shaping Indian perceptions of, and reactions to, British rule. There were, broadly speaking, two key elements influencing Indian opinion of the Company's government: firstly, the personal reputations of key public figures, in this case the governor-general and councillors and, secondly, what might be termed 'institutional reputation' – the military prestige garnered from the successes of the Company's army, or the bureaucratic reputation formed by the conduct of myriad Company servants, observed on a daily basis by Indian society. The dividing line between personal and institutional reputation was frequently blurred, particularly in the figure of the governor-general, whose personal conduct, as has been seen with both Hastings and Cornwallis, influenced popular perceptions of the character of colonial rule. It is in the particular aspect which they each stressed – the personal or the institutional – that we see the chief distinction between the administrations of Hastings and Cornwallis, and, indeed, the change over time in their assumptions regarding reputation mirrors the changes taking place within the administrative structures of the Company state.

Robert Travers has identified the key difference between the administrations of Hastings and Cornwallis as being that Hastings's 'reforms looked back to the imagined order of an earlier age of Mughal imperium',[93] and in contrast, 'the old legitimizing language of the Mughal constitution lost its purchase in the new regime' of Cornwallis.[94] While this is true, it is also important to consider why each man chose either to embrace or to reject indigenous forms and why they placed their reliance more on a personal or a broader 'institutional' reputation.

From the very outset, Hastings found himself in a tenuous position: the state was in the middle of a colossal financial crisis; he was attempting to govern a population which was 'often hostile and antagonistic', and he lacked the effective official powers necessary to force through his measures.[95] He was frequently subjected to personal attacks from within his own government, and the example of Madras governor George Pigot's deposition by his council in 1776, followed by his death in confinement, can never have been far from his thoughts.[96] Consequently, lacking any other substantial legitimacy, Hastings embraced Mughal forms to lend his precarious administration some weight in the public eye. He was also keenly aware that in addition to the protection afforded by this cloak of indigenous institutional tradition, his personal reputation could either help or harm the standing of the government. Hastings's insistence that his personal reputation directly affected that of the government can be seen as a product of his vulnerability, with a prime example being at the culmination of Francis's vendetta against him when he declared that personal attacks against him amounted to an attack on 'the public interests'.[97] His attempts to forge this link between himself as an individual and something far larger and stronger – the collective, corporate whole of the Company's government – may be seen in the same light as his attempts to bolster that very same government by linking it in turn with something older, grander and more 'legitimate': the Mughal empire.

This is not to imply that he was entirely objective, viewing personal prestige solely as an instrument of rule. Clearly, his actions were not always taken on the basis of cold calculation or a 'rational process of maximising returns' for the Company, and his duel with Francis was an obvious case of personal enmity, proclaiming disunity within the council, and, in his own opinion, encouraging Chait Singh's resistance to the Company.[98] Likewise, his decision to take only a small bodyguard with him to Benares, relying on his personal magnetism to compel the raja's obedience, displays an astonishing level of arrogance. Even though the consequences were not fatal to him personally, they were still damaging to the security of the Company's position in India.

Cornwallis, on the other hand, began in a far stronger position. He was a peer, the possessor of a professional reputation established well before his arrival in Calcutta, and, as a result of the 1786 India Act and his dual appointment as governor-general and commander-in-chief, the wielder of official powers far more robust than those of Hastings. Consequently, he had less reason to fear for his personal standing and was free to concern himself with broader concepts of the Company's institutional reputation which found expression in his anxiety over indigenous perceptions of Europeans in India. That said, Cornwallis was not wholly free of vanity with regard to his personal prestige which, on occasion, could lead him to make decisions which were not in the best interest of the state. His decision to take the field against Tipu in person, with the resulting failure at Seringapatam in 1791, can also be seen as personal pride clouding professional judgement. Although he played down the reverse, the head of the Company's government should have been overseeing the administration of the Indian empire from Fort William, not intervening personally in one localised conflict, however serious. The necessity of projecting a positive image for the colonial regime was easily subverted by visceral, personal considerations.

The growing concern with broader, institutional identities, characteristic of the administrative changes under Cornwallis was also shared by Hastings (attested by his appropriation of a corporate Mughal identity), but it was manifested to a far lesser degree, being subsumed by his profound concerns about the effect of personal reputation on the public business of government. Hastings placed a greater reliance on personal status partly because the notion of a government based on anything other than personal reputation was not fully developed in either Europe or India at this time and because the limited official powers of the governor-general during his period of office left him with little choice. Further, the state institutions which should have served as a prop to his rule – the civil service, the judiciary and the armed forces – were not yet fully developed, and uncertainty remained as to the precise form which they would ultimately take. The shift towards a greater concern with wider notions of institutional reputation under Cornwallis, with that attached to Europeans in India generally and to the colonial government as a monolithic whole, was a product of his personal position. As Cornwallis was not constantly lurching from crisis to crisis, and dissipating his energy in parrying attacks from within his council, he had the capacity to build, and under his stewardship, the mechanisms of the state began to be stabilised and strengthened.

Hastings was faced with the task of constructing workable systems of administration for the fledgling state through a process of trial and error, and in the face of persistent opposition from his colleagues. For example, he was compelled to experiment radically with several systems of revenue assessment throughout the 1770s: the tax yield of lands was only properly gauged for the first time by the Amini Commission between 1776 and 1778, and the necessity for European collectors to determine the value of each district was hotly debated following their withdrawal in 1773. In effect, the fundamental nature of local government was in flux during Hastings's administration, with various mechanisms for the extraction of territorial revenue, central to the existence of the Company state, being tested and discarded.

Cornwallis, however, entered the Indian arena after this basic principle of local government, the presence of a supreme European official in each district, had been established. Consequently, freed from the necessity for drastic experimentation and buoyed up by his augmented powers as governor-general and commander-in-chief, he was able to refine the existing system and attempt the stabilisation of rural society through the class of 'improving landlords' which he hoped to create with the Permanent Settlement of Bengal in 1793. This is not to say that there was absolutely no experimentation under Cornwallis: during the early years of his first administration there is ample evidence of schemes being implemented and rapidly abandoned. A prime example of this may be seen in his judicial reforms which united the powers of magistrate and civil judge in the person of the district collector in 1787, only to divide them again shortly afterwards.[99] However, his later restructuring of the *daroga* (police constable) network (1793) and of the Indian Army (1796, implemented in a modified form by his successor Sir John Shore), built on Hastings's pioneering work, and were evidence of the gradual maturing of the state.[100] They signified a move away from the enforced improvisation of Hastings's personality-driven administration in which the relative positions of the state's components had yet to be firmly established and in which ad hoc measures were perpetually needed, towards a more professional and impersonal bureaucracy.

The most recent substantial scholarship on the period has argued that in the years before Cornwallis's arrival in India the form of the Company state was 'fluctuating and uncertain', and that it was the new governor-general's brief 'to introduce stability and solvency to the regime'.[101] This is not to say that by the end of Cornwallis's first administration the infrastructure of the Company state was fully formed or that subsequent governors-general didn't continue to place emphasis on reputation as an instrument of rule. They did so, but the preoccupation with personal standing became less marked, the concern being more for the reputation of the office itself. Cornwallis's successor, Richard Wellesley, for example, expressed a determination from the outset 'to entrench myself with forms and ceremonies', essentially to bolster the institutional – rather than personal – aspect of governor-generalship.[102] Likewise, 'in conformity with the oriental concept of imperial dignity', Wellesley spent considerable sums on the construction of a new Government House and a luxurious residence for the governor-general, as well as on lavish official ceremony.[103] The personal was not wholly eradicated, though: in 1799, he was bitterly disappointed only to be offered what he termed the 'double-gilt potato' of an Irish peerage.[104] Writing to the prime minister William Pitt, he complained that

> in India, the disproportion between the service and the reward would be imputed to . . . some personal incapacity . . . I leave you to judge what the effect of such an impression is likely to be on the minds of those whom he [the governor-general] is appointed to govern.[105]

The shift from personal to institutional reputation was gradual, then, and each variety would persist and overlap to a greater or lesser extent, but from the turn of the 19th century, the focus became ever more institutional.

Regardless of whether it was concern with the broadly institutional or the narrowly personal sources of prestige which was foremost in the minds of governors-general and their councillors, throughout the period covered by this chapter there was a very clear sense at Fort William that Indian society was intensely watchful, closely monitoring the actions of the Company's servants, and that Indian public opinion needed to be courted at every possible opportunity through conduct which strengthened impressions of the Company's competence, justice and overwhelming military force. Such is the view apparent in the upper echelons of government.

Yet important though the conduct of these senior central figures was in shaping Indian perceptions of British rule, as subsequent chapters will seek to demonstrate, the Company's local officials, whose priorities were often not in accord with those of their superiors, were arguably of equal, if not greater, significance in forming Indian public opinion. These individuals were, by virtue of their role in local administration, exposed to the immediate gaze of large sections of the population on a daily basis, through the hearing of civil and criminal cases, deciding on boundary disputes and levels of revenue assessment, and, in short, from the routine operation of the district's governmental apparatus. The way in which they interacted with local society, how they administered the collections and dealt with armed threats and even their personal foibles, were all observable by the district's inhabitants and provided a rich source of discussion. In the more rural areas of the Company's territory, where those inhabitants had very limited contact with Europeans, the public acts of this tiny handful of administrators had a disproportionate influence on grassroots perceptions of the Company's government. As with the governors-general, although on a much reduced scale, one or two isolated European officials in a district became the exemplars of Company rule for its inhabitants, and, again in common with their superiors, the personal conduct of these local officials could, in turn, be interpreted as the official policy of the government.

The Company's district administrators were hugely influential in forming Indian opinion of colonial rule as a whole. However, their capacity to present the image desired by Fort William – that of forceful military government applied with justice – was very much dependent not only on the limited knowledge of Indian governance which the nascent civil service was able to accrue, but also on the financial support and, crucially, the military material which was allocated to them. As will be argued in the next chapter, the resources allotted to local officials with which to administer their districts and enhance the standing of their employers in Indian society were seriously, deliberately and counterproductively limited by the central government.

Notes

1 Malcolm, *Political History*, I, p. 144.
2 *Ibid.*, p. 145.
3 Select Committee on the East India Company, PP, 13 (1831/2), LV, cit. Peers, *Between Mars and Mammon*, p. 63.
4 Malcolm, *Political History*, I, p. 144.
5 B. Wegener, 'Concepts and Measurement of Prestige', *Annual Review of Sociology*, 1992 (18): 258.
6 Peers, *Between Mars and Mammon*, p. 62.
7 James C. Scott, 'Prestige as the Public Discourse of Domination', *Cultural Critique*, 1989 (12): 146.
8 Malcolm, *Political History*, I, p. 7.
9 Scott, 'Prestige as the Public Discourse of Domination', p. 147.
10 Edmund Burke, *Works*, VI, p. 147, cit. A. B. C. Cobban, 'Edmund Burke and the Origins of the Theory of Nationality', *Cambridge Historical Journal*, 1926, 2 (1): 39.
11 Bayly, *Empire and Information*, p. 204.
12 Marshall, *Making and Unmaking of Empires*, p. 44.
13 'A Narrative of the Insurrection Which Happened in the Zemeendary of Banaris in the Month of August 1781 and of the Governor-General in that District', in G. W. Forrest (ed.), *Selections from the State Papers of the Governors General of India: Warren Hastings*, Vol. 2, Oxford: Blackwell, 1910, p. 130.
14 *Ibid.*, pp. 132–133.
15 *Ibid.*, p. 133.
16 *Ibid.*, p. 160.
17 *Ibid.*
18 The ruler of Awadh was referred to as the 'nawab-wazir' in recognition of the hereditary role of *wazir* (chief minister), which was conferred on that house by the Mughal emperor in 1740.
19 R. Burn, J. S. Cotton, W. W. Meyer and H. H. Risley (eds.), *Imperial Gazetteer of India, Vol. XIX, Náyakanhathi to Parbhani*, Oxford: Clarendon Press, 1908, p. 282.
20 'A Narrative of the Insurrection', Forrest, *Hastings*, II, p. 173.
21 *Ibid.*, p. 173.
22 *Ibid.*, p. 160.
23 Marshall, *Making and Unmaking of Empires*, p. 265.
24 Fort William circular, 3 October 1781, W. K. Firminger (ed.), *Bengal District Records: Rangpur, Vol. II, Letters Received 1779–1782*, Calcutta: Bengal Secretariat, 1920, p. 161.

25 'A Summary Abstract of Mr Hastings' Government and Present Situation' [Endorsed: '1781'], Dodwell, *Letters to Sir John Macpherson*, p. 72.
26 Nasser Hussain, *The Jurisprudence of Emergency: Colonialism and the Rule of Law*, Ann Arbor: University of Michigan Press, 2003, p. 80.
27 *Ibid.*, p. 80.
28 *Ibid.*, p. 82.
29 *Ibid.*
30 W. Hastings to J. Macpherson, 15 October 1781, Dodwell, *Letters to Sir John Macpherson*, p. 90.
31 *Ibid.*
32 *Ibid.*, pp. 90–91.
33 Hussain, *Jurisprudence of Emergency*, p. 82.
34 W. Hastings to J. Macpherson, 15 October 1781, Dodwell, *Letters to Sir John Macpherson*, p. 92.
35 Recent work on the Majority has portrayed it as a split between the Company's interests, represented by Hastings and Barwell, and the interests of the British home government, represented by Clavering, Francis and Monson. See Travers, *Ideology and Empire*, p. 145.
36 'A Summary Abstract of Mr Hastings' Government and Present Situation', [Endorsed: 1781], Dodwell, *Letters to Sir John Macpherson*, p. 73.
37 *Ibid.*
38 Fisher, *Indirect Rule in India*, p. 134.
39 G. R. Gleig (ed.), *Memoirs of the Life of the Right Hon. Warren Hastings, First Governor-General of Bengal*, Vol. 1, London: Richard Bentley, 1841, p. 474.
40 *Ibid.*, p. 475.
41 Forrest, *Hastings*, I, p. 81.
42 W. Hastings to the Court of Directors, 20 March 1783, Forrest, *Hastings*, II, p. 41.
43 Circular of the governor-general, 3 October 1781 [signed J. Auriol], *BDR: Rangpur*, II, p. 161.
44 Even in an age generally notable for duelling in the higher echelons of society, some contemporary Europeans considered Britons to be extreme in this regard. Frederick the Great, for example, was not attracted by the Anglomania of the 1770s and 1780s, since 'he disliked the English for their . . . political faction, and their inclination towards physical violence'. C. Duffy, *Frederick the Great: A Military Life*, London: Routledge & Kegan Paul, 1985, p. 259.
45 Secret Select Committee's Proceedings, 20 July 1780, pp. 711–12, cit. Forrest, *Hastings*, I, p. 187.
46 *Ibid.*, p. 188.
47 'A Narrative of the Insurrection', Forrest, *Hastings*, II, p. 130.
48 *Ibid.*
49 Marshall, *Bengal: The British Bridgehead*, p. 101.
50 W. Hastings to J. Macpherson, 12 October 1781, Dodwell, *Letters to Sir John Macpherson*, pp. 86–87.
51 Forrest, *Hastings*, II, p. 1.
52 C.A. Bayly and K. Prior, 'Cornwallis, Charles, first Marquess Cornwallis (1738–1805)', in L. Goldman (ed.), *Oxford Dictionary of National Biography*, Oxford: Oxford University Press, 2004.

53 Malcolm, *Political History*, I, p. 115.
54 G. W. Forrest (ed.), *Selections from the State Papers of the Governors General of India: Lord Cornwallis*, Vol. 1, London: Blackwell, 1926, p. 19.
55 W. Palmer to D. Anderson, 12 November 1786, BL Add MSS 45,427, ff. 196–197.
56 Editor's commentary in Forrest, *Cornwallis*, I, p. 61.
57 *Ibid.*
58 C. Cornwallis to the Court of Directors, 7 September 1791, Forrest, *Cornwallis*, I, p. 33.
59 *Ibid.*, p. 38.
60 *Ibid.*, pp. 23–24.
61 C. Cornwallis to G. Foster, 5 January 1787, C. Ross (ed.), *Correspondence of Charles, First Marquis Cornwallis*, Vol. 1, London: John Murray, 1859, p. 252.
62 C. Cornwallis to Tipu Sultan, 19 May 1791, Ross, *Correspondence*, II, p. 94.
63 W. Hastings to J. Macpherson, 1 November 1781, Dodwell, *Letters to Sir John Macpherson*, pp. 86–87.
64 C. Cornwallis to the Secret Committee of the Court of Directors, 19 August 1787, Forrest, *Cornwallis*, II, p. 169.
65 'The State of India', Forrest, *Hastings*, II, p. 67.
66 'A Narrative of the Insurrection', Forrest, *Hastings*, II, p. 67.
67 J. W. Kaye, *Lives of Indian Officers: Lord Cornwallis: Sir John Malcolm; Mountstuart Elphinstone: Henry Martyn: Sir Charles Metcalfe*, London: W. H. Allen, 1869, p. 109. Cit. Forrest, *Cornwallis*, I, pp. 29–30.
68 C. Cornwallis to the Court of Directors, 16 November 1786, Ross, *Correspondence*, I, p. 242.
69 C. Cornwallis to W. Fawcett, 12 August 1787, Ross, *Correspondence*, I, pp. 279–280.
70 C. Cornwallis to H. Dundas, 16 November 1787, Ross, *Correspondence*, I, p. 311.
71 C. Cornwallis to the Duke of York, 10 December 1787, Ross, *Correspondence*, I, p. 317.
72 Forrest, *Cornwallis*, I, p. 67.
73 General Order of Lord Cornwallis, 26 February 1791, Forrest, *Cornwallis*, I, pp. 67–68.
74 Secret Select Committee's Proceedings, 23 May 1774, I, p. 104, cit. Forrest, *Hastings*, I, p. 48.
75 W. Hastings to A. Champion, 27 May 1774, Gleig, *Memoirs*, p. 425.
76 P. J. Marshall, *The Impeachment of Warren Hastings*, Oxford: Oxford University Press, 1965, p. xiv.
77 W. Hastings to N. Middleton, 27 May 1774, Gleig, *Memoirs*, p. 438.
78 Forrest, *Hastings*, I, p. 49.
79 Circular of the governor-general, 3 October 1781 [signed J. Auriol], Firminger, *BDR: Rangpur*, II, p. 161.
80 *Ibid.*
81 'Warren Hastings', T. B. Macaulay, *Lays of Ancient Rome and Selections from the Essays*, London: Ward Lock, 1884, p. 219.
82 *Ibid.*
83 Forest, *Hastings*, I, p. 25.
84 *Ibid.*

85 P. J. Marshall, 'Britain and the World in the Eighteenth Century, IV: The Turning Outwards of Britain', *Transactions of the Royal Historical Society*, 2001, 6 (11): 9.
86 M. Martin (ed.), *The Despatches, Minutes and Correspondence of the Marquess Wellesley, K.G.*, Vol. 4, London: John Murray, 1837, p. 153, cit. C. A. Bayly, *Indian Society and the Making of the British Empire*, Cambridge: Cambridge University Press, 1988, p. 16.
87 C. Cornwallis to C. W. Malet, 18 December 1789, Ross, *Correspondence*, I, p. 566.
88 *Ibid.*
89 *Ibid.*
90 *Ibid.*, p. 383.
91 C. Cornwallis to H. Dundas, 4 April 1790, Ross, *Correspondence*, II, p. 15.
92 C. Cornwallis to the Bishop of Salisbury, 27 December 1788, Ross, *Correspondence*, I, pp. 397–398.
93 Travers, *Ideology and Empire*, p. 139.
94 *Ibid.*, p. 233.
95 Bayly, *Origins of Nationality in South Asia*, p. 62.
96 Particularly so, given that Hastings had spent two years on the Madras council prior to becoming the governor of Bengal in 1771. See Travers, *Ideology and Empire*, p. 101.
97 Secret Select Committee's proceedings, 20 July 1780, II, p. 711/12, Forrest, *Hastings*, I, p. 187.
98 Wegener, 'Concepts and Measurement of Prestige', p. 255.
99 Forrest, *Hastings*, I, p. 320.
100 Chatterji, 'The Darogah and the Countryside', pp. 19–20.
101 Wilson, *Domination of Strangers*, p. 45.
102 R. Wellesley to C. Greville, 18 November 1798, L. S. Benjamin (ed.), *The Wellesley Papers: The Life and Correspondence of Richard Colley Wellesley, Marquess Wellesley, 1760–1842*, Vol. 1, London: H. Jenkins, 1914, pp. 85–86.
103 Misra, *Central Administration*, p. 47.
104 R. Wellesley to W. Pitt, April 1800, Benjamin, *Wellesley Papers*, p. 121.
105 *Ibid.*

3 'A gendarmerie of last resort'? The roles of armed force, 1760–1820[1]

The origins and role of the Company's army

Both modern historians and contemporary Anglo-Indian commentators have placed great emphasis on the role of the Company's army in establishing and consolidating colonial authority over a vast Indian population, and particularly its importance in countering violent resistance from within civil society. This chapter aims to refine that view through an examination of the Company's deployment of its regular and paramilitary forces in Bengal during the half century after 1765, the year in which the Mughal emperor granted it the diwani of Bengal. It seeks to demonstrate that the regular army was not widely used to police Indian society and that this role was principally undertaken by a variety of paramilitaries who have largely been ignored in the modern historiography. It will examine the reasoning behind the Company's desire to limit the forces available to its district officials, investigating the consequences of this policy on the nature of local administration in late 18th- and early 19th-century Bengal, and on the development of the early Company state more widely.

The grant of the diwani revolutionised the Company's standing as a territorial power, presenting it with the opportunity of accumulating vast wealth through the taxation of Bengal's inhabitants. Simultaneously, it necessitated the provision of far larger armed forces, both regular and paramilitary, than had previously been required. These were needed to ensure the steady generation and collection of territorial revenue by protecting the province's frontiers from external threats, and its hinterland from the disruption caused by internal resistance. The Company's regular army was initially an insignificant body, only a few hundred strong and tasked simply with protecting its factories and outposts from opportunistic bandits and the depredations of commercial rivals and Indian powers.[2] From the middle of the 18th century, however, these small garrisons swiftly grew into a very substantial and efficient armed force. During the late 1740s, the Company began to regulate its troops through the introduction of a system of martial law based upon that used by the contemporary British (Crown) army.[3] The units hastily raised and organised by Clive following the recapture of Calcutta in 1757 formed the core of what was to become the Bengal Army, but it was only as the Company developed as a territorial power in northern India after 1765 that this force began to be seriously augmented.[4] Approximately 25,000 troops, mainly sepoys, were enrolled in the army of the Bengal Presidency by 1768. By 1805, that figure had risen to 64,000, at which point the Company's Indian Army (the combined armed forces of the Bengal, Bombay and Madras presidencies) numbered more than 150,000 men.[5]

This rapid expansion of the Company's military establishment occurred in tandem with its massive acquisition of territory through a series of conflicts with Indian powers, notably the Maratha Confederacy and Mysore, over the course of the late 18th and early 19th century. Having defeated the forces of these powers, it was necessary for the army to pacify the region, to ensure the smooth running of local government until the populace grew more accustomed to, and compliant with, the Company's rule.

Writing on the Company's forces in the late 18th century, Raymond Callahan has observed that 'even in times of nominal peace the strength of the Indian Army remained high' because 'hunting down and dispersing bands of plunderers . . . coercing refractory local chieftains, and "revenue work" made continual demands upon the Company's forces'.[6] It is the purpose of this chapter to critique the idea that the late 18th-and early 19th-century Indian Army was a de facto military police force, imposing the Company's will on its newly acquired, and fractious, civil population. Obvious though the link would appear to be, the simple fact of the army's existence does not equate to it having been the key instrument in combating low-level indigenous resistance within the colonial state. As the next section will demonstrate, in contrast with the practice common to British India after the late 1810s – by which point the Company's military and political dominance had been established – from the late 1760s until the early 1800s the central authorities at Fort William consistently shied away from using their regular army to suppress disorder and resistance among their Indian subjects.

Douglas Peers, in his analysis of the Company's military dispositions in India after the 1810s, has observed,

> The army's role as a gendarmerie of last resort is attested to by the geographical distribution of troops and garrisons . . . troops were

> not concentrated along India's vulnerable frontier. Instead they were scattered across India in small garrisons, where they were in a position to monitor local society and if needs be stamp out any signs of resistance.[7]

The annual Bengal military statements of the late 1810s confirm this view of the army as scattered piecemeal across the subcontinent and support the idea that its widespread deployment was designed to expose as much of the population to it as possible, thereby maximising its power as a deterrent against civil insurrection. Throughout the period after 1765, the overwhelming majority of the Company's armed forces were regular sepoy infantry, with a small number of European battalions[8] and limited cavalry and artillery.[9] An examination of the regular sepoy and the few European (Company and Crown) foot regiments serving with the Bengal Army during 1820 reveals that the 60 battalions serving in mainland India[10] were distributed between 71 different posts in garrisons ranging from one company to a maximum of just four battalions (Barrackpur);[11] only 13 of the garrisons were more than a battalion strong, and, of these, only six were composed of more than two battalions.[12]

These statistics clearly support Peers's observations on the widely dispersed distribution of the Anglo-Indian military after the later 1810s. However, they contrast strongly with the marked trend in military dispositions apparent during the previous 50 years. Although in the regular infantry figures for 1815, 1810 and, to an extent, 1805, one may observe a similarly diffuse pattern of distribution, for the period between the early 1760s and the early 1800s, a rather different set of principles appears to have determined the siting and composition of garrisons.[13]

The deployment of the Bengal Army

In 1763, the Company had 9,494 sepoys and 632 European infantrymen in Bengal, based at 11 posts, of which six contained approximately 1,000 or more men, and the remainder (with the exception of the battalion at Chittagong) were outposts of companies or half-companies.[14] The Bengal Army's infantry corps grew rapidly, reaching 25,158 in 1772.[15] By 1777, its hugely increased size makes clearer the pattern, suggested by the ratio of soldiers to posts in 1763, in which a considerable part of the army's strength was concentrated in a few, very large garrisons. The returns of that year show that the army's 30 battalions of infantry (Indian and European) were distributed between 14 posts. Nine of these were garrisoned by single battalions, leaving 21 battalions (70 percent of the Bengal Army's infantry strength) concentrated at just five posts, while eight battalions (nearly 30 percent of the infantry) were stationed at just one post (Bilgram in Awadh).[16]

This pattern of distribution continued with the growth of the army in the following decade. In 1785, there were 44 battalions of infantry (Indian and European) on the Bengal establishment, distributed between 19 posts, none of which was garrisoned by less than a battalion.[17] Two-thirds of this infantry were based at just five posts: the cantonments of Baharampur, Barrackpur and Kanpur, and the two forts of Chunar and Fatehgarh. The distribution remained nearly identical for 1787.[18] In 1792, 18 of the 43 infantry battalions were based at just four posts: Baharampur, Barrackpur, Dinapur and Kanpur, with a further six battalions away serving against Mysore. The remaining 19 battalions were distributed either singly or in pairs at 13 posts.[19] The pattern continues in the figures for 1800, although with a lessening in the troop concentration: of 30 battalions, one-third was based at just three posts (Chunar, Kanpur and Midnapur), with the remaining 20 battalions distributed between 18 posts.[20] By 1805 the distribution shifts towards the pattern observed by Peers,[21] with a move towards the deployment of many more, smaller garrisons which were dispersed across north India, as was to become the norm for the Bengal Army over the subsequent decades.[22]

Even allowing for the detachment of large sections of the Bengal Army on foreign service, the statistics for the period between the early 1760s and the early 1800s indicate Fort William's distinct preference, as far as circumstances permitted, for relatively few, but large, garrisons across northern India. During the first 50 years of Company rule, frequent conquests massively increased the territory under its control. Necessarily, the size of its army increased in tandem: in 1805, the Company's Indian Army was more than eight times larger than its predecessor of 1763.[23] Yet it was now being deployed in smaller and smaller garrisons. Indeed, if one looks at the 1820 figures, five of the six largest posts had fewer than four battalions each, and these were deployed not in the Bengal Presidency, but in or immediately adjacent to the central western territories recently seized from the Marathas, which still required a relatively high concentration of troops for pacification, and which now formed the Company's north-west frontier.[24] More than two-thirds of the Bengal Army's infantry were deployed across the presidency in formations of less than two battalions, and one-third of its total infantry strength was deployed in sub-battalion groupings. The argument for the later period is that the wider dispersal of troops in smaller garrisons was an indicator of Fort William's desire to monitor Indian society more closely and to enhance public exposure to its military might. If this is accepted, then it raises questions regarding the rationale behind the earlier policy of concentration and the reasons for the shift away from it during the first quarter of the 19th century. In answering those questions, it is necessary to examine both the physical positioning of the garrisons and their composition.

A geographical analysis of the deployment of the Bengal Army and its embedded Crown forces between the 1760s and the early 1800s demonstrates a clear bias in favour of positioning large garrisons on, or in very close proximity to, the river Ganges and its major tributaries. The six largest, and most consistently used, military posts during this period were on the Ganges itself (Chunar, Fatehgarh and Kanpur), on its Hugli tributary (Barrackpur and Fort William), or on its source stream, the Bhagirathi (Baharampur). The overwhelming majority of the smaller posts, such as Allahabad, Anupshahr, Benares and Mungher were similarly located. It is notable that a significant proportion of the Bengal Army's force was actually deployed beyond the geographical boundaries of the Bengal Presidency in this period. In 1763, nearly a third of the Company's infantry was concentrated at Bilgram in Awadh; in 1785, three of the five largest posts were Kanpur and Fatehgarh in Awadh, and Chunar, to the south at Benares. Again, in 1800, the largest garrison (including four regular sepoy battalions and the Crown's 78th Highlanders) was at Kanpur, and in 1805, even without counting the battalions serving in the forces assembled against the Marathas, over three-quarters of the Bengal Army's total regular infantry strength was deployed outside the presidency.

Such deployment suggests a concern with a strategy to protect the presidency from external threats, principally the Marathas, against whom the Company fought three wars between 1775 and 1818, rather than with the internal policing of Bengal. Of course, the presence of large bodies of Company troops in adjacent client states did help to ensure the loyalty, or at least the acquiescence, of their rulers, but this was more of a diplomatic manoeuvre, designed to subdue potentially recalcitrant rajas, rather than to prevent the criminal misbehaviour of their subjects. As G. J. Bryant has shown, for example, the proximity of the Company garrison at Chunar helped guarantee the nawab-wazir of Awadh's continued payment of the war indemnity imposed on him following the Buxar campaign in 1764; it also served to maintain Awadh as a 'cost-free barrier to the restless "country" powers further into Hindustan'.[25]

The defence of Bengal, beyond its frontiers, on the line of the Ganges as it passed through Awadh and Benares, suggests that the potential for using the presidency's waterways to supply troops and to enable their mobilisation was thoroughly appreciated by the Company's military planners. The course of the Ganges describes an arc from the north to the south-east as far as Chunar, facing, during this period, the Maratha territories to the west. Beyond Chunar it goes on to bisect Bengal, although it still provided a baseline from which operations could be undertaken against the Maratha province of Berar to the south. In north-eastern and north-central India, where the overland transportation of large bodies of troops was severely hampered by poor roads and supply difficulties, the capacity to move its forces rapidly across the province by river afforded the Company a crucial strategic benefit.[26] The Ganges served a dual function, both as both a medium of military transportation and as a natural barrier which could hamper hostile forces moving eastwards.[27] This, combined with the (notionally) stabilising influence of Company garrisons in client states, helps to explain why, and how, the Bengal Presidency was being defended, to a great extent, beyond its western frontier.

The high concentration of troops at relatively few posts, and the physical location of these garrisons, suggests that, during this early period, Fort William did not intend that the Bengal Army should act as a military police force, quelling civil unrest across the presidency's rural hinterland. Prior to the first quarter of the 19th century, it was not dispersed across the Company's territory in a multitude of small garrisons 'to monitor local society'; in fact, a very substantial proportion of it was not actually based in the Company's territory at all. While the Bengal Presidency's borders with Bhutan, Burma and Nepal to the north and east were rendered comparatively secure by the difficult local terrain and the reasonably good diplomatic relations which Fort William enjoyed with those states, the 'vulnerable frontier' on the line of the Ganges was not. The concentration of the Bengal Army clearly indicates that, at least until the Company's decisive victory in the Second Anglo-Maratha War (1803–05), regular operations against Indian powers to the west and south were to be its prime occupation.

Drawing attention to the proliferation of many, small garrisons scattered across India after the 1810s, Peers has argued, 'The army was the means through which peasant resistance could be checked, either through direct punitive actions, or more usually by displays of force designed to impress upon rural society the omnipotence of colonial rule'.[28] As has been shown earlier, this army distribution pattern was in marked contrast to that which had prevailed during the previous

50 years; its concentration during the earlier period minimised that section of the Indian population routinely exposed to theatrical displays of military power. The difference in patterns of deployment before and after the 1810s suggests that Fort William's thinking with regard to the policing of civil society, or at least the priority it accorded to that function, was also different. The policy of concentrating the army, apparently preserving it for regular warfare, casts much doubt on its importance as an instrument of 'military policing' during this period. If it was preserved chiefly for regular operations, then this, in turn, prompts the question of what, if any, forces were employed by the Company for the routine coercion of Bengal's rural population.

'Provincial duties' and the Company's paramilitaries

As the Company gradually increased its administrative control in Bengal after 1765, it had to take responsibility for suppressing violent disorder within its new territory in order to secure the steady flow of taxes into its coffers. Ostensibly, this policing function remained within the remit of the nawab of Bengal – with whom, in theory, the Company shared governmental power – but it rapidly became apparent that neither the nawab's government nor the local zamindars were able to guarantee the security of the *mofussil* (countryside) at a level acceptable to the Europeans.[29] Consequently, the Company was drawn into a policing role, which entailed the provision of armed forces to prevent resistance and disorder among the rural population from disrupting the district administrations' collection and remittance of territorial revenue. Troops were needed to act as guards for local treasuries and government offices, to escort convoys of species and to combat any disorderly groups that threatened the largely agrarian economy of Bengal's districts. They were also required to enforce the collection of taxes from obstructive landowners.

The Company's large standing army might have seemed an obvious body for this work, but Fort William was steadfastly against that solution, and as late as 1795, the governor-general Sir John Shore observed that such a practice was 'pregnant with Evils of a most serious nature'. For the upper echelons of the colonial administration, the deployment of regular troops in support of the district authorities was undesirable on several counts. As has been seen, the Company's regular army was kept concentrated on the vulnerable frontier in western Bengal to facilitate its rapid deployment against rival powers, distributing it piecemeal across Bengal would greatly reduce the Company's capacity to respond in strength to any threat moving eastwards from within

Hindustan. Furthermore, it was feared that the discipline of troops split up into small parties on detached duties would suffer, and some would be tempted to take advantage of their independence to oppress the local populace by extorting money and goods. Such problems had emerged among the first troops which the Company had raised for this revenue service in 1766, Robert Clive's *pargana* battalions.[30]

The revenue service had initially been performed by bodies of armed cultivators, which, in the words of Warren Hastings, were 'variously composed of Footmen armed indiscriminately with Bows, Lances, Swords, Matchlocks and Bamboos, and a few ill-appointed horsemen for Shew intermixed'.[31] This motley collection of seasonal mercenaries was deemed unequal to the needs of revenue duty, and Clive's pargana troops were expected to be a significantly more reliable replacement. A corps of 11 pargana battalions, composed of approximately 9,000 men, was formed along regular lines, with the standard Bengal Native Infantry complement of European officers, NCOs and sepoys to each battalion.[32] Almost as soon as the force was established, however, the corrosive effect of provincial duties on discipline began to be realised. Finding themselves largely independent of any effective higher military authority, the detachments of pargana battalion sepoys deployed across the districts took to extorting the populace on their own account. Nor was such behaviour confined to the private soldiers; their European officers were also quick to seize on the 'opportunities of their remote situation and the temptation of unresisted power'.[33] They frequently ignored the civilian district officials, to whom they were theoretically subordinate, and often became racketeers, lending public money to zamindars – at ruinous rates – and torturing those who failed to make their repayments. Officers could rapidly become rich through such activities, and consequently, in spite of the unmartial nature of revenue duty, postings to these lucrative battalions became a source of jealousy throughout the service. As Hastings noted,

> The Contagion spread . . . for the same officers belonged to each Establishment [pargana battalions and the Company's regular army], some returning with disgust from a field of Emoluments to the moderate pay and scanty Perquisites of the Army, and others envious and eager to succeed them.[34]

So widespread was the abuse of power on the part of these officers, that in later years Fort William found it necessary to issue strict instructions that the officers of revenue troops were not permitted to 'punish or confine' individuals arbitrarily, to 'lend or borrow money . . . or to have any Dealing of any kind whatever with any Dewan, Zamindar, Farmer, Ryot or other Dependent officer of the Revenue'.[35]

Ultimately the failure of the pargana battalion model became too scandalous to be ignored. Their disbandment followed in 1770, and from then, until the increasingly widespread deployment of the Bengal Army subsequent to the Company's decisive victory over the Marathas in 1805, the collectors of Bengal's districts were supported by a heterogeneous assortment of paramilitaries. Units acting in this capacity were commonly referred to as 'revenue troops' and were placed at the immediate disposal of the district's civilian authorities. These forces were composed of militia (drawn from a range of sources, including invalided regular sepoys) until 1784, when they were replaced with cheaper 'sebundy' (*sibbandi*) revenue troops, poorly trained and ill-equipped bodies of irregulars.[36] Hereafter, until the establishment of better quality 'provincial battalions' and wider regular deployment during the early 1800s, the troops assigned to this revenue duty were usually the unreliable sebundies, or, infrequently, regular Bengal Army formations. Auxiliary armed forces could be levied by collectors (if Fort William approved the expense, which it rarely did) through the local recruitment of *barqandazes* (mercenaries, occasionally armed with matchlock muskets) or armed cultivators.[37] In addition to being of variable, and often dubious, quality, these revenue troops were also frequently very few in number, with two companies (operationally, a total of perhaps 180 men) typically being assigned even to major districts. Some collectors received no allocation of militia or sebundies at all and were wholly reliant on recruiting whatever mercenary troops were available locally as the exigencies of their district demanded. An example of the paucity of the forces allocated to the districts may be seen in the fact that by the mid-1780s – at which point the infantry strength of the Bengal Army stood at some 40,000 of all ranks – the paramilitary infantry allocated for revenue service was scarcely one-tenth of that number.[38]

Moreover, in a colonial state held together by the successful manipulation of popular opinion, appearances mattered as much as numbers, if not more so. Given that the Company's ability to govern was so reliant on overawing Indian society with its military reputation, the widespread use of largely untrained, irregular troops in the districts was a potentially dangerous policy. Reflecting on the militia in 1783, Hastings wrote, 'They are cloathed with the Military Garb, and armed with firelocks of which they know but the practice common to the rest of the people, because these Engines of their occupation are found to command respect'.[39] That 'respect' properly belonged to the

Company's well-drilled and effective regular sepoys, to encourage the population at large to conflate the Company's mediocre paramilitaries with its regular troops – while economical – was to risk undermining the military reputation which enabled the state's continued existence.

The delegation of military power within the early Company state

While the urgent necessity of reducing overheads profoundly shaped Fort William's policy towards provincial revenue duties, it is clear that there were other forces at work too. Concerns over internal security and the Company's military reputation also provided arguments both for and against the strengthening of the paramilitary corps, but these considerations alone do not entirely account for the weakness of the establishments permitted by the Company to its local officials in the rural hinterland and on the fringes of its territory. A further explanation for the consistent under-resourcing of these district officials may be found in Fort William's desire to exert greater restraint on its diffuse and over-extended state mechanisms.

The desire for the increased centralisation of armed forces went beyond the strategic deployment of the army at a provincial level and into the internal ordering of the few revenue troops that were stationed in the districts. For the central government, the lesson of the pargana battalions had been clear: the dispersal of troops in small parties throughout the mofussil hampered the maintenance of discipline and, frequently, resulted in bands of sepoys extorting bribes and otherwise mistreating the population in the more remote parts of the Company's territory. The practice of dispersal continued, however, during the 1770s, in which period revenue duties were being performed by the militia. By 1783, the government was so incensed at its continuance that the Committee of Revenue was forced to circulate a notice throughout Bengal, exhorting the concentration of each district's forces and threatening severe punishment if district chiefs and their military officers did not attend to the injunction.

> The Honble Board having remarked that Seapoys are Often employed in . . . trifling . . . Services & in Small Detachments & Suffered to remain Singly or in small Parties for a . . . [length] . . . of time at fixed-Stations without use or necessity . . . have positively forbidden this practice, & have declared their Censure & disapprobation of it, with a Resolution to punish in an . . .

> [exemplary] . . . manner every . . . [deviation] . . . from the above prohibition.[40]

The harshness of this circular, and the frequency with which the issue was referred to in correspondence from the central government, indicates the importance attached to the centralisation of force by Fort William.[41] However, it met with little immediate success, since the various threats to the districts from border raiders, dakaits, sannyasis and faqirs, often occurred simultaneously. It was usually not possible to bring the whole of the district's body of revenue troops to bear on one threat without dangerously weakening the local government's grip on another part of the district, perhaps even its administrative headquarters. The paucity of military resources available to district officials meant that, even if their attempts to counter threats were limited to preventing only the most significant disruptions to the revenue stream, it was still necessary to distribute their troops among a number of small independent commands.

The prohibition of this practice by Fort William was an attempt to apply the policy of centralising its armed forces at a subcontinental level to the microcosm of the district. This was intended to reduce the number of individuals in the Company's hierarchy who enjoyed the capacity for undertaking significant, independent, violent action. A compromise had to be found between the desirability of attempting to suppress all instances of resistance within a district and the risk inherent in allowing so many individuals to exercise command of armed forces in the Company's name without the direct supervision of a higher authority. Fort William preferred that command be concentrated in the single person of the district chief, rather than dispersed piecemeal among the junior officers and NCOs of his revenue troops by virtue of their isolation at distant outposts. Yet at the same time, it expected that the district revenues would be realised, meaning that, at the very least, the more threatening instances of armed resistance had to be countered, and this often demanded the dispatch of troops to several sectors of the district simultaneously, thereby forcing the collector to juggle the conflicting directives of his superiors.

The principle of concentration, which preferred command of the district's armed forces to reside with the collector, as head of the district, also extended to the place of that official within the Company's military hierarchy as a whole. The district administration's capacity to extract revenue efficiently could be seriously hindered by only allowing local authorities a handful of inferior quality troops for the immediate security of their territory. Yet there was an equal, if not greater, danger in allowing these officials to have control of significant bodies of soldiers. It was necessary to pitch the delegation of command at a level which allowed the revenue stream to be secured while minimising the harm that could be done through the actions of overambitious or incompetent district administrators. A public reverse inflicted on a large formation of soldiers engaged in revenue duties, whose officers were subordinate to the district collector, would be especially damaging to a government heavily reliant on its military reputation to maintain order. But by allowing that collector only a small body of second-rate troops, Fort William limited the scale of operations he would be likely to undertake, and, at worst, the loss of a handful of paramilitaries in a skirmish would be proportionately less harmful to the government's capacity to impose rule. It was a question of choosing between suffering a multitude of what were, on a pan-Indian scale at least, relatively minor affronts to the government from perpetrators of low-level resistance, or delegating greater power to covenanted servants, who might sensibly defend the Company's interests, but who might equally be prone to use armed force on a whim, without considering the wider implications of their conduct. The general line of policy pursued by Fort William throughout the period can be interpreted not simply as an attempt to reduce overheads by restricting the quantity and quality of troops made available to district administrations, but by so doing, also to limit the capacity of its largely amateurish and unreliable local officials for significant autonomous action.

Unsurprisingly, given Fort William's preferred policy, the annals of early colonial Bengal abound with examples of militarily under-resourced collectors struggling to impose the government's authority, with the Company's wider interests suffering as a consequence. However, the reckless decisions taken by some district collectors on the rare occasions when they found themselves in possession of a substantial armed force go some way to explaining Fort William's anxiety. A prime example of this may be seen in the unauthorised invasion of Nepal, in pursuit of raiders, ordered by Rangpur's collector D. H. McDowall, following the reinforcement of his district by a battalion of regular Bengal sepoys in 1786.[42] Yet at the same time, some collectors were wary of disbanding their local paramilitaries and using regular troops when the army was employed on provincial duties, as there was considerably less flexibility in the way in which the regular forces could be used. Collectors could at least exert a measure of control over their paramilitary troops, whereas the army was answerable primarily to the central government, and these regular detachments might be suddenly withdrawn to meet a crisis elsewhere.

However, if Fort William was reluctant to employ the regular Bengal Army as a force for the pacification of its territory, then the same could not be said of its attitude towards its ex-servicemen. From the 1780s onwards, much attention was directed towards the role of the Company's invalid *thanahs* in securing rural areas against unrest. These thanahs were the stations where Company sepoys were settled with their families after retiring from service, either through age or infirmity. Such settlements of military pensioners served a twofold purpose. They were a very public demonstration of the Company's worth as an employer, identifying it closely with the Mughal practice of assigning rent-free *jagirs* (land grants) to imperial retainers, and thereby lending it legitimacy in the eyes of its Indian subjects.[43] The settlements also represented 'pockets of influence' for the Company and were particularly useful 'for policing Company territory and training its new recruits' in frontier areas and in the recently conquered Maratha domains.[44] As with its employment of paramilitaries, this was a key way in which the Company minimised the costs arising from the pacification of Bengal and retained its army for regular operations. The auxiliary function of the thanahs – as a demonstration of the benevolence of the colonial authorities towards collaborating groups – proved so valuable that the scheme was still being fostered, indeed augmented, well into the 1820s, by which time its importance as an instrument of policing had been much reduced by the recent redeployment of the Bengal Army.[45]

The function of the regular army within the structure of armed bodies which supported the Company's government in Bengal during the 50 years after 1765, was not, then, principally, or even significantly, that of a military police force. Nor were these duties yet fulfilled by an effective system of civil police, extending upwards from *paiks* and *dusadhs* (village constables) to *kotwals* (town police), and faujdars or, after the Cornwallis reforms, darogas. Throughout this period, the burden of combating serious armed threats at a local level was borne by a provincial paramilitary body, which, in its various incarnations, occupied a position somewhere between the regular army and the pre-Company police network in the maintenance of the colonial state's security.

Throughout the second half of the 18th century, Bengal's police network was in disarray, and the effects of Cornwallis's sweeping police reforms of the 1790s would take years to be fully felt. Moreover, as has been seen, there was considerable reluctance on the part of Fort William to spread the Bengal Army across the presidency on policing operations, particularly while major Indian powers continued to threaten the Company's heartland. Until the 1810s, it was concentrated principally in a few large garrisons in the west and south, leaving the northern and eastern districts of Bengal, from Rangpur in the north to Chittagong in the south-east, comparatively lightly defended. It was not until the 1810s, at which point the Company's most powerful Indian opponents, the Maratha Confederacy and Mysore, had been comprehensively defeated, that the colonial government could exert something approaching a monopoly on the use of arms over its Indian subjects. It is surely no coincidence that, in parallel with the Company's rise to political and military supremacy, we see the greater dispersal of the army in many, relatively small and scattered posts, explained by Peers as the army's redeployment as a police force 'to monitor local society'. With the removal of the last great Indian power which could seriously contend with the Company for the subcontinental hegemony, there was no immediate threat which required the routine concentration of the army in readiness for mobilisation, so now the secondary function of policing local society could be attended to. This is not to imply that the regular army was now charged with enforcing the law; the development of a more effective civil police force after the 1810s, and the government's long-standing reluctance to use the army in that way, combined to ensure that this was not the case. Rather, with the Company's paramount status confirmed, it was, in the view of Fort William, both safe and fitting to disperse the army throughout the presidency in a multitude of garrisons as a highly visible symbol of the colonial state's coercive power. The suppressing influence which the widespread dispersal of troops had on Indian society certainly benefitted district administrators.

However, until this point in the early 19th century, the Company's reluctance to dilute the strength of the Bengal Army in low-level 'pacification' operations meant that district officials had to make do with a secondary corps, variously composed of militia, sebundies or provincial battalions, supported by whatever armed peons and barqandazes could be recruited without incurring the wrath of Fort William. It was with this force – undermanned and, in the main, badly trained and equipped – that they were expected to impose the colonial government's authority, guaranteeing the operation of the civil, and later criminal, courts and, most importantly, safeguarding the revenue stream from the disruption brought about by various kinds of civil unrest.

Conclusions

The military context of the Company's colonial bureaucracy is central to understanding the nature of early British rule in India, and the interaction between the colonial military and bureaucratic arms in this instance is perhaps surprising. Rather than using its large, well-organised army as an instrument for the coercion of civil society in support of government (as might have been expected), the Company actually under-resourced its local government militarily, for reasons of economy, frontier defence and to impose checks upon the activities of its far-flung network of isolated officials. This exacerbated a professional culture of extreme competition for potentially huge financial rewards and led to a heightened concern among local officials with their personal standing in the Company's hierarchy, rather than with tackling the problems of governing a population which was, at best, ambivalent towards them. While many of these district collectors were daring in their efforts to enrich themselves personally, they were also, for that very reason, often risk averse in their governmental practice. They needed, above all, to hold onto their posts in order to benefit from their illicit perquisites. District collectors frequently ignored serious unrest among the local populace when this seemed safer than hazarding a chancy armed intervention, which might incur the wrath of their superiors were it not completely successful. Such considerations led to the widespread suppression of unpalatable information by local officials, who, fearing censure and loss of position, were reluctant to let the central government know too much about district affairs. This practice – strongly informed by Fort William's military dispositions – acted against the penetration of Indian society by any effective colonial bureaucracy until well into the 19th century, hindering the accumulation of the 'colonial knowledge' needed to refine governmental systems and procedures. It also continues to present problems today for scholars using the often disingenuous and incomplete records of the Company's early district bureaucrats.

Notes

1 This chapter is substantially based on J. Lees, 'Sepoys and Sebundies: The Role of Regular and Paramilitary Forces in the Construction of Colonialism in Bengal, c. 1765–c. 1820', K. Roy and G. Rand (eds.), *Culture, Conflict and the Military in Colonial South Asia*, Abingdon: Routledge, 2018, pp. 45–63. The material is reproduced with the permission of Routledge India.

2 The 'Indian Army' consisted of 500 men and 20 officers by the middle of the 18th century. Marshall, *East Indian Fortunes*, p. 15.

3 G. J. Bryant, *The Emergence of British Power in India, 1600–1784: A Grand Strategic Interpretation*, Woodbridge: Boydell Press, 2013, p. 45.

4 *Ibid.*, p. 126.

5 Callahan, *East India Company*, p. 6.

6 *Ibid.*, p. 7.

7 Peers, *Between Mars and Mammon*, p. 11.

8 In this period, the infantry battalion had a nominal strength of approximately 700 officers and other ranks, although in practice disease and injury rendered large numbers unfit for duty. Indian service was particularly hard for the Company's Europeans and the Crown regiments: on average, between 1783 and 1787, the Company European battalions were 33 percent under their nominal strength, and their British Army counterparts 53 percent under strength. See Callahan, *East India Company*, pp. 75, 148–149.

Until Cornwallis's military reforms were (partially) implemented, each battalion was numbered as a separate unit, but between 1796 and 1824, when the structure reverted to the pre-1796 system, they were paired off to form two-battalion regiments. This made very little difference in operational terms, as the battalions rarely served together. The main effect of the Cornwallis reforms was hugely to increase the number of European officers serving with regular Indian infantry units. Previously, it was common for battalions to be commanded by a captain and an adjutant, with most of the companies under the charge of Indian officers and NCOs (*subedars* and *jemadars*). After 1796, regiments were commanded by colonels, and lieutenant-colonels commanded battalions which were composed of 10 companies and staffed by a major, four captains, 11 lieutenants and five ensigns.

9 For example, in 1815, 75 battalions of regular infantry were serving with the Bengal Army, but only 10 cavalry regiments (eight Company and two Crown) and three battalions of foot artillery. See the Bengal Military Establishment Annual Statement 1814–15, IOR, L/MIL/8/24, pp. 1–13. This ratio between the three arms of the service is fairly typical of the early Company period, if with rather more cavalry than had been usual in the preceding decades. In 1767, the Bengal establishment contained 2,712 European privates and NCOs (with 217 commissioned officers) and 22,087 sepoys (with 1,176 Indian NCOs and 30 European commissioned officers), but only 42 European cavalrymen and 298 *sowars* (Indian troopers). There were also only 298 European gunners in the Bengal Army in 1767, with Indian artillerymen not being employed until 1771. In that year there were 2,291 Indian gunners (with 296 Indian NCOs) and 330 European gunners (with 41 commissioned officers and NCOs). See 'Ninth Report from the Secret Committee, appointed to enquire into the state of the East India Company' (1773), *Reports from Committees of the House of Commons, Vol. IV, East Indies, 1772–1773*, London: House of Commons, 1804, p. 506. The extra expense of maintaining cavalry regiments as compared to infantry battalions, and the fact that it was not until the early 1800s that the Company began to control territory capable of producing large bodies of high-quality horsemen, seriously limited that arm in the Company's service. See Callahan, *East India Company*, p. 4.

10 There were actually 61 regular infantry battalions on the strength of the Bengal Army in 1820 (30 double-battalion sepoy line regiments and the single battalion 1st Bengal Europeans). However, the second battalion of the 20th Bengal Native Infantry Regiment was serving overseas: of its 10 companies, six were at Prince of Wales Island, two at Bencoolen and two

at Singapore. Bengal Military Establishment Annual Statement 1819–20, IOR, L/MIL/8/29.

11 At this time, a company of infantry on active service might be expected to number some 100 men.

12 Bengal Military Establishment Annual Statement 1819–20, IOR, L/MIL/8/29.

13 In 1810, for example, there were some 60 battalions of Company and Crown infantry in mainland India, covering 62 posts in garrisons of between one company and five battalions. See the Bengal Military Establishment Annual Statement 1809–10, IOR, L/MIL/8/19, pp. 5–171. In 1805, the figures seem to hint at an early adoption of the widespread deployment described by Peers. However, the figures are skewed by the absence of 25.5 infantry battalions, away on service with the army assembled for the Second Anglo-Maratha War. The remaining 41.5 battalions were distributed between 35 posts, and, other than the four battalions on service in Bundelkhand, only 10 of these posts were more than a single battalion strong and none had more than two battalions.

14 In 1763, Bengal's regular sepoys were distributed as follows: Fort William (1,090), Gauhati (1,080), Patna (2,822), Burdwan (969), Midnapore (1,456), Chittagong ['Islamabad'] (686), on service in Manipur ['Meckly'] (971), Lakhipur (121), Dhaka (121), Malda (57) and Kasimbazar (121). 'Ninth Report from the Secret Committee', p. 509.

15 *Ibid.*, p. 506.

16 Bengal Military Consultations, 22 January to 31 December 1777, 'Dispositions of all troops under the Presidency of Fort William. Abstract of officers from the returns of the army, August 31st 1777' encl. 24 September 1777, pp. 161–162, IOR, P/18/44.

17 Bengal Military (incomplete) and Civil Statement, 1784–85, pp. 122–172, IOR, L/MIL/8/1.

18 Bengal Military and Civil Statement, 1786–87, pp. 194–258, IOR, L/MIL/8/2.

19 Bengal Military and Civil Statement, 1791–92, pp. 1–6, IOR, L/MIL/8/6.

20 Bengal Military and Civil Statement, 1799–1800, pp. 2–6, IOR, L/MIL/8/10.

21 In 1805, there were 68 battalions of regular infantry (Company and Crown) on the Bengal establishment: 25.5 were serving in the army fighting the Maratha Confederacy, a further four were on service in Bundelkhand, and the remaining 38.5 were distributed over 36 posts, ranging from five companies to two battalions in strength. See the Bengal Military Establishment Annual Statement 1804–05, pp. 214–221, IOR, L/MIL/8/15.

22 Peers, *Between Mars and Mammon*, p. 247.

23 Callahan, *East India Company*, p. 6.

24 In this period, the Bengal Presidency was composed of the province of Bengal (present day West Bengal and Bangladesh), as well as Assam, Bihar, Orissa and Tripura.

25 Bryant, *Emergence of British Power in India*, p. 180.

26 Bryant, 'Pacification in the Early British Raj', p. 3.

27 In this regard, the Company was continuing the pre-colonial defensive system of the *subah* (Mughal province) on its western frontier. Bryant, *Emergence of British Power*, p. 155.

28 Peers, *Between Mars and Mammon*, p. 11.
29 Bryant, *Emergence of British Power*, p. 182.
30 Governor-general's minute, 2 October 1783, IOR, F/4/8/709. The pargana was an administrative sub-unit consisting of several villages which was used for revenue assessment purposes.
31 Governor-general's minute, 2 October 1783, IOR, F/4/8/709.
32 R. Clive to H. Verelst, 19 April 1766, BL Eur MSS. E231, cit. Bryant, 'Pacification in the Early British Raj', p. 8.
33 Governor-general's minute, 2 October 1783, IOR, F/4/8/709.
34 *Ibid.*
35 Extract of Bengal Revenue Consultations, 12 August 1783, IOR, F/4/8/709.
36 The term 'sebundy' (plural 'sebundies') was an Anglo-Indian word used loosely during the 18th century to describe a body of troops employed on revenue service, originating in the Persian *sihbandi*, (*sih* meaning 'three') and signifying three-monthly (quarterly) payments. After the turn of the 19th century, it became identified less with revenue service than with the irregular (and often inferior) quality of troops. As late as 1869 a corps of labourers raised at Darjeeling was denominated 'The Sebundy Corps of Sappers and Miners'. See H. Yule and A. C. Burnell, *Hobson-Jobson: The Definitive Glossary of British India*, K. Teltscher (ed.), Oxford: Oxford University Press, 2013, p. 456.
37 Although the term 'barqandaz' (lit. 'lightning-thrower') originally referred to the early musketeers of the Mughal imperial armies, by the later 18th century, it had also come to signify these mercenary troops who were variously armed and trained. Their poor quality may be inferred from an incident during the 1783 Rangpur peasant rebellion in which a Company subaltern disguised his militia sepoys with white cloth, after which 'the Ding allowed them to come very nigh taking them for Burgundasses, whom they are not affraid of'. A. Macdonald to R. Goodlad, 22 February 1783, W. K. Firminger (ed.), *Bengal District Records: Rangpur, Vol. III, Letters Received: 1783–85*, Calcutta: Bengal Secretariat, 1920, p. 13.
38 Sebundy returns for 1785 in Bengal Military (incomplete) and Civil Statement, 1784–85, pp. 75–77, IOR, L/MIL/8/1.
39 Governor-general's minute, 2 October 1783, IOR, F/4/8/709.
40 Revenue Committee Circular, 25 August 1783, Firminger, *BDR: Rangpur*, III, p. 70.
41 Injunctions from Fort William to keep troops centralised were a common feature of district correspondence in this period, often appended to any communiqué concerning armed force, however tangentially. For example, a letter to the collector of Dhaka on a vaguely related subject ends as follows: 'We also desire that you will strictly adhere to the late Regulations as to the mode of deputing Sepoys into the Mofussil'. Committee of Revenue to M. Day, 12 April 1784, S. Islam (ed.), *Bangladesh District Records: Dacca District, 1784–1787*, Vol. 1, Dhaka: Dhaka University Press, 1981, p. 68.
42 D. H. McDowall to the Board of Revenue, 14 May 1786, W. K. Firminger (ed.), *Bengal District Records: Rangpur, Vol. VI, Letters Issued: 1786–87*, Calcutta: Bengal Secretariat, 1928, pp. 52–54.
43 S. Alavi, 'The Company Army and Rural Society: The Invalid Thanah, 1770 to 1830', *Modern Asian Studies*, 1993, 27(1): 154–156.
44 *Ibid.*, p. 157.
45 Alavi, *The Sepoys and the Company*, pp. 135–143.

4 Rangpur district, 1770–c. 1800

The opening chapters of this book have argued that Indian society closely monitored the conduct of Company servants at the highest levels of government and that it gauged its reaction to that government according to its perception of their capacity to act decisively against dissidents. Further, the previous chapter has established that, while the Company possessed a large standing army, until the 1810s that army was deployed almost exclusively in the west of Bengal, and in large garrisons, strategically sited to defend Company territory against external threats from rival Indian powers. It was not much used for the internal policing of Indian society and it was rarely at the disposal of the Company's collectors, who were routinely allowed only very small numbers of inferior quality troops to secure their districts. The district case studies which follow are intended to detail the scale and character of the resistance which these local officials encountered, and how their reactions to it changed in the decades following the grant of Bengal's diwani.

Rangpur's physical and political geography

Rangpur district, covering an area of some 3,000 square miles in northern Bengal, came under the Company's jurisdiction through the assumption of the diwani in 1765.[1] The district was bounded to the north and north-east by the semi-independent state of Koch Bihar and the district of Jalpaiguri, to the east by the Brahmaputra River, and to the south and west by the Company's districts of Bogra and Dinajpur, respectively.[2] Rangpur's topography was extremely flat with no significant natural elevations of any kind; the soil was fertile and the terrain dotted with numerous small marshes or *bheels*.[3] This saturated landscape provided Rangpur with a particularly rich agricultural economy based primarily around the cultivation of rice, although there was also significant production of indigo, opium and tobacco.

The major characteristic of Rangpur's political geography in this period was its position as a frontier district. Koch Bihar, which became a feudatory of the Company in 1774, acted as a partial buffer against Bhutan to the north-east, but the remainder of the eastern frontier was entirely exposed, and the kingdom of Nepal adjoined Rangpur to the north-west.[4] Boundary disputes with these powerful neighbours were frequent, but the most significant difficulty Rangpur experienced with adjacent states in this period was the series of major incursions made into the raja of Baikanthapur's zamindari in the north of the district by Nepalese border raiders. Perhaps exacerbated by the appearance of governmental incapacity caused by Hastings's detention at Benares in 1781, these incursions became almost an annual occurrence throughout the 1780s, and at their peak, Baikanthapur was harrowed several times in the space of a year. The most serious of these disturbances was the Nepalese subahdar Gungaram Thapa's prolonged occupation during 1786 of the area of Baikanthapur close to the border with Purnea. Further cause for concern lay in the activities of armed religious orders, the Hindu sannyasis and, to a lesser extent, the Muslim faqirs. Organised into a hierarchy under a leader (the *mohunt*) and his principal followers (the *chelas*), the sannyasi mendicants travelled through the province in large bands, seeking employment as mercenaries with local zamindars and forcibly extracting alms from raiyats. Some settled in fortified hermitages in Rangpur's northern thanahs,[5] where they combined banditry and extortion with trade and money-lending.[6] These activities – largely centred around Murshidabad and the forested areas of Baikanthapur – have become collectively known as the Sannyasi Rebellion, although numbers of faqirs were also involved. The drivers behind the disturbances are unclear, but the hardships caused by the great Bengal famine of 1770 and the competition between the Company and the mendicants for the fruits of the raiyats' labour – for revenue and alms, respectively – doubtless played their part. The presence of this large, and potentially violent, body of men, outside the government's control, was perceived as a direct threat by Rangpur's authorities from the 1770s onwards. Until the 1790s, sannyasi resistance remained a serious problem across Bengal, and as late as 1794 the Company's commissioner at Koch Bihar was reporting conflict with bodies of mendicants.[7] Indeed, the discontented peasantry of Rangpur made ready converts to the sannyasa cause, as did those unemployed soldiers who had formerly been retained by local magnates until the Company's attempts at demilitarisation began to take effect. Evidence of this process occurring was apparent in Rangpur from as early as 1770, and, in this way, the ranks of the sannyasis were swelled.[8] The incorporation of former soldiers also meant that the fighting quality of these bands improved markedly over the period, with the collector of Purnea observing in 1795 that the sannyasi bands now contained a strong element 'of Pathans, Rajputs and disbanded sepoys'.[9]

While it could be a violent district by the standards of contemporary Bengal, Rangpur was also considered a very lucrative posting by Company officials. It was made so, not only because of its position on the network of caravan routes between northern India, Bhutan and Nepal, which presented an opportunity for officials to trade, against Company regulations, on their own account, but also because of the district's generous revenue yield, a share of which could be misappropriated by unscrupulous collectors.[10] Indeed, it was such a prized position in the nascent Anglo-Indian civil service that in 1779 an unsuccessful attempt was made to buy out the incumbent collector, George Bogle (better known for his mission as Hastings's ambassador to Tibet in 1774–75), by a would-be successor, Richard Goodlad, for the enormous sum of a *lakh* of rupees.[11] Goodlad clearly considered this to be a sound investment, expecting, with some justification, to make significantly more than 100,000 rupees from the collectorship were it awarded to him.[12] Certainly, Bogle must have felt the same. With his patron Hastings fettered by the Majority in the supreme council, Bogle had struggled to find employment after his return from Lhasa in 1775, and his later appointment to bountiful Rangpur was intended by Hastings as 'a remunerative post' to help him recover his fortunes.[13]

The levying of additional cesses by early Company servants in order to maximise their personal profit was a serious problem across Bengal's districts, particularly prior to Cornwallis's first term as governor-general, when some attempt was made to restrain the avarice of collectors, and Rangpur was no exception to this pattern. In 1770, officials in Rangpur notoriously levied the *mahtaut* (a tax which was originally extorted from the populace for the personal benefit of the nawab's revenue officers), an act which caused outrage when it was reported in Britain.[14] Equally worrying for Fort William was the fact that local Company servants often used the public purse to make private loans, usually to zamindars, profiting from the crippling rates of interest which they could impose. In 1769 and 1770, Captain David Mackenzie, the commander of Rangpur's detachment of pargana sepoys, made loans to local magnates at 60 percent interest (5 percent a month) rising to 169 percent (14 percent a month).[15] Clearly, his position of authority over this body of troops was a distinct advantage in that he could both loan out a portion of the money intended for his men's pay and use the sepoys to enforce the collection of repayments.

Government armed forces in Rangpur

No regular army garrison was present in Rangpur between the 1760s and 1810s, the district being allotted a small number of revenue troops, normally two companies of militia sepoys, or, later, sebundies, augmented by a contingent of varying size, formed of barqandazes. These troops were employed as guards on government buildings and commercial factories, and as escorts to treasure convoys transporting revenue payments. A further part of their role was plugging the gap, caused by the decline of the civilian police, in suppressing banditry, dealing with bands of sannyasis and faqirs, and acting as guards on the district's borders.

The district correspondence reveals that in 1770, a Company force, most likely composed of pargana sepoys, was sent to Rangpur in response to the threat posed by a large group of sannyasis.[16] In 1772, the raja of Baikanthapur made an abortive attempt to wrest control of Koch Bihar from the incumbent raja, which prompted the Company to dispatch two regular battalions of sepoys to Rangpur. One of these, under Captain James Jones, succeeded in driving a considerable body of sannyasis (hired as mercenaries by the raja of Baikanthapur) over the border into Bhutan; the other, under a Captain Stuart, defeated the body of troops under the immediate command of the raja. The emergency being over, the sepoys were then withdrawn.[17]

After this, the security of the district appears to have been neglected for several years, with the barqandazes the only force consistently available to the authorities. In 1778, the collector, Charles Purling, complained that there were no troops with which to counter Nepalese border raiders who had started to harry the population of Baikanthapur.[18] The impression that Rangpur's defences had long been overlooked is reinforced when, upon a force of militia sepoys being assigned to Rangpur in the following year, Purling's assistant, the ambitious Richard Goodlad, observed that because it had been so long since any troops had been based in the district, there were no quarters available for them.[19] In the period between Purling's letter and Goodlad's, the district seems to have been under the sole protection of a small detachment of militia sepoys from Purnea, which Goodlad was soon obliged to return to its original station.[20]

The arrival of the two companies of militia sepoys in August 1779 marked the beginning of a period in which the district authorities could finally call upon the services of a body of at least moderately able troops. The militia, mostly composed of sepoys invalided out of the regular army through age or disability, was disbanded across Bengal in early 1784 and replaced by a roughly equivalent number of less well-trained sebundy sepoys, the Rangpur detachment being in position by May 1784.[21] The deficiencies of the sebundy corps led to it being disbanded within a year and replaced in northern Bengal by a brigade of regular sepoy infantry,[22] with one company of Rangpur's sebundies being taken directly into the service of the rani of Koch Bihar.[23] As the peasant rebellion of 1783, the bloody Rangpur *dhing*, began to take hold, the district was also permitted an allowance, closely monitored by Fort William, for the maintenance of approximately 200 barqandazes as a supplement to the militia.[24] The district correspondence indicates that a number of additional quasi-military forces were employed by the Rangpur authorities throughout the period, either barqandazes or kachari peons, but their numbers were insignificant in comparison with those mobilised during the dhing. Finally, in 1795, the regular army was withdrawn, and from then on the Rangpur garrison was reduced to a single company of sebundy sepoys,[25] until they were replaced by a detachment of the Purnea provincial battalion in 1809.[26]

The armed forces routinely allocated to the Rangpur authorities by Fort William in this period were, then, frequently both meagre and of doubtful quality. With the aim of charting the effects of that under-resourcing on the practice of local government, this chapter will now examine the responses of Company officials in Rangpur to the extensive violent disruption from both internal and external sources which wracked the district during the final quarter of the 18th century.

Internal threats: the Rangpur dhing of 1783

The violent episode for which the district is perhaps best known – the dhing which occurred in the early months of 1783 – reveals conflicting concerns on the part of Rangpur's collector, Richard Goodlad, for both the government's local authority and for the security of his professional standing with his superiors. The trigger for the revolt by Rangpur's peasantry was the extortionate tax levied on them by the Company's revenue farmer in Rangpur, Devi Singh. Between 1765 and 1793, the Company trialled several systems in its attempts to realise fully the revenues of Bengal, and revenue farming was one such experiment. The Company had contracted Devi Singh to collect Rangpur's revenues for a three-year period commencing in 1781. He was given 'both practical and political authority to manage the process of revenue collection and juridical responsibility for ensuring that the cash the Company demanded was delivered each year'.[27] As an outsider to the district, however, Devi Singh had little understanding either of Rangpur's rural politics or the realistic level of its tax yield, and this ignorance was not helped by his frequent absences from the district. According to Goodlad, Devi Singh 'never was in Rungpore but for five weeks before the Disturbances broke out. It was always underfarmed by him to the zemindars'.[28] In 1782, he and his subordinates had managed to collect less than three-quarters of the total revenue anticipated when the tender was made to Fort William.[29] With the government pressuring him for money, he sought to extract all he could from the district's cultivators, allegedly using the most brutal methods of torture to achieve his aim.[30]

In response to this provocation, from the end of December 1782, the outraged cultivators began to combine against Devi Singh's assistants to withhold tax. Many left the fields and assembled in camps outside revenue kacharis in a number of Rangpur's parganas to protest against their treatment. As the dhing grew in strength, the rebels organised their own governing body, appointing a nawab, diwan and other assorted officials from among their ranks. They also levied a 'strike tax' to meet the costs of their protest.[31] After storming several outlying revenue kacharis, the raiyats imprisoned a number of zamindars and forced Devi Singh's revenue officers to flee for their lives. Many of these collectors were then seized and tried by the dhing's leaders.[32] One particularly notorious official, Gourmohan Chaudhuri, was captured alive by the insurgents and taken to their encampment near Dimla, where he was later decapitated and his body mutilated.[33] After a brief lull, in which Goodlad unsuccessfully attempted to restore order by addressing the raiyats' grievances, these events were replicated across the district, with Devi Singh's representative at Kankina being killed by the dhing when he attempted to disperse protesters there by force. The violence continued until the end of February 1783, at which point the district's contingent of sepoys was reinforced by other Company units and the rebellious cultivators were finally suppressed and dispersed.

It has been argued by modern commentators that, for the raiyats, this rebellion was not an attack on the government per se, but rather 'an attempt to assert their ability to negotiate within a flexible political order'.[34] Regardless, it was perceived by the Company's senior administrators as a direct threat to their authority which had to be treated with hostility. Indeed, Fort William was, as much during this period as at the height of its power in the 19th century, 'most firmly resolved to punish in the most exemplary manner' any acts of rebellion.[35] The basic tenet of Anglo-Indian military government was that negotiation implied weakness and that 'swift, decisive action was the only response to armed resistance from within indigenous society'. In this context, the readiest interpretation of 'action' must be the application of armed force. Yet, despite the clear message emanating from the higher echelons of government, the first response of the Rangpur collector to disturbances within his district was not a vigorous, crushing blow, but rather an attempt at negotiation with the insurgents. Richard Goodlad wrote of the rebellious cultivators that 'I should have deemed it cruel to have submitted them to military Chastisement without first hearing what they had to say'.[36] Indeed, in his attempts to quell the dhing through negotiation, he undertook to protect the raiyats from any person who levied unjust taxes on them,[37] and later he went so far as to reduce the levels of taxation to those of a previous assessment.[38] Although he ultimately 'found these lenient measures ineffectual' it is interesting to speculate on why he chose leniency as his first response to the unrest, and why he turned to a more aggressive policy only towards the end of the rebellion.[39]

Even if Goodlad could have immediately suppressed the revolt by armed force, the enormous damage which military operations would (as they ultimately did) cause to the district's agrarian economy, with huge numbers of cultivators killed or forced to flee, made a peaceful, non-disruptive resolution an attractive option. Although it could not sanction resistance to the government's authority, Fort William would not thank a collector for decimating the district's workforce, however rebellious it might be, and thereby throwing the revenues into turmoil for years to come. The collector, his superiors would argue, should never have allowed the raiyats to become so discontented as to have revolted in the first place, overlooking the fact that the Company's servants in Rangpur were under enormous pressure from the Committee of Revenue to realise the maximum possible tax yield for remittance to Calcutta.

In addition to his concern that violence be avoided so as to protect the district's profitability as far as possible, both to appease Fort William and perhaps to ensure a healthy slice of the revenues for himself, Goodlad must have been painfully aware of the limitations of Rangpur's military resources. His initial preference for negotiation can be explained by a belief that the armed force present at Rangpur (two companies of militia and a band of barqandazes) was not equal to the task of putting down a district-wide uprising unaided. This conviction is testified to by his appeal to Purnea for the loan of an additional company of militia and Fort William's agreement with Goodlad's assessment is evident in their dispatching, unrequested, 200 militia sepoys to Rangpur at the end of February 1783.[40] Indeed the precarious nature of the Rangpur administration's military capacity is highlighted by a report from Alexander Macdonald, the lieutenant commanding the government forces operating against the dhing.

> They [the district's militia sepoys] came up with the ding about dawn of the Day, who wer[e] very numerous, and the greater part of them armed with Bows and Arrows, lances & spears, as I advised the Sepoys to disguise themselves, by [c]overing themselves over with white cloths, the Ding allowed them to come very nigh taking them for Burgundasses, whom they are not affraid of.[41]

Although this particular party of insurgents was successfully dispersed, Macdonald's letter casts doubt on the 'moral authority' which the Rangpur administration could expect to draw from its military establishment. The standing force in the district at the onset of the dhing consisted of the two companies of militia under Macdonald augmented by some 300 barqandazes.[42] If, as Macdonald asserts, the peasantry was 'not afraid' of the barqandazes, then it is reasonable to suppose that the gangs of dakaits, sannyasis, faqirs and border raiders which beset the district held them in equal contempt. It is also possible that it was not simply a lack of martial skill and equipment that emboldened the rebels. As the barqandazes, being raised locally, were known to the raiyats, and perhaps also were periodically cultivators themselves, it is likely that they were to some degree sympathetic with the dhing's aims. In any case, Goodlad must have realised that more than half of Rangpur's armed forces, the prop of the local government, were of a very doubtful quality, and, more importantly, the behaviour of the insurgents suggests that the local populace were aware of it. This reasoning helps explain his actions during the previous summer, when he recruited 100 more barqandazes than Fort William permitted.[43] If he could not request regular troops without jeopardising his credit with the government, then his next best resort was to strengthen the locally raised contingent. While this may have risked harbouring elements with questionable loyalty, it at least took them out of circulation for a time and placed them on the district's payroll, rather than leaving them among the ranks of its potential adversaries.

The weakness of Rangpur's armed forces at the onset of the dhing made it clear to Goodlad that external aid was urgently required to end the rebellion, but an appeal to Fort William for military relief would have been viewed as an admission of failure by both the collector and the central government. The collector's early negotiation with the rebels, stemming from his inability to put down the dhing swiftly and convincingly with his immediate armed force, can be seen as an attempt to resolve the crisis quietly before it had the chance to adversely affect his standing in Fort William by disrupting the revenue stream. It is notable that even when his dialogue with the insurgents had failed, as was obviously the case by the middle of February, he appealed to the neighbouring district of Purnea for military aid, but still made no direct requests to the central government. Although the proximity of Purnea meant that its company of militia would have arrived in the troubled area well before any force sent by Fort William, the scale of the unrest, described by Goodlad as 'the most formidable that ever happened in Bengal', clearly warranted greater reinforcement than Purnea alone could muster.[44] It would certainly be taking the point too far to suggest that any notable level of camaraderie, arising from the shared experience of the difficulties of local administration, existed between collectors in different districts. These men were rivals in the Company's service, with the welfare of their own districts, and careers, to consider, and nothing more than a calculated provision of the minimum of assistance could be expected. However, Rangpur's collectors were far readier to ask their neighbours in Purnea for a loan of troops than they were to appeal to Fort William for aid, a preference demonstrated not only during the dhing, but, as will be seen, in many other cases of violent unrest throughout the period. The primary concern of the collector was the nurturing of his reputation for competence and self-sufficiency with his superiors, and avoiding calls for help to Fort William was a crucial part of his strategy.

The maintenance of this reputation, with the forces immediately to hand, was not an easy task. Fort William's attempts to curb the local autonomy of the collectors went beyond restrictions placed on troop numbers and deployment, which have been examined in the previous chapter: the executive powers which the collector could legitimately exercise in an emergency were also kept in check by the central government, as Goodlad made clear in a letter to Macdonald at the height of the unrest.

> If I adhere strictly to the Letter of my authority, it will be impossible for us to remain in the district, and as a disturbance so violent never before happened in Bengal, and is consequently not provided against by Government, I am obliged of my own accord to adopt such measures as I deem most essential for the Public safety, and as I have tried every plan that could be dictated by humanity for quieting this disturbance, and all in vain, I must now see what effect [severity] will have on them . . .[45]

As with the Committee of Revenue's circular of August 1783, which railed against the common practice of scattering a district's troops in small, widely dispersed garrisons, there is evidence here of a pronounced gap between the theoretical authority which Fort William was prepared to delegate to the collector and the pragmatic exercise of power which the collector judged necessary to keep the district functioning.[46] In his letter to Macdonald of 13 February, Goodlad authorised the hanging of insurgents without any legal process whatsoever 'as a public Example';[47] a policy which his lieutenant wasted little time in implementing.[48] Clearly, the imposition of summary executions exceeded the collector's authority. However, Goodlad was forced to choose between acting within the limits of Fort William's sanction and allowing his district (and his career) to be ravaged, or to use his initiative and perhaps save his district, but by means which would damn him in the eyes of his superiors if they were not immediately successful. In justification of his conduct to the Committee of Revenue, Goodlad talked of the necessity of taking 'the most active and vigorous exertions' while hampered by the 'little authority invested in me', but the fact remained that Fort William's attention had been drawn to his mishandling of the crisis before he could present them with a *fait accompli*.[49] The necessity of his resorting to such measures when the restraining of Devi Singh's excesses during 1782 might have prevented the rebellion, or the early use of punitive military action halted it less violently, incurred the government's extreme disapproval.[50]

With the whole district in an uproar, and by the second week of February 1783, Goodlad was forced to abandon the pretence that normal administrative functions could be carried on. As he observed in a letter to Macdonald, 'It is needless in the present state of the Country to look for any more revenue'.[51] He also ordered Macdonald to concentrate his forces, even though this amounted to the public relinquishment of the government's control over large parts of Rangpur.[52] In that climate of open rebellion, maintaining the revenue troops in scattered outposts invited either their desertion or destruction in detail by the incensed raiyats, and the slightest hint of a military reverse would have encouraged the dhing, damaged the government's prestige and dealt a significant blow to Goodlad's professional prospects.

The collector could, then, misrepresent the scale of his district's problems for his own sake until the point where they began to impact seriously on the revenue stream. It was at that juncture, when concealment of the financial disruption became impossible, that Fort William would begin to take an increasingly close interest in events and were the status quo ante not immediately restored, an increasingly critical stance towards their agent. Goodlad's admission in mid-February that events were effectively moving beyond his control was met with a letter from the Committee of Revenue stating, 'We are of opinion that the Disorders which have arisen may be easiest obviated by your personal Interposition'.[53] This reply suggests that Goodlad was right to consider a request to Fort William for military aid as professionally damaging to himself: the Committee judged that Goodlad had badly neglected his duties and that his implicit appeal for reinforcements was both an unnecessary extravagance and proof of his professional incompetence. This impression is reinforced by the Committee's letter of the following week, announcing the appointment of a special commissioner, John Paterson – whose reports on the causes of the Rangpur dhing were later to furnish useful material for Edmund Burke's impeachment of Warren Hastings[54] – to bring the district back under control and to determine the causes of the dhing.[55]

This move was a pointed expression of Fort William's lack of confidence in Richard Goodlad's professional abilities and was, one imagines, precisely the kind of development that he had originally hoped to avoid by resolving the unrest through negotiation. His only hope of maintaining his position had lain in a comparatively quiet resolution of the uprising; the sanguinary punitive operations which followed sealed his fate. As far as Fort William was concerned, the end justified the means. Whether Goodlad had been innocent or complicit in causing the dhing, whether his conduct as violence erupted around him had been professional or partial, responsibility for that end – the mayhem which paralysed Rangpur's administration in the winter of 1783 – would be laid at his door.

Goodlad's principal concern throughout much of the dhing seems to have been to portray himself to Fort William as a competent district administrator acting in a manner which would meet with his superiors' approval. His desire for a favourable public appraisal is revealed in his post-dhing entreaty to Hastings's close friend and confidant David Anderson: 'I have a Character to lose – a Character dearer to me than all the appointments under the sun'.[56] While this sentiment may be genuine, the vehemence with which he pursued the Rangpur collectorship and the violence which he displayed in trying to retain it suggest that in reality Goodlad was principally concerned with the way in which his public character would affect his professional career, and his subsequent capacity to accrue wealth. However, his reluctance to draw Fort William's attention to his shortcomings by appealing for help at the start of 1783, far from safeguarding his reputation, actually allowed the dhing to grow in strength and ultimately invited the censure of his superiors.

Goodlad, who had been so very keen to buy out George Bogle for the collectorship, now found that his tenure of this coveted post was to be seriously curtailed. The Board of Revenue decided it was convenient to treat him as if he had been complicit in Devi Singh's reign of terror or, at best, a 'patient witness of all these cruelties', content to receive the revenues from the farmer's hands without inquiring closely enough as to his methods.[57] Indeed, upon receipt of Paterson's initial findings, the Board peremptorily dismissed Goodlad from office and replaced him with his erstwhile assistant Peter Moore, who was charged with examining the events surrounding the dhing and verifying Paterson's discoveries. Given that the new collector, in addition to being no friend of Goodlad's, was Devi Singh's 'most inveterate enemy', it was exceedingly unlikely that he would present his predecessor's conduct in a favourable light, particularly if it might lead to Goodlad's reinstatement in the prized Rangpur collectorship.[58]

Goodlad railed against his accusers, declaring that Devi Singh's crimes were much exaggerated ('I cannot answer for things I never heard of, that I believe did never exist')[59] and defending his conduct with indignation.

> I know not upon my word what the Board can call on me to answer. I can tell them that I supported D' Sing and that it was my Duty so to do; that he the first year paid his rents with regularity that highly pleased Government. I myself had nothing to do with the minutiae of the Collections of either district. D Sing was farmer and dewan – nobody complained of him, he paid up his rents and I supported him.[60]

Unfortunately for Goodlad, after the fiasco of the dhing, no defence could have saved him from the censure of the Board, and he was soon reconciled to being 'held forth as . . . Collector of the District where enormities were committed unheard of in the annals of Time'.[61] Once the Rangpur commission had been set in motion, he remained unemployed until 1787, when he was briefly posted as collector of Goraghat. Then, after another period of unemployment he worked as the Company's salt agent at 24 Parganas throughout the 1790s, until, finding himself without employment yet again, he returned to Europe in 1800.

However, even if Goodlad's career was not exactly sparkling after the dhing, it is notable that he was not prosecuted, nor even dismissed from the Company's service. Indeed, he remained prosperous enough to maintain an estate and country house at Baruipur in the district of 24 Parganas (painted by the celebrated artist Balthazar Solvyns in

1793),[62] and on his return to England, he took up residence in a 'capital modern mansion' in Hampshire[63] and retained enough influence to later be made Sheriff of the county.[64] In contrast, Judge John Paterson, upon returning to Fort William from Rangpur, discovered that it was he, rather than Goodlad, who was more likely to face trial. The very people who had engaged him to head the commission now questioned his veracity. Employed, one suspects, simply to smooth matters over, Paterson's revelation of widespread corruption in Rangpur found little favour at the highest levels of government. Warren Hastings himself publicly declared that the collector was innocent of any crime: 'I entirely acquit Mr Goodlad of all the charges . . . I so well know [his] character'.[65] In 1781, Goodlad had been recommended to David Anderson by George Bogle as a suitable person to join the governor-general's circle of intimates, and this patronage may account for his relatively mild treatment.[66] In contrast, Paterson was made the subject of forgery charges laid against him by Devi Singh, who claimed that the judge had falsified testimony to secure a conviction. In the words of Edmund Burke, addressing Parliament during the later impeachment of Warren Hastings, Paterson was reduced by degrees from 'a Commissioner to report; then an accuser to make good his charge; then a party accused', and so the findings of the commission were gradually discredited.[67]

Although Goodlad was widely deemed culpable for having permitted Devi Singh's atrocities, perhaps in return for bribes, and was censured in Parliament for his brutal suppression of the dhing – his 'conduct was terrible indeed', declared Burke[68] – the embarrassment of his superiors at having allowed such a state of affairs to develop as occurred in Rangpur may have afforded him a degree of indirect protection. Just as Goodlad feared the wrath of his employers, and was reluctant to appeal for help to put down the dhing, so too did Fort William fear the scrutiny of the Court of Directors and the British government. The concealment of unpalatable facts from superiors seems to have occurred at all levels of the Company's service, and had Warren Hastings done any less than clear Goodlad unconditionally, this would have been seen as an implicit admission of the inadequacy, and brutality, of the Company's provincial government in Bengal.

External threats: Nepalese raids into Baikanthapur, 1778–86

While the dhing of 1783 posed a serious threat to the Company's authority in Rangpur through its attack on the internal structures of cultivation and revenue collection, it took place in the context of a period of wider disruptions in the district, caused by external elements from neighbouring Nepal. These were the incursions into Baikanthapur, a zamindari covering more than 300 square miles in the north of the district, by Nepalese border raiders between 1778 and 1786. The first reference made to Nepalese raiders on the borders of Baikanthapur occurs in a letter of March 1778 from Rangpur's collector, Charles Purling, to the governor-general Warren Hastings.[69] This first encounter exposed a serious deficiency in the local administration: Purling was writing to complain that there were no armed forces based at Rangpur with which to oppose the raiders. The petition of the raja of Baikanthapur's diwan neatly sums up the case.

> The zemindars of Putcheem Bootgong have, for this year past, been plundering the country and enticing away ryots. On which account the Company's revenue has not been collected. I petitioned you several times for a few sepoys to drive the people away, but no attention has been paid to my applications. You ordered me to entertain some burkundoses for the defence of my country. I therefore built a little fort or place of defence upon the borders of my country to keep them out [the raiders] took the fort [and] afterwards plundered four or five villages . . . I am a poor zemindar. I cannot entertain a sufficient number of people to contend with them.[70]

The complaint that there was no armed force present at Rangpur with which to defend the raiyats against the depredations of various groups was repeated by Richard Goodlad, in his capacity as assistant collector, in 1779.[71] The immediate withdrawal of the raiders appears to have precluded any decisive action that the central government may have felt inclined to take, but shortly afterwards, in 1780, another collector of Rangpur, George Bogle, again referred to problems in that quarter.[72] Gungaram Thapa, the Nepalese subahdar of a border district near Gorakhpur,[73] had not only raided Baikanthapur but also occupied the Company's territory.[74] As a frontier subahdar, Gungaram enjoyed a degree of autonomy from the government at Kathmandu. According to a later collector of Rangpur, he had abused this autonomy and was 'a low man of a bold and [daring] Disposition', who had 'wrested several districts from their rightful Owners and by that means rendered himself in some shape independent' from the Nepalese raja.[75] Keen to enrich himself, and finding that he was unable to pay his establishment of 700 soldiers from the resources of his own district, Gungaram authorised several raids into Baikanthapur so that they might 'pay themselves by plunder'.[76] A dispute between a group of border zamindars (headed by the raja of Baikanthapur) and a local faujdar had presented the subahdar with this prospect of further territorial aggrandisement. The feud had resulted in the death of the faujdar, and now his son, one Munzaram, had brought a mercenary force to Baikanthapur's borders and was laying waste to the zamindars' estates. In desperation, the zamindars had appealed to Kathmandu for aid (it says much about local perceptions of the Company's lack of capacity to intervene that no appeal was made to Rangpur town), and Gungaram was ordered to the area. Seeing an opportunity for gain, the Nepalese subahdar drove out Munzaram, but then promptly occupied the zamindars' territory on the grounds that they had not remunerated him sufficiently for his services. A sternly worded correspondence ensued between Bogle and Gungaram, with the subahdar finally withdrawing into his own territory, motivated, one suspects, more by fear of a counter-attack from the allied forces of Munzaram and the zamindars – newly reconciled by the presence of a common enemy and reinforced by 1,000 men under the raja of Baikanthapur – than by the prospect of direct action by the Company.[77] Bogle took advantage of the stand-off between the two groups to send a company of militia sepoys, half of Rangpur's garrison, to occupy a position on the Mahananda River and to keep the peace between Gungaram and his opponents, but the district's limited forces could not be tied up like this indefinitely, and they were soon withdrawn. In early 1786, William Amherst, the acting collector of Rangpur, received complaints that Gungaram was again raiding Baikanthapur in earnest. The woeful inadequacy of a force commanded by a junior Company officer which was sent to oppose him encouraged his belligerence and it was only at this point, after some eight years of plundering Company subjects, that a battalion of regular sepoys was ordered to pursue him into Nepalese territory and put an end to his activities.

It could be argued that the military prestige necessary to limit resistance to the Rangpur administration was supplied by the Company's regular army, which, although not stationed in the district, was an ever-present threat, held over the heads of the population, and which could be used in times of crisis, as it was in Baikanthapur during 1786. However, this ignores questions about the extent of the local population's knowledge of an army which it rarely, if ever, came into direct contact with, as compared with the scanty revenue forces actually based in the locality.[78] It also overlooks the fact that a situation damaging to the reputation of the Company's government in Rangpur had been allowed to carry on for several years before the regular army was deployed there. In the intervening period, the authority of the Rangpur administration was based primarily on the actions of its officials in dealing with the Nepalese threat. These actions were dictated to a great extent by the forces available for their immediate use, and these forces were, in the main, a paltry number of militia sepoys or sebundies augmented with ill-equipped barqandazes.

The failure to deal with the raiders when the pillaging began in 1778 set a precedent which effectively guaranteed an escalation in their activities. The government had failed to protect its subjects and in so doing had not safeguarded its prime interest in generating revenue. The raja of Baikanthapur was able to withhold revenue payments from the Rangpur authorities on the grounds that his lands had been devastated and his raiyats 'enticed away' by the raiders.[79] Whether or not he exaggerated his difficulties – and several collectors in this period suspected that he did – the Company's weak local administration, by its failure to protect Rangpur's inhabitants, had allowed him to argue such a case convincingly. It also encouraged him to claim later that he should be given a large tract of land on the border with Bhutan in compensation for his losses.[80]

It is not unreasonable to suppose that, as well as the revenue, the prestige of Rangpur's toothless government suffered from these raids, both in the eyes of its subjects in Baikanthapur and its enemies across the border. In 1778, Charles Purling was unable to assert the Company's authority as a ruler because he had nothing to assert it with. The bluff involved in creating a facade of military strength might be brought off with very few troops, but with absolutely no material to work with the Company was made to look timid, unable to protect either its subjects or its territory. Nor, apparently, did Purling's appeal to Fort William for aid meet with any immediate success, as it was not until the August of the following year that two companies of militia sepoys were ordered to be stationed in the district.[81]

Neither can the actions of Purling's successor George Bogle have greatly enhanced local opinion of the Company's power in Rangpur. When a renewal of hostilities between Gungaram and the faction headed by Munzaram threatened in April 1780, Bogle was unable to intervene convincingly in the dispute. The troops at his disposal, rather fewer than 200 militia sepoys, were simply not enough to overawe the protagonists. The combined forces of Munzaram, the raja of Baikanthapur and Gungaram appear to have run into the thousands, and Bogle's available force was further weakened by the detachments which were required throughout the district.[82] The two companies of militia could not be concentrated at Baikanthapur without dangerously weakening the government's grip on the rest of Rangpur, especially the area immediately around the district headquarters at Rangpur town. In addition to this, the failure to meet Gungaram's menacing demands for money from the northern zamindars with a display of force can only have weakened the raja's faith in an administration that had already demonstrated either an inability or unwillingness to protect him.[83] From this position of weakness, Bogle was forced to adopt a feeble neutrality in response to a situation which threatened the further invasion of Company territory and renewed armed conflict involving its subjects. Intelligence that the raja of Baikanthapur had raised a force to attack Gungaram in conjunction with Munzaram and that Nepalese forces were marching to the subahdar's aid, forced Bogle to attempt to halt the escalation of this conflict. Clearly, with the forces at his disposal he could not hope to contend for control of the district in the fluid, not to say chaotic, environment of open warfare, and so he desperately needed to keep the peace. However, when he ordered Munzaram in the name of the Company to disband his army he was, unsurprisingly, ignored.[84] Bogle lacked the force to make him disarm, and he could not undertake to protect Munzaram and the Baikanthapur raja if he did comply. Bogle's next action was to dispatch a company of militia sepoys under a subedar to Baikanthapur with orders to prevent either party crossing the Mahananda River with hostile intent.[85] The inadequacy of this measure is testified to by his immediate appeal for support to the neighbouring district of Purnea, but the administration there was also troubled by Nepalese incursions,[86] this time on the Morung border, and the reply demonstrates an equally poor state of defence.

> The few Seapoys stationed in this Division will not admit of our detaching [at] present a Force sufficient to have any immediate good Effect; but we have issued a Perwannah agreeable to your Intimation to the Surjapore Zemindar directing him to watch the motions of the Nepaul People, & to give us the earliest Information of their Approach . . . also to resist any Attempts they may make to cross the Mahanada, and as far as lies in his Power to prevent any Incursions & Disturbances on the frontier Purgunnahs.[87]

The weakness of the force available to the Rangpur collectorate was clearly not an isolated case among the frontier districts. Furthermore, having publicly failed to protect the raja of Baikanthapur from attack, the government was now reduced to appealing to another of its subjects, the zamindar of Surjapur, to take responsibility for the defence of the Company's own territory against the aggression of the Nepalese raiders. As if the credit of the Company in Rangpur could fall no lower, the long-suffering population of Baikanthapur were attacked from a different and unexpected quarter: the subedar in charge of the sepoys sent by Bogle for their defence had taken advantage of his independent command to wreak havoc throughout the region, as a petition forwarded to the collector illustrates.

> [The] Subahdar without any occasion has sent for and taken several Ryotts, and commits great Oppression & he has beat several of them. On which Account [many] of the Ryotts have Absconded, and the rest are [much] alarmed and on the point of following the Others example. The Subahdar is sent for the Protection of the Ryotts and the Boundaries, but instead of that he himself commits the most Extravagant Oppression.[88]

This was by no means an isolated incident, and complaints were frequently made about the conduct of Rangpur's unruly sepoys towards the district's population.[89] It seems rather ironic that what little force the Rangpur administration was able to spare for the defence of Baikanthapur actively damaged the Company's interests there, adding to the raiders' activities in disrupting the agrarian workforce and perhaps turning the popular image of the Company's government in that place from what was already that of a weak or indifferent ruler into one of a despot. Certainly, the presence of this negligible border guard can have played little part in the suspension of hostilities between Gungaram and Munzaram, which occurred shortly afterwards. This seems to have owed more to there being no very decided advantage of numbers on either side and to the onset of the rainy season swelling the Mahananda River to the extent where an opposed crossing would have been extremely hazardous.

The inability of both Purling and Bogle to take decisive action against the raiders stemmed from the key problem of a lack of government armed force in the district. Purling's inaction set a dangerous precedent that encouraged future raids and Bogle's position was undermined by this. It is not unreasonable to suppose that Purling's inability to support the raja in 1778 had a bearing on Munzaram's disobedience to Bogle's order in 1780. In this, it is possible to see the earlier damage to the government's prestige impacting on its capacity to control later events. Bogle, with both an insufficient force and unreliable subordinates, attempted to impose the Company's authority as a sovereign power in Baikanthapur and found himself largely discounted as a player in this dispute. The display of force necessary to offset the earlier damage to the administration's local prestige was quite beyond his resources. His order to Munzaram, nominally a subject of the Company, to disband his forces was ignored because it was obvious that the collector had no power to make him do so or to safeguard him if he did. The raja of Baikanthapur, the 'poor zemindar' who, having been bested by the Company's army over his bid for Koch Bihar in 1772, had submitted himself to its protection and been failed, had now been obliged to levy a force for his own defence which was, if the reports are accurate, some five times larger than that which Bogle could muster for the entire district. The statement that this made about the Company's lack of capacity for local intervention must have been obvious to all parties concerned.

Although several years passed in which the collectors reported no really significant disturbance in Baikanthapur, the Nepalese raiders had not been permanently deterred. By 1786, the militia and sebundy revenue troops had been disbanded, and, apart from a small force of barqandazes stationed at Rangpur town, the business of securing the frontier districts had fallen to the army, which kept three infantry battalions circulating in the region. In February of that year the acting collector, William Amherst, received complaints of renewed and very serious attacks on Baikanthapur by Gungaram and by a large number of sannyasis and faqirs. The Nepalese raiders had committed their most serious attack yet, carrying off 100 raiyats and 400 cattle, and killing a number of people who tried to resist them.[90] Accordingly, Amherst dispatched William Duncanson, the ensign commanding Rangpur's small detachment of irregulars, to the border with orders to 'act, as you may deem proper' and with a public 'letter of encouragement' to boost the morale of the raiyats of Baikanthapur.[91] Upon his arrival, Duncanson found that there were some 800 faqirs and 300 of Gungaram's troops in the immediate vicinity, in addition to a group of adherents who supported a rival claimant against the current raja as ruler of Baikanthapur.[92] To meet this threat, Duncanson had 17 sepoys, of whom only 12 possessed firearms, and 20 barqandazes, who were armed only with spears. As he admitted frankly to his chief, the enemy 'would make but a mouth full of me'.[93] The presence of so many seemingly disparate groups – armed mendicants, bandits, raiders and would-be usurpers – in company with each other, united by nothing except contempt for the Rangpur authorities, indicates that the Company's failure to deal with the raiders had resulted in the fringes of its territory being filled with a multitude of discontented individuals.[94]

Gungaram, by his indifference to the Rangpur collectors, had advertised that the district's northern borderland was a safe haven for all those unhappy with their lot under the rule of the Company or that of neighbouring states, and who wished to enrich themselves at the expense of local society.

Upon discovering that Duncanson's force was in the vicinity, the Nepalese subahdar wrote to him, threatening to attack if he did not deliver up Munzaram and Mohadif, his opponents in 1781, who were still taking refuge in Baikanthapur.[95] He further insisted that Duncanson should meet him in person and alone to hear his demands.[96] Despite the fact that this meeting, which Duncanson later described with some understatement as 'a disagreeable situation' was clearly very dangerous indeed, he decided that a display of confidence was the best way to deal with the raiders.[97]

> [I] rode across but no sooner had I gone into the River but 150 of his Men [ran down] to me . . . I rode through them without pretending to heed them to where he was, they all crowded about me with their pieces presented . . . I desire[d] he would make them go back while I spoke to him, but he seemed to have no Command . . . I then again told him he had done wrong in going into the Companys Country seizing and murdering Reyots . . . I told them the Company would not permit it, that the Bykuntpore Reyots were theirs & must be protected.[98]

His insistence that Munzaram and Mohadif were subjects of the Company and must be tried in a Company court made the statement that the Company was a power in the region, and that by cooperating with it, Gungaram could achieve his ostensible purpose, while avoiding the risk inherent in armed conflict. Without the backing of a significant armed force, Duncanson's implied threat was an empty one, but it was the only course of action open to the Rangpur administration since attempts to appease the Nepalese subahdar would have been useless. As Duncanson related to his chief, 'I believe if those men were Delivered to them tomorrow they would have something farther to demand & that nothing but a Regt [would] bring them to terms'.[99] The extent to which this bold front would have been successful in forestalling Gungaram's aggression cannot be known because the presence of the regular army in the region finally led to a battalion of Bengal Native Infantry being detached for service in Baikanthapur.

The district having been denied any sizeable armed force for so long, the collector of Rangpur, D. H. McDowall, newly promoted in January

1786 to the collectorship from his post as Company resident at Tripura, seized upon the temporary presence of the battalion to resolve a number of outstanding issues.[100] Nathan Alexander, the captain in charge of the detachment sent to Baikanthapur, was ordered to expel the raiders from the Company's territory and to seize the ringleaders, while at the same time, for the purpose of revenue assessment, he was to determine the legitimacy of the raja's claim that his lands had been comprehensively devastated by the occupation. After the resolution of this conflict, which had now dragged on for eight years, he was to deal with another perennial problem, that of sannyasi depredations, and was ordered to pursue a large band, headed by one Musa Shah,[101] and drive them out of Rangpur,[102] while further detachments were detailed to counter other bodies of sannyasis at Kazirhat and Ghoraghat.[103]

McDowall's aggressive conduct marked a distinct break with the policy of Rangpur's previous collectors and was informed by several converging factors. In the first instance, he had, for the time being, a body of regular troops at his disposal, which was both of a much higher quality and significantly larger than the paramilitary garrison that had been the main resource of his predecessors; this in itself provided him with a great deal of confidence to stamp his authority on the district. Furthermore, he was newly arrived at a post with a serious, perennial problem, a problem which previous collectors had been unable to tackle for want of military resources. In Captain Alexander's sepoys, McDowall now had the necessary resources, but he had no way of knowing for how long the battalion would remain. Therefore, he had to act at once, to strike a decisive blow against Gungaram while he had Alexander with him, or else risk the battalion's withdrawal and then be forced to spend the rest of his term of office at Rangpur adopting the unsatisfactory, passive stance of his predecessors. Added to this already potent motivation was the question of his standing within the Company's hierarchy. His career in India had been steady rather than stellar; the promotion to Rangpur had been hard won after 11 years as an assistant collector in Burdwan, a stint as an investigator for enforcing revenue collection in the same district, and then the residency of Tripura. Therefore, in Gungaram Thapa and Nathan Alexander he had the elements necessary to improve his position in life. The routing of Gungaram would, in theory, be easily effected; this would attract the good opinion of his superiors at very little risk to himself, improving his career prospects in proportion to his improved standing at Fort William, while at the same time lending him a degree of martial glory, which, from both a social and professional point of view, was highly desirable.[104]

In his communication with Gungaram, McDowall's actions and the tone of his language demonstrate an aggression that was absent with the earlier collectors, and this aggression was mirrored by the battalion's commanding officer, Nathan Alexander. Unlike Duncanson, the captain was not inclined to negotiate with Gungaram or to try to convince him of the wisdom of pursuing his aims through the Company's courts, as his letter illustrates.

> The Honble Company has been pleased to order me with my Battalion to require satisfaction. I therefore on the part of the Honble Company demand that you do immediately deliver over to me all the Ryots, cattle &c you have carried off from the Honble Company's provinces. I shall Expect your answer by the Evening of this Day, in failure of which I shall consider you as an Enemy by invading your country; and retaliate the insults offered the Honble Company.[105]

In their correspondence, both the collector and the captain frequently referred to the demanding of 'satisfaction' and the avenging of 'insults'. Indeed, McDowall seemed almost incapable of writing a letter without endlessly repeating those very words. Although it is applicable to the perceived loss of prestige on the part of the Company caused by the unchecked raids, this language is also strongly reminiscent of an affront to personal honour and suggests that McDowall saw this as something more than simply a scheme calculated to remove a hindrance to the Company's government in Rangpur. The tone of the Nepalese subahdar's reply, in keeping with that of Alexander and McDowall, also has more the quality of a personal feud about it than of correspondence between the representatives of two local powers.

> [You] mean to put me in confinement and carry me before the presence of the Company. This may be done – but on that day you will see what colour will be produced when iron is beat against iron – I am not like the fumes of the poppey that ascend and dissipate – Neither am I like unto a Cucumber to be taken and eaten . . . 'I hold the bridle and will not turn out of my road, I will sacrifice my Head or Seize your Crown'.[106]

Even before he received this 'insolent' and 'extraordinary' reply,[107] McDowall had stated, 'It is absolutely Necessary that . . . conduct of this Nature be not passed over with Impunity'.[108] This was a notion that previous collectors might also have been willing to support, had they enjoyed, as McDowall did, the means to respond forcefully. As it was, it had been safer for them to ignore Gungaram's provocation. The language used by both Alexander and McDowall was intemperate, in marked contrast with that of Bogle, who, well aware of the weakness of his military position and not needing to improve his already high standing at Fort William by any dangerous, drastic action, had merely sought to be assertive. He had never gone so far as to make specific threats or to take decisive measures which may have miscarried and left him in a worse position. The increased aggression of McDowall's official correspondence, arising from the confidence generated among the Company's servants by the presence of the battalion in Baikanthapur, provoked the Nepalese subahdar's colourful and unequivocal statement of hostility. This provided further grounds for McDowall to take the action that he deemed necessary. On the 1 March 1786 he ordered Alexander to cross the border and 'take satisfaction' for Gungaram's 'reiterated insults' to the government.[109] This invasion led to the storming of a Nepalese border fort by Alexander's men and Gungaram's hurried retreat deeper into Nepal.[110] It also brought down charges of wanton aggression on McDowall's head from both Kathmandu and Calcutta.

The cases of Purling and Bogle demonstrate the danger caused to the Company's governmental authority by an immediate lack of armed force, which allowed public slights to the Company to go unpunished. The case of McDowall exhibits the corresponding danger in allowing the man on the spot access to significant military resources. McDowall's triumphant letter reporting the 'reparation of the Insults which had been offered to the Government'[111] did not meet with the expected response from the Board of Revenue, which hurriedly replied that 'as we are not authorised to commence hostilities we disapprove of this Order and desire you will forthwith countermand it – at the same time directing Captain Alexander to confine his operations to the defence of your province'.[112]

In justification of his actions, McDowall argued that surely the government's intention in sending the battalion was not simply to drive out the raiders, but to 'prevent a repetition of the enormities which had been Committed'.[113] As Alexander reported soon after his arrival in Baikanthapur,

> Many of the Riots have returned to their Villages and again employ themselves in cultivating the lands, But they seem to dread the consequence of the Troops being withdrawn without chastising the Goorkas who they say will again invade them, and the consequence will be that the Country will be entirely deserted.[114]

The principle of concentrating the regular army, as outlined in the previous chapter, was well established, and the government was unwilling to station a battalion in the threatened area indefinitely. Once it had been withdrawn, Rangpur's barqandazes alone would not be sufficient to defend Baikanthapur from the Nepalese raids. Therefore, McDowall decided to put an end to the matter at once by defeating the raiders, in their own territory if necessary, while he had the capacity to do so. To have acted otherwise would have been to put himself in the unenviable position of his predecessors: desperately trying to maintain enough stability with his scanty district forces to persuade the cultivators to remain and thereby ensure the satisfactory remittance of revenue to Calcutta. His actions demonstrate assumptions about the use of armed force which, far from being rooted in the calculating strategy for state security which would later characterise the Empire of Opinion school, were actually informed by a visceral, emotional response to the Nepalese threat and a desire to protect his personal position within the Company's hierarchy. Rangpur's previous collectors were constrained by the absence of armed force sufficient to put down this low-level raiding. McDowall, provided with the means to stop the raids had, within a week of his arrival in Rangpur, potentially elevated the situation from a border disturbance to a full-scale war with a sovereign power. Alexander's sepoys were perfectly capable of defeating the raiders, but they could not protect Rangpur from a concerted attack by the raja of Nepal, who might quite justifiably have viewed Alexander's invasion as a declaration of war. Indeed, the battalion having retreated into Baikanthapur, there was a build-up of Nepalese forces along the border which caused Alexander to send for help[115] and committed the government to sending the remainder of the regular army in the frontier districts to his aid.[116]

The maintenance of prestige in a situation where the Company's forces were so thinly spread required a careful calculation of whether the benefits of defeating Gungaram, and thereby reassuring the population of Baikanthapur and securing the revenue, justified the risk of being drawn into an expensive and arduous campaign in Nepal.[117] Clearly, they did not, but, fortunately, the raja of Nepal 'fully disavowed the conduct of Gungaram Tappah',[118] who was reported by the Company's battalion commander in the area to have been put 'in Irons and close confinement',[119] and let McDowall off with a mild reproof for invading his country.[120] The collector, ever sensitive to matters touching his prestige, would not tolerate even this criticism. Choosing, presumably for the benefit of his employers, to lend his personal concerns a more acceptable, national colouring, he replied that the raja should understand that 'the English Nation has never yet suffered an indignity to them to pass with impunity'.[121] Following this episode, however, his career in the Company's service hardly went from strength to strength; indeed, it was terminated a very few years later. Although he was permitted to remain in post at Rangpur, he retired in 1790 (being replaced by Rangpur's former collector Charles Purling) and returned to England.[122] Although his unauthorised invasion of Nepal in 1786 had caused the Board of Revenue to censure him, McDowall's actions found favour with the acting governor-general, Sir John Macpherson, and this may explain why he was allowed to continue at Rangpur despite having perpetrated a highly embarrassing, and potentially costly, diplomatic blunder. Macpherson announced to the Board that he was 'entirely approving of the conduct of Mr McDowall', although he included the caveat 'that you cannot too strongly recommend to Mr McDowall to preserve in future a good understanding with the Goorka Government'.[123] The Board of Revenue was deeply unimpressed with McDowall's self-aggrandising behaviour throughout the crisis, and it seems that, were it not for the good offices of Macpherson, he would have suffered a much more severe reprimand than he ultimately received. While his return to England after only four years in the lucrative collectorship of Rangpur could have been prompted by ill health or any number of personal reasons, his renouncement of that hard-won promotion is also suggestive of a career terminated prematurely as a result of disapproval in the higher echelons of government.

District armed forces and the collector's representation of resistance

By examining the conduct of the Company's officials in Rangpur throughout the period of these raids, it is possible to draw some conclusions regarding commonly held assumptions on the use of armed force in local government. While the conduct of these individuals varied chiefly according to the size and quality of the force immediately at their disposal, it is possible to see their prime motivation as the maintenance of reputation. However, the demarcation between the government's reputation and concerns with their own personal prestige was hazy. Certainly, there is at least one very definite example in McDowall of a personal, emotional response which ran counter to what Malcolm termed the 'wise and politic exercise of . . . military power on which the whole fabric [of the Company's government] rests'.[124] Finding himself unable to act in defence of Baikanthapur in 1778, Purling did at least bring the situation to the attention of Fort William, but he made no direct appeal for aid, merely a statement of the situation. Bogle's conduct displays a realisation that the local indifference to the government could only be countered by a display of armed force, the absence of which in 1778 had damaged local perceptions of the Company's ability to influence events in Rangpur. However, the forces at his disposal did not allow him to intervene convincingly, and his was necessarily a token demonstration of force. But, as with Purling, despite the fact that it was the absence of armed force which undermined his position, he made no appeal to Fort William for aid. The comparative scarcity of correspondence with the central government about the raids, combined with the mild tone of what little there was, seems to indicate a desire to play down the importance of the unrest. Although they were of a different variety, the actions of Purling and Bogle share McDowall's more obvious motivation of personal standing with Fort William. The absence of appeals for help on their part speaks volumes. It could have a number of causes: the correspondence may not have survived in the archive, although this period seems relatively complete in the district records; it may have been that the collectors were indifferent to disruptive strife within their districts, although the pressing need to maximise revenue extraction makes that highly unlikely, or there may have been a realisation that an appeal to the parsimonious Calcutta government would be futile. Yet there is at least one further explanation, namely that a request for aid would be viewed by both Fort William and the collector himself as an admission of failure. Ultimately, a collector who cried out for the army whenever he was faced with a problem would not be suffered to remain long in his post. Military intervention was expensive and the collector was expected to govern his district with the forces allocated to him. Therefore, it is possible to see that the local availability of military force had a direct impact on the district official's representation of the seriousness of armed resistance. If the threat was too great to be tackled by the district's garrison, but was not yet significantly disrupting the revenue stream, it was preferable for a collector to conceal it from his superiors. Military intervention under these circumstances could result in a career-ending reverse, whereas, if ignored, the threat might resolve itself. The raiding of Gungaram provides a case in point. There was, initially at least, no attempt to occupy the Company's territory permanently, and Baikanthapur, the area affected, was located on a distant fringe of the district. The disruption could be safely ignored until it reached a level which began to cause sustained damage to the district's profitability, which would inevitably attract the attention of the Committee of Revenue.

When Bogle turned to the use of armed force it was as a last resort. He would not risk his few sepoys until it became apparent that the district's economy would suffer hugely if the conflict between Gungaram and Munzaram were to escalate. In this event, his credit with Fort William would suffer anyway from the impact which large scale unrest would have on the revenue stream, so now the gamble of deploying Rangpur's revenue troops became worth taking. Having suppressed for some time the scale of the violence being committed, it was desirable that, in the event of Rangpur's profitability falling and Fort William's attention being attracted, Bogle should be able to show his superiors that he had at least made some attempt to engage as a player in the district's affairs, be it ever so feeble. Even when he chose to commit his armed forces, it was certainly not a quick, vigorous and effective pursuit of the Company's enemies, but rather an attempt to forestall a conflict from which the Rangpur administration could not hope to emerge with credit. The single company sent to the area was ordered to stand on the defensive; it was a token gesture, which would allow Bogle to claim he had taken action to protect the Company's interests while minimising the chances of the sepoys suffering a defeat. This can only have confirmed the Nepalese raiders' belief that they could act with impunity and further convinced the Company's subjects that the government was not to be relied on. By dispatching so small a force to Baikanthapur, Bogle did not create an impression of strength in the region, but rather advertised the Company's local weakness – a weakness exacerbated by the fact that not only was the collector unable to impose his will on either allies or aggressors, but apparently even his own troops, who had turned on Baikanthapur's raiyats, were beyond his control.

This idea that representations of a threat were coloured by the force available to counter it is also apparent in the actions of McDowall. Provided with a battalion he characterised the raids as deserving a campaign encompassing the invasion of a sovereign state, whereas his predecessors, backed by little or no armed force, had portrayed them as minor border disturbances. While Purling and Bogle found that they had too few troops to intervene and subsequently seem to have played down a situation which could call into question their professional abilities, McDowall saw an opportunity for personal distinction because he had the means to act offensively.

The maintenance of the revenue-extracting mechanisms in these circumstances, where the district administration was often supported by very little armed force, required a delicate judgement of whether the possibility of damage to the government's authority in the long term justified risking a possible, even likely, defeat in the present. However, such an attitude required the collector to be prepared to sacrifice his own professional reputation within the Company's service, and with it his chances of advancement should he suffer a serious military reversal in trying to levy what Fort William considered to be an acceptable amount of revenue. The widespread unwillingness to make this sacrifice nurtured a risk-averse culture among the Company's collectors, which militated against wider, institutional concerns, and often led to passivity and the concealment of unpalatable information from their superiors for as long as possible. Military intervention was rarely contemplated other than when the district's revenues were very seriously threatened; a failure to meet Fort William's financial expectations would significantly damage a collector's professional standing, and so the risk of defeat inherent in the use of his scanty armed forces then became one which it was necessary for the collector to take.

The effect on the Company's pan-Indian reputation of the Nepalese raids may seem trifling, even when compared to other contemporary events in Rangpur, such as the dhing, whose repercussions were felt at Westminster, but when it is considered that Indian society's common perception of the government came from the routine administration of the districts, rather than from grand campaigns against rival powers, the cumulative significance of these local incidents becomes apparent. Until the early 19th century at least, the isolated position of Rangpur's collectors, and the slender resources allocated to the district, caused them to adopt a defensive posture in their administrative practice. They were not mere automata executing a set strategy dictated by Fort William and were perpetually conscious of the need to conciliate their superiors. It was necessary to maintain an appearance of control in order to preserve their position within the Company and the perquisites to which their posts allowed them access. However, the concealment of potentially career-damaging occurrences from Fort William often led to an unchecked escalation of resistance to the government's authority. This culture of concealment, therefore, had significant, detrimental consequences for the Company's revenue-extracting interests and for the quality and scope of the knowledge it was able to accrue about the state it purported to govern.

Notes

1 The district's administrative headquarters, Rangpur town, lay approximately 225 miles north and a little east of Calcutta.
2 Hunter, *Imperial Gazetteer of India, Vol. XI*, p. 488.

3 See E. G. Glazier, *The District of Rungpore* (1872), cit. W. K. Firminger (ed.), *Bengal District Records: Rangpur, Vol. I, 1770–1779, Letters Sent and Received*, Calcutta: Bengal Secretariat, 1914, p. 1.
4 S. Ray, *Transformations on the Bengal Frontier: Jalpaiguri, 1765–1948*, London: Routledge, 2002, p. 30.
5 Ray suggests that these groups also maintained a permanent stronghold in the forests of Morung between 1772 and 1794, from which they would emerge at regular intervals to pillage northern Rangpur. See Ray, *Transformations*, p. 34.
6 *Ibid.*, p. 31.
7 *Ibid.*, p. 35.
8 R. Becher to J. Grose, 1 September 1770, Firminger, *BDR: Rangpur*, I, pp. vii–viii.
9 Collector of Purnea to Board of Revenue, 9 January 1795, *ibid.*, p. 33.
10 Marshall, *East Indian Fortunes*, p. 193.
11 R. Goodlad to G. Bogle, 24 September 1779, Mitchell Library, Bogle MSS, cit. Marshall, *East Indian Fortunes*, p. 198.
12 Elements of this chapter concerning Richard Goodlad are reproduced with the permission of Cambridge University Press from J. Lees, '"A Character to Lose": Richard Goodlad, the Rangpur *Dhing*, and the Priorities of the East India Company's Early Colonial Administrators', *Journal of the Royal Asiatic Society of Great Britain & Ireland*, 2015, 25 (2): 301–315.
13 R. Wenger, 'George Bogle, Part 3: Into Bhutan and Tibet', *The Journal of the Families in British India Society*, 2006, 16: 27.
14 Marshall, *East Indian Fortunes*, p. 194.
15 *Ibid.*, p. 197.
16 J. Grose to R. Becher, 24 April 1770, Firminger, *BDR: Rangpur*, I, p. 1.
17 Ray, *Transformations*, pp. 34–35.
18 C. Purling to W. Harwood, 28 March 1778, Firminger, *BDR: Rangpur*, I, pp. 33–34.
19 R. Goodlad to W. Hastings, 19 August 1779, *ibid.*, p. 98.
20 R. Goodlad to M. Barnewall, 24 August 1779, *ibid.*, p. 98.
21 'Review of the 2 Companies of Sebundy Sepoys attached to Rungpore under the Command of Captain Daniel MacGregor for May 1784', Firminger, *BDR: Rangpur*, III, p. 170.
22 P. Moore to W. Cowper, 19 March 1785, W. K. Firminger (ed.), *Bengal District Records: Rangpur, Vol. IV, 1779–1785, Letters Issued*, Calcutta: Bengal Secretariat, 1921, p. 206.
23 P. Moore to W. Cowper, 20 February 1785, Firminger, *BDR: Rangpur*, IV, pp. 204–205.
24 W. Haverkam to R. Goodlad, 20 January 1783, Firminger, *BDR: Rangpur*, III, p. 7.
25 See Rangpur sebundy monthly returns, NAB, Rangpur District Records, January 1799–December 1799 (Letters Sent) A12.2/299 to NAB, Rangpur District Records, November 1809–March 1811 (Letters Sent) A12.2/306.13.
26 J. Digby to Capt. Maling, 14 December 1809, NAB, Rangpur District Records, May 1805–April 1806 (Letters Sent) A12.2/305.
27 J. E. Wilson, '"A Thousand Countries to Go to": Peasants and Rulers in Late Eighteenth Century Bengal', *Past & Present*, 2005, 189: 87.

28 R. Goodlad to D. Anderson, Rangpur, 14 April 1784, British Library, Anderson Papers, xx, Add MS 45436, f. 47.
29 Wilson, '"A Thousand Countries"', p. 87.
30 'Report of the Rungpore Commission', 23 March 1786, cit. McLane, *Land and Local Kingship*, p. 84.
31 Wilson, '"A Thousand Countries"', p. 87.
32 Ray, *Transformations*, p. 37.
33 Wilson, '"A Thousand Countries"', p. 88.
34 *Ibid.*, p. 84.
35 Circular from Fort William, 3 October 1781, Firminger, *BDR: Rangpur*, II, p. 160.
36 R. Goodlad to Committee of Revenue, March 1783, Firminger, *BDR: Rangpur*, IV, p. 151.
37 R. Goodlad to 'The Ryots of the Chucklas of Cargeehaut, Kankneah and Tepah', February 1783, *ibid.*, p. 138.
38 R. Goodlad to 'The Ryots &ca of the Pergunnahs of, Kankneah, Cargeehaut & ca', February 1783, *ibid.*, p. 142.
39 R. Goodlad to Committee of Revenue, March 1783, *ibid.*, p. 151.
40 W. Rooke to R. Goodlad, 15 February 1783, Firminger, *BDR: Rangpur*, III, p. 13.
41 A. Macdonald to R. Goodlad, 22 February 1783, *ibid.*, p. 20.
42 W. Haverkam to R. Goodlad, 20 January 1783, *ibid.*, p. 7.
43 *Ibid.* Goodlad appears to have maintained an establishment of 300 barqandazes (100 above his permitted complement) between May and July 1782. It seems probable that this remained the case until his warning from the Committee of Revenue in January 1783, and, with the onset of the dhing, likely that it continued for some time after.
44 R. Goodlad to Committee of Revenue, [. . .] March 1783, Firminger, *BDR: Rangpur*, IV, p. 151.
45 R. Goodlad to A. Macdonald, 13 February 1783, *ibid.*, p. 133.
46 Committee of Revenue Circular, 25 August 1783, Firminger, *BDR: Rangpur*, III, p. 70.
47 R. Goodlad to A. Macdonald, 13 February 1783, Firminger, *BDR: Rangpur*, IV p. 133.
48 A. Macdonald to R. Goodlad, 21 February 1783, *ibid.*, p. 135.
49 R. Goodlad to the Committee of Revenue [. . .] March 1783, *ibid.*, pp. 151–152.
50 Committee of Revenue to R. Goodlad, 28 February 1783, Firminger, *BDR: Rangpur*, III, p. 22.
51 R. Goodlad to A. Macdonald, 13 February 1783, Firminger, *BDR: Rangpur*, IV, p. 133.
52 *Ibid.*
53 Committee of Revenue to R. Goodlad, 20 February 1783, Firminger, *BDR: Rangpur*, III, p. 16.
54 See H. Furber (ed.), *The Correspondence of Edmund Burke, Vol. V, July 1782 to June 1789*, Cambridge: Cambridge University Press, 1965, pp. 381–386; P. J. Marshall (ed.), *The Writings and Speeches of Edmund Burke, Vol. VI, India: The Launching of the Hastings Impeachment, 1786–1788*, Oxford: Oxford University Press, 1991, pp. 423–435.
55 Committee of Revenue to R. Goodlad, 28 February 1783, Firminger, *BDR: Rangpur*, III, p. 22.

56 R. Goodlad to D. Anderson, 14 April 1784, 'Anderson Papers', XX, ff.49, BL Add MS 45, 436.
57 In his impeachment of Warren Hastings, Edmund Burke declared that Richard Goodlad 'had been a patient witness of all these cruelties, to say no more', Marshall, *Edmund Burke*, VI, p. 422.
58 R. Goodlad to D. Anderson, 14 April 1784, 'Anderson Papers', XX, ff.49, BL Add MS 45, 436.
59 *Ibid.*, ff.48.
60 *Ibid.*, ff.46.
61 *Ibid.*, ff.48.
62 See 'The Residence of Richard Goodlad at Baruipur', Balthazar Solvyns (1793; oil on wood panel) in the collection of the Victoria Memorial Hall, Kolkatta.
63 The *Times*, London, 5 July 1822 (no. 6566).
64 *The Royal Kalendar and Court and City Register for England, Scotland, Ireland, and the Colonies*, London: J. Almon, 1819, p. 239.
65 'Opening of the Impeachment, 19 February 1788', Marshall, *Edmund Burke*, VI, p. 434.
66 'I have a good opinion of Goodlad's sense, & I told him to have full confidence in talking with you. Get him to pass a Saturday & Sunday with you at Hooghly and make *him* be very free with you, which I desire him to be. I told him how trusty a man you were. The great point to my mind appears to be to get every able man', addendum, G. Bogle to D. Anderson, 11 November 1780, Anderson Papers, v, BL Add MSS 45,421, f. 118.
67 Marshall, *Edmund Burke*, VI, p. 428.
68 *Ibid.*, p. 434.
69 C. Purling to W. Hastings, 28 March 1778, Firminger, *BDR: Rangpur*, I, p. 33.
70 Petition from Kinker Bucshee, encl. C. Purling to W. Harwood, 30 March 1778, *ibid.*, pp. 34–35.
71 'The dacoits keep in such large bodies that no force I have here could effect anything against them. I am, therefore, under the necessity of requesting that you will be pleased to order some seapoys to be stationed here, that by their assistance the inhabitants may be relieved from so great a calamity'. R. Goodlad to W. Hastings, 24 May 1779, *ibid.*, p. 79.
72 Charles Purling had left Rangpur in 1779 to become the Company's resident at Awadh. Firminger, *BDR: Rangpur*, II, p. iii.
73 Initially, Bogle was unsure 'whether to call [Gungaram Thapa] a freebooter or an Officer of the Nepaul Government'. It later transpired that he was a combination of the two. See G. Bogle to D. Anderson, 4 May 1780, f. 107, BL Add MSS 45, 421.
74 G. Bogle to W. Rooke, 7 April 1780, Firminger, *BDR: Rangpur*, IV, pp. 31–32.
75 D. H. McDowall to J. MacPherson, 17 March 1786, Firminger, *BDR: Rangpur*, VI, p. 28. The raja of Nepal later disavowed the subahdar's conduct to the extent of describing him as 'that Traitor Gungaram Tappah' and imprisoning him. See 'Translate of a Letter from the Rajah of Napaul to Mr McDowall, Collector of Rungpore, received at Rungpore the 13th May 1786' encl. D.H. McDowall to Committee of Revenue, 14 May 1786, *ibid.*, pp. 52–53.
76 D. H. McDowall to Committee of Revenue, 12 April 1786, *ibid.*, p. 39.

77 G. Bogle to W. Rooke, 5 May 1780, Firminger, *BDR: Rangpur*, IV, pp. 35–36.

78 As G. J. Bryant has observed, 'The Army was far less in evidence in the countryside, though its presence in an emergency could be felt more rapidly after the building of the first stage of the Grand Trunk Road between Calcutta and Benares in 1780'. Bryant, 'Pacification and the Early British Raj': 16.

79 Given the value attached to labour in the depopulated Bengal of this period, some trouble may well have been taken by Gungaram to entice the raiyats away with the promise of improved conditions of service, although, as a commodity of some importance, those who could not tempted to leave were doubtless induced to do so by force.

80 'Extract of the Proceedings of the Collector of Rungpore in the Business of the Settlement for 1193 B.S.', 5 June 1786, Firminger, *BDR: Rangpur*, VI, p. 73.

81 R. Goodlad to W. Hastings, 19 August 1779, Firminger, *BDR: Rangpur*, I, p. 98.

82 G. Bogle to W. Rooke, 5 May 1780, Firminger, *BDR: Rangpur*, IV, pp. 35–36.

83 G. Bogle to W. Rooke, 7 April 1780, Firminger, *ibid.*, pp. 31–32.

84 *Ibid.*, pp. 33–34.

85 In this context, 'subedar' signifies an Indian infantry officer with a rank corresponding to that of a captain in the British army, rather than a governor.

86 W. Rooke to G. Bogle, 15 April 1780, Firminger, *BDR: Rangpur*, II, pp. 44–45.

87 E. Fenwick and J. Lowe to G. Bogle, 16 May 1780, *ibid.*, pp. 47–48.

88 Petition of the Zamindar of Surjapur, encl. E. Fenwick and M. Dawson to G. Bogle, 11 July 1780, Firminger, *BDR: Rangpur*, II, p. 55.

89 For example, Goodlad was informed in 1782 that a *jemadar's* party of Rangpur militia sepoys 'have in attempting to plunder from the people . . . occasioned much disturbance'. J. Christie to R. Goodlad, 31 October 1782, Firminger, *BDR: Rangpur*, II, p. 283.

90 N. Alexander to D. H. McDowall, 19 March 1786, NAB, Rangpur District Records, January to December 1786 (Letters Received), A12.1/21, p. 129. Thapa had also raided Purnea, carrying off from that district'126 people and a great number of cattle', D. H. MacDowall to Committee of Revenue, 12 April 1786, Firminger, *BDR: Rangpur*, VI, p. 59.

91 W. Amherst to W. Duncanson, 7 February 1786, *ibid.*, p. 4.

92 W. Duncanson to W. Amherst, 17 February 1786, *ibid.*, p. 20.

93 *Ibid.*

94 This situation had also prevailed on the borders of Rangpur throughout the previous decade. 'To the west of Baikanthapur, between the rivers of the Mahananda in the east and the Mechi in the west, lay an area known as east Morung under the nominal control of Sikkim but virtually a no-man's land from where the *sannyasis*, *faqirs* and later Gurkhas made inroads in the Company's territories in Rangpur district'. Ray, *Transformations*, p. 30.

95 N. Alexander to B. Singh, 4 March 1786, W. K. Firminger (ed.), *Bengal District Records: Rangpur, Vol. V, 1786–87, Letters Issued*, Calcutta: Bengal Secretariat, 1921, p. 31.

96 W. Duncanson to W. Amherst, 17 February 1786, *ibid.*, p. 20.

97 *Ibid.*, p. 18.
98 *Ibid.*, pp. 19–20.
99 *Ibid.*, p. 20.
100 Board of Revenue to D. H. McDowall, 3 January 1786, NAB, Rangpur District Records, January 1786–May 1789 (Letters Received), A12.1/23, p. 2. The intention was that McDowall should restore order to the district administration in the wake of the Rangpur Commission under John Paterson. See Board of Revenue to D. H. McDowall, 6 February 1786, NAB, Rangpur District Records, January 1786–May 1789 (Letters Received), A12.1/23, p. 107.
101 The same sannyasi leader who had been active in the district four years previously. See Committee of Revenue to R. Goodlad, 19 December 1782, Firminger, *BDR: Rangpur*, II, p. 297.
102 W. Amherst to N. Alexander, 16 February 1786, Firminger, *BDR: Rangpur*, VI, p. 17.
103 Ray, *Transformations*, p. 35.
104 His apparent desire for military distinction was seen again in 1789, when he conducted, in person, a campaign against a party of sannyasis in Baikanthapur. During the course of this campaign, he surrounded the raiders in a densely wooded tract and compelled their surrender, with 549 of them being brought to trial. Hunter, *Imperial Gazetteer of India, Vol. XI*, p. 492.
105 N. Alexander to G. Thapa, 23 February 1786, Firminger, *BDR: Rangpur*, V, p. 24.
106 G. Thapa to N. Alexander, enclosed in D. H. McDowall to Board of Revenue, 1 March 1786, Firminger, *BDR: Rangpur*, VI, p. 13.
107 D. H. McDowall to N. Alexander, 1 March 1786, *ibid.*, p. 11.
108 D. H. McDowall to N. Alexander, 23 February 1786, *ibid.*, p. 9.
109 D. H. McDowall to N. Alexander, 1 March 1786, *ibid.*, p. 11.
110 N. Alexander to R. Sloper, 11 March 1786, *BDR: Rangpur*, V, p. 39.
111 D. H. McDowall to Board of Revenue, 4 March 1786, Firminger, *BDR: Rangpur*, VI, p. 16.
112 Board of Revenue to D. H. McDowall, 6 March 1786, NAB, Rangpur District Records, January – December 1786 (Letters Received), A12.1/21, p. 193.
113 D. H. McDowall to Board of Revenue, 14 March 1786, Firminger, *BDR: Rangpur*, VI, p. 23.
114 N. Alexander to W. Amherst, 26 February 1786, Firminger, *BDR: Rangpur*, V, p. 23.
115 N. Alexander to R. Sloper, 11 March 1786, *ibid.*, p. 39.
116 J. Baujeneer to D. H. McDowall, 13 March 1786, *ibid.*, p. 41.
117 According to the report of a Company agent sent by McDowall to Kathmandu, the Nepalese army was a very substantial force. In the summer of 1786, it numbered approximately 30,000 men, about a third of whom were barqandazes, with a further 14,000 swordsmen, and a corps of 6,000 musketeers. In addition, there was an artillery park of 24 light cannon. The Company's Bengal Army at this time numbered approximately 40,000 men, few of whom were stationed in the northern districts, and a conflict with Nepal would have meant an extremely arduous campaign (as happened some 30 years later). See 'Account of Napaul given by a

very intelligent Person who was sent into the Country (Disguised as a Fakir) by the Collector of Rungpore in Consequence of a report that the Napaul Government was collecting together a large army', encl. D. H. McDowall to J. MacPherson, 23 July 1786, Firminger, *BDR: Rangpur*, VI, pp. 92–94.

118 R. Aplin to D. H. McDowall, 1 August 1786, encl. Extract of a letter from the Honble Governor-General and Council 26 July 1786. NAB, Rangpur District Records, April – September 1786 (Letters Received), A12.1/20, p. 77.

119 J. Buchanan to D. H. McDowall, 14 April 1786, *ibid.*, p. 4.

120 'Translate of a Letter from the Rajah of Napaul to Mr McDowall, Collector of Rungpore, received at Rungpore the 13 May 1786', encl. D. H. McDowall to the Board of Revenue, 14 May 1786, Firminger, *BDR: Rangpur*, VI, pp. 52–54.

121 'Answer to the Napaul Rajah's Letter', encl. D. H. McDowall to the Board of Revenue, 14 May 1786, *ibid.*, pp. 52–54.

122 Shortly afterwards, however, Purling went on sick leave and was replaced by his assistant James Graham, who had been appointed as the district's assistant collector when MacDowall arrived in 1786. C. Purling to Board of Revenue, 21 September 1790, NAB, Rangpur District Records, May 1790–April 1791 (Letters Sent), A12.2/288, p. 210.

123 Extract of a letter from the Honble the Governor-General and Council, 19 July 1786, encl. Board of Revenue to D. H. McDowall, 28 July 1786, NAB, Rangpur District Records, April–September 1786 (Letters Received), A12.1/20, p. 73.

124 Malcolm, *Political History*, I, p. 245.

5 Chittagong district, 1760–c. 1800

Chittagong's physical and political geography

In 1760, the district of Chittagong in eastern Bengal, together with those of Burdwan and Midnapur farther to the west, was ceded to the Company by Mir Kasim in recognition of the Company's role in establishing him as nawab of the province. This territory, a narrow coastal strip nearly 165 miles long, hemmed in by Arakan and Burma to the east and the northern reaches of the Bay of Bengal to the west, was both fertile and well situated to benefit from sea-borne trade.[1]

Despite Chittagong's mercantile contacts within the world of the Indian Ocean, and the abortive attempt by the British to wrest the district from Mughal control in 1686, it was at this time still relatively unknown territory for the Company, in terms of both its physical and political geography. Upon the appointment in 1760 of Harry Verelst, the Company's first commercial chief at Chittagong,[2] two sloops had to be dispatched to make soundings and gauge the draught of a vessel which could undertake the navigation of the Karnafuli River as far as Islamabad, the district's administrative centre.[3] Moreover, Verelst's first task was to fortify the town to the fullest extent which the district's resources would allow as a precaution against possible local aggression;[4] and the wisdom of this measure was soon made apparent by the activities of the Arakanese *Maghs*.[5] Following their defeat by the Mughals at the battle of Chittagong in 1666, the Arakanese had lost much of the maritime power they had enjoyed in the 16th and 17th centuries, yet they remained a force to be reckoned with.[6] Large numbers of Magh vessels conducted annual raids on Chittagong's coastal areas throughout the 1760s and 1770s, and were a source of great alarm for the Company's administration. Together with the external threats to the district, such as the incursions of the Burmese following their invasion of Arakan in 1785 and the depredations of armed mendicant sannyasis, there was also considerable internal resistance to the government's authority throughout the period.[7] This was carried on by bands of discontented raiyats and tribal peoples, as well as local zamindars.[8]

In the period under examination, the local economy was based principally on agriculture, particularly the cultivation of rice, cotton and capsicum.[9] The district was also an important source of timber, wood-oil, salt and wax. Its fertility is testified to by the fact that it regularly produced a large rice surplus, even during Bengal's great famine of 1770. Islamabad and its immediate environs, near the mouth of the Karnafuli in the west, were home to a sizeable urban population. However, in his account of a journey through Chittagong in 1798, Francis Buchanan, the Scottish geographer and botanist, described a countryside which was remarkably under-populated.[10] The insatiable demand for agricultural labour remained the defining economic feature of the region, even though nearly three decades had passed since the Bengal famine, and the eastern districts had been much less severely affected than those farther west.[11] The need to promote settlement, thereby bringing wasteland 'under the plough' featured heavily in the correspondence of the district's administrators throughout the latter half of the 18th and well into the 19th century. Greater productivity would lead to increased tax yields, but this was not the sole consideration; a densely settled Chittagong would also provide the Company's territories with a stable eastern frontier, discouraging the gradual encroachment of the local powers which lay beyond its borders. Even during the early years of its governmental presence, the Company was well aware of the pressing need to increase the local labour pool. The earliest extant letter sent from Fort William to Harry Verelst, in December 1760, emphasised the importance of enhancing the prestige of the local government as a key step in encouraging immigration and subsequent economic development.

> We must recommend to you that you carry yourselves towards the natives & Inhabitants at Chittagong in such a manner as to give them a good & favourable Idea of the English Government & thereby encourage others to come and settle under your protection.[12]

However, the settling of immigrants was not to be an easy process; the raiyat was an immensely valuable commodity and local powers would go to great lengths to retain their cultivators and to acquire new ones. Much of the border conflict between the Chittagong authorities and Burma from 1785 onwards can be ascribed to a desire on the part of the latter to force the return of groups which had fled Arakan following the Burmese annexation. Some of these refugees had political ambitions and waged a guerrilla campaign against their Burmese conquerors from bases in the Company's territory, but the aggressive military response of the Burmese was not prompted solely by the necessities of counter-insurgency.[13] Literally thousands of people, an economic force of considerable potential in labour-hungry eastern Bengal, spilled across the Chittagong border during the late 18th century.[14] The Burmese were anxious to compel their return, realising that the benefits arising from their conquest of Arakan would be lessened if so sizeable a portion of the local workforce was allowed to abscond and leave the land uncultivated. In this way, a series of events was set in train which would ultimately result in the outbreak of the first Anglo-Burmese war in 1823.[15]

The local government in Chittagong during the opening decades of the Company's rule was, then, plagued by armed challenges to its authority both from powers beyond its borders and from disruptive elements within. It was also a district in which, as Buchanan reported, 'the Grand object of the Zemeendars is to keep the English in as much ignorance as possible', refusing to give 'the least information on any subject'.[16] While it was valuable, it was also vulnerable: its eastern frontier was open to attack through Arakan, and its western extremity, resting on the Bay of Bengal, was exposed to coastal raids by the Maghs. Chittagong's accessibility to hostile external groups added to the difficulty of imposing rule on the district, a task problematic enough in areas farther away from the Company's frontiers. This placed a heavy burden on the nascent Anglo-Indian civil service which, even towards the end of the period, was still far removed from the homogenous bureaucracy of the 19th century. It was under these desperate conditions that district officials were expected, with limited military and financial resources, to impose the Company's governmental authority.

Government armed forces in Chittagong

From the outset, the Company's servants in Chittagong had been enjoined by their superiors in Calcutta to look to the government's local prestige, and this implied not only the fair treatment of the district's inhabitants but also the proper use of armed force to put down internal resistance and to defend the district against external threats. Throughout the later 18th century, Chittagong enjoyed a military establishment larger than that of many other districts, even other frontier districts. The size of the garrison was a testimony to Fort William's desire to protect a key trading port which lay in an exposed position, but it was by no means an overwhelming force and sometimes it was spread very thinly indeed, with serious consequences for the district's security and economic growth. The responses of local officials were conditioned by the level of armed force which they could afford to mobilise against any given threat and, crucially, when economic growth was reliant on the stable settlement of cultivators, a failure to guarantee the security of the population was a serious impediment to the development of the district's agricultural economy. From the 1760s onwards, Chittagong's usual garrison seems to have been a regular battalion of sepoy infantry nominally based at Islamabad;[17] although, particularly in the 1760s and 1770s, much of its strength was dispersed throughout the district in outposts ranging from several companies to a naik's guard.[18] The employment of locally raised barqandazes to augment this force was rare. Chittagong's civil authorities seem to have considered that the expense was not commensurate with the service provided, even when this clashed with the advice of their military officers.[19] The struggle between economy and efficiency is a frequent theme in the local correspondence, with the district's chief hectoring his subordinates over often minor and well-justified expenditure, in the fear that he would be censured by Fort William for the wanton extravagance of his administration.

The town of Islamabad was 'better built than the generality of places in Bengal', and its security appears to have been taken seriously from the start of the Company's occupation.[20] Even though it was garrisoned by 'only a small military force', it was considerably better supplied with military materials than the administrative centres of comparable northern frontier districts, such as Purnea and Rangpur.[21] The surviving ordnance returns for the town's garrison of May 1771 indicate a significant artillery complement, with a dozen iron 12-pounder cannon, nine brass field pieces of smaller calibre and a howitzer.[22]

However, not all the threats to the district could be countered by static defences and land forces. The low-level raids of the Maghs demanded the improvisation of an additional riverine and naval force, to prevent attacks on fishing vessels and coastal villages. Again, the activities of these raiders draw attention to the value placed on labour by regional groups, with Chittagong's chief reporting in 1776 that Maghs had 'enslaved' the crews of captured fishing vessels, presumably returning with them to their bases in Arakan.[23] The defence against these raids seems to have been organised on an ad hoc basis, with Company sloops being detached for short, preventative cruises when available.[24] Despite the implication that the raids were both a serious nuisance and an almost annual occurrence from the 1760s,[25] it was not until they peaked in the mid-1770s that any significant attempt was made to establish a standing anti-Magh force of small craft, loaded with sepoys, to act in conjunction with a permanently based sloop at Chittagong.[26] Even then the stress was on economy, with the chief declaring, 'The Boat will never be Manned but in persuit',[27] a measure which would reduce operational costs, but which would also give the sloop little opportunity to work up to a state of efficiency.[28]

Internal threats: discontented zamindars and popular resistance[29]

Chittagong possessed an extremely porous land border and coastline, making it difficult to defend against raids by external groups, particularly the Burmese. Moreover, as was the case with much of the Company's territory in this period, it was also beset by individuals from within the district, who were driven by a range of motives to resist the government's authority. An important figure in this regard was the 'Refractory Zamindar' Ranu Khan, who waged a military campaign against the authorities at Islamabad between 1776 and 1787.[30] He was described by Francis Law, the Company's chief at Chittagong at the beginning of this episode,[31] as a subordinate landowner in the eastern hill country.[32] Contact between the local authorities and the peoples of the hill tracts had been extremely limited up to this point, and the chief's letter to Warren Hastings in April 1777 is the earliest record of interaction between the two groups.[33] Largely ignorant of the people in this sector of his district, Law was at a loss to explain the landholder's behaviour, attributing it to a general 'disposition to revolt' or perhaps to his dissatisfaction with the behaviour of the Company's revenue farmer at the pargana of Rangunia.[34] Ranu Khan had, Law complained, been extorting money from other Company landholders and committing 'great violence' upon them.[35] News of his activities seems to have been filtering into Islamabad for several months prior to Law's letter of April 1777 without any action being taken, but the chief's hand was forced when Ranu Khan ordered the beating of two Company sepoys, who had been sent to the area on a government errand, and tore up the *parwana* (warrant) which they carried. It was only gradually that the district officers came to realise that this flouting of the Company's governmental authority in the hill tracts was, in fact, a fully fledged rebellion of the *Chakma* people, instigated by their 'powerful and turbulent' raja, Sher Daulat Khan, and prosecuted by his diwan, and now general, Ranu Khan.[36]

The immediate cause of this uprising was the Company's taxation of the estate at Chakla Rangunia which the Chakma raja had obtained from the Mughal government in 1733.[37] Since they considered Chittagong to be primarily a military outpost, shielding Bengal from Magh raids, the policy of the Mughals had been to co-opt local groups, such as the Chakmas, through the liberal allocation of *lakheraj* or 'rent-free lands', and thereby incorporate them into a system of border defence.[38] The primary concern of the Company, however, was to increase the district's immediate financial profitability. From as early as 1770, the Chittagong authorities had been eyeing these rent-free land grants with resentment; it was estimated that fully two-thirds of the district's prime acreage was tied up in this way.[39] Accordingly, during the next seven years, rent-free status was withdrawn from various zamindaris, the level of rent was increased, and Rangunia pargana, which included the hereditary estate of the Chakma raja, was sold to a revenue farmer who oppressed the raiyats by levying a number of illegal cesses.[40] Provoked by the withdrawal of the autonomy to which they had grown accustomed, the Chakma leadership finally embarked upon a guerrilla campaign against the Company in Chittagong.[41]

In the early spring of 1777, a party of 50 regular sepoys was dispatched from the Islamabad garrison to capture Ranu Khan and put an end to his depredations,[42] but it met with fierce resistance from a large body of tribal peoples from the hills whom the Chakma general had gathered about him and 'who, tho' ill armed, harassed the few Sepoys on the Expedition'.[43] Eventually, the party had to be reinforced to the strength of more than a full company (115 men) in order to make any headway against the *Kuki* hillmen who formed this band.[44] Despite the sizeable force sent against him, Ranu Khan contrived to escape into the hills of the interior. Realising the futility of pursuing the Chakma general with the limited resources available to him, the chief embarked upon a policy of starving Ranu Khan into submission by punishing any people found to be supplying him and 'depriving the Chowdries or Zemindars of their Lands who connive at such Practises'.[45]

For several years after this, Ranu Khan continued to wage his campaign against the Company in a way which clearly indicated that he was not just a glorified dakait chief: his aim was Chakma political autonomy. In June 1778, the chief at Chittagong received a complaint from several zamindars that Ranu Khan had raised *nishans* (flags of independence) on the Company's land and that he had compelled them to pay their revenue to the Chakma raja and to withdraw their loyalty from the Company.[46] He had also forced the zamindars to pay him and his raja tribute (in the form of nazrs), and had seized raiyats, employing them in cultivating Chakma territory and punishing and fining them as he saw fit. This was not simply resistance to the government's authority; it was a usurpation of it.

Ranu Khan rapidly made the whole of the hill tracts independent of Company rule, compelling Islamabad to send three separate military expeditions to the area between 1777 and 1781 in an attempt to bring the population back into the Company's fold. Neither side, however, was able to strike the decisive blow, and in August 1781, Ranu Khan changed tack and attempted to negotiate with the Chittagong authorities. He reportedly offered to release one of the Company's *sezawals* (Indian revenue officers), whom he had 'in confinement and in heavy Irons',[47] and to live peaceably under the Company's rule, if the sepoys who were attempting to blockade him in the hills were called off, and if he were granted a 'Pardon for his Crimes'.[48] John Buller, the acting chief, referred the matter to the Committee of Revenue, as he did not consider himself authorised 'to recall a force detached by Orders of Mr Sumner (the district's chief) to bring a Rebel to Justice who has for some Years past bid Defiance to the orders and Perwannahs of Government'.[49] The situation remained unresolved, however, as in October of the same year Buller had to ask the garrison commander at Islamabad, Major Edward Ellerker, to provide an escort for a sezawal, whom he wished to send to Rangunia, 'to protect him from any Violences or Obstructions that may be offer'd to him from the People of Runnoo Cawn'.[50] His plea for a pardon having been rebuffed, in April of 1782, Ranu Khan remained in conflict with the Chittagong authorities; Buller pleaded with Ellerker to maintain his outposts in the affected area, fearing that the Chakma general's depredations would escalate if the sepoys were withdrawn.[51] As late as 1785, Chittagong's chief was still requesting armed escorts for revenue officers travelling in Rangunia pargana. At the same time, Ranu Khan and the Chakma raja, Jan Baksh Khan, who had by this time succeeded Sher Daulat, continued to evade the local authorities: they had 'approached the Skirts of the Hills where they keep themselves concealed'.[52]

Islamabad's efforts to starve out the Chakma guerrillas proved ineffective, as supplies clearly found their way to the fighters in spite of Law's proclamation of April 1777, and the damage caused to the government's salt manufacture in the district, which was dependent on access to the fuel provided by the wooded hill tracts, also militated against a strategy of drawn-out blockade.[53] Finding this measure ineffective, the Company attempted to sow discord among the rebels, in the first instance by impressing on the Kukis that they were ethnically different from the Chakmas, and that their allies were using them to further their own ends; and, in the second, by employing agents to convince Jan Baksh that Ranu Khan was growing in popularity as a result of his military successes, and that he might at any moment usurp him as raja.[54] The first approach failed, but the second prompted Jan Baksh to enter into a secret dialogue with the government. Without Ranu Khan's knowledge, he travelled to Calcutta in February 1787 and signed a peace treaty, under which the Company recognised him as the legitimate raja of the Chakmas and he agreed to live in conformity with the Company's rule, paying a tribute of cotton to the government each year.[55] His position now being extremely insecure, Ranu Khan apparently went into hiding, and after this point, he vanishes from the historical record.[56]

The reactions of the Company's chiefs and collectors at Chittagong to the recurring problem of Ranu Khan during the period 1776 to 1787 illustrate a powerful concern with the maintenance, under very difficult local conditions, of their personal reputation within the Company's professional hierarchy. The first correspondence on Ranu Khan in April 1777 was an unconvincing attempt at self-justification, which, towards the end of the letter, took on an anxious, almost pleading, tone. It began with the claim that, like an alert and dutiful servant, the chief, Law, was providing Fort William with 'an early Intimation of a Circumstance of some Moment',[57] a claim which was almost immediately contradicted by the admission that Ranu Khan had 'for some Months past committed great violence on the Company's Land holders'.[58] It was also undermined by the fact that there had been time for the chief to organise, after some considerable delay, a local military expedition. The opening implication that he had reacted swiftly and vigorously against the threat was completely undermined before the end of the first paragraph, when he felt the need to excuse his sluggish response:

> Many have been the complaints presented to me by the Cotton Farmer against this man, but I judged private Interest might have been in good part the cause, I refused embroiling the Companys officers on this account.[59]

Law had been aware for some time that there was disruption within his district and that Ranu Khan was implicated, but he had apparently remained inactive throughout this period. It is certainly possible that a heavy workload and a dearth of reliable subordinates prevented him from investigating in detail every report which reached his kachari in Islamabad, but he would have at least tried to determine the truth of such serious claims. This suggests that, after investigating, he was either still unaware of the severity of the situation, or, that he knew and chose to conceal that knowledge from his superiors. If he had been unable to obtain definite information, that would only serve to highlight the difficulty of district administration during the early years of Company rule, with the chief isolated in an urban centre and attempting, with only a partial understanding of local society, to govern a scattered population, among which were many individuals ready to use violence in realising their ambitions. Indeed, Law's ignorance of Chittagong's rural politics is rendered all the more understandable by the fact that had only been appointed to Chittagong the previous year, having spent the previous 12 years serving in various capacities at Dhaka. If, however, as seems more likely from the admission that he had received many complaints over several months, he was aware of Ranu Khan's activities and chose to remain passive, then this inaction implies either a lack of concern for the business of government, or motives of personal interest; several months of complaints suggests ample time in which to make comprehensive enquiries. This consideration was to the forefront of the chief's mind as he closed his letter:

> I am really concerned Hon'ble Sir & Gentlemen that there should be the least Commotion during my Chiefship, & I can assure you with strict honor & truth, no private motive has by passed me in my publick Conduct, but I looked on the Man . . . with too despicable an Eye to make him formidable or worthy your Notice.[60]

The chief claimed to be unable to identify precisely why Ranu Khan had been transformed from an apparently peaceable landholder into a notorious rebel, suggesting that it may have been 'through ill Usage from the farmer' or from a general 'disposition to revolt'.[61] This dual explanation is in itself telling. Rangunia pargana, which was a major source of raw cotton for the Company,[62] had been farmed out to 'an oppressive bania from Calcutta', suspicion of whose self-interested profiteering had caused Law to disbelieve the complaints he had preferred against Ranu Khan.[63] The levying of illegal cesses had played a significant part in provoking the Chakma uprising and Law had clearly been aware of the farmer's character but had taken no action. He had also completely underestimated the scale of the threat posed by Ranu Khan, viewing him with 'too despicable an Eye'. A lack of judgement and the sustained ignorance of important events taking place within his district were uncomfortable things for Law to have to reveal to Fort William, but worse still was the imputation of a dishonest 'private motive', that he had either colluded with the farmer of Rangunia in return for a bribe or concealed these events to protect his own position in the Company's service. Now, forced to hint at the farmer's unjust behaviour by way of explanation for the disturbances, he attempted to mask it with the rather weak alternative that Ranu Khan may have been disposed by his natural inclinations to resist the Company's authority. The chief wished to reduce the seeming importance of the farmer's oppression as a factor in provoking the outbreak of violence, while at the same time removing any suspicion of his collusion with the farmer through an explicit denial of personal interest.[64]

Law's fear that, whether through ignorance or complicity, his failure to put a check on the farmer's activities would be discovered provides a plausible explanation for why he took no action against the initial Chakma violence, choosing instead simply to conceal events from Fort William. The revolt's modest opening phase, which caused Law to take the unrest too lightly, encouraged this passive approach. The chief was aware of stirrings within his district, but initially the Chakma general's 'daily encroachments' remained at a level which he could safely ignore, whereas the use of the district's slender armed forces was potentially fraught with risk. The perils of a more robust response were clearly demonstrated by the experience of the party finally sent to take Ranu Khan. Even against an enemy who did not have 'the use of firearms', the district's sepoys suffered an initial reverse; the Company's local military presence was far from overwhelming and, under such circumstances, seeking to quell resistance by armed force was a hazardous undertaking. An altogether more appealing alternative to this uncertain intervention was for the chief to keep his distance, hoping, perhaps not unreasonably, that Ranu Khan would meet a violent end at the hands of a vengeful zamindar or a jealous member of his own circle. The removal of his outstanding leadership would probably have brought about the disintegration of his *palwans* (armed companies) and put an end to their disruption.[65]

A desire to avoid reporting 'the least Commotion' to Fort William led to the disturbances being concealed for as long as possible, in the hope that the situation might quietly resolve itself without any direct action by the Chittagong authorities. Their isolated position certainly enabled district officials to hide a good many unpalatable events from their distant superiors, but, once those events impacted negatively on the amount of revenue being remitted from the district, concealment became impossible. Francis Law 'found that the Companys Revenues [were] suffering from the mass Insolvence' brought about by Ranu Khan's activities. The disruption was now on a scale which could not be ignored, as the chief would be betrayed by the next set of district accounts. It was preferable that he should attempt to put a gloss on his conduct with a pre-emptive explanation, rather than simply allow the Revenue Department to discover from the monthly returns that Chittagong's finances were in serious disorder:

> I judged it no longer adviseable to remain a Tranquil spectator or hearer of Acts Derugatory to the Companys honour & Interest, and as the Man had been all along looked on as one of no rank, or consideration, I was flattered with the hopes of securing his Person, & thereby at once putting an End to his evil designs & practices.[66]

The existing damage to the district's revenues was compounded by the likelihood that the situation would only deteriorate; the beating of the two sepoys and the destruction of their parwana signalled Ranu Khan's growing disregard for the Chittagong authorities. These pressures compelled the chief, reluctantly, to make a military response. He was perfectly aware that Ranu Khan had both observed and been encouraged by his remaining a 'Tranquil spectator' – by his own admission until now Law could scarcely have been considered even as an actor, let alone the dominant figure, in his district's affairs – and that the Chakma general had attributed his prolonged inactivity 'to a Weakness in the Government'.[67] Nevertheless, lacking the military strength to intervene with confidence, it had seemed safer to wait for Ranu Khan to bring about his own downfall over time by alienating an ever-larger number of powerful local magnates, each of whom maintained armed establishments. Now, faced with the necessity of removing Ranu Khan immediately so he could present Fort William with a *fait accompli* when the sorry state of Chittagong's revenues became apparent, the chief had to gamble on the use of his armed forces.

Ranu Khan's escape is a testament to the fact that this military intervention was abortive, with the Company publicly failing to punish a rebel, but perhaps equally damaging to its interests was the conduct of the sepoys under Major Ellerker.[68] In pursuing Ranu Khan and his original party, the sepoys of the Chittagong garrison 'burnt 2 or 3 Hillocks & Villages' where the band had taken refuge, and this highlights another risk which was inherent in utilising soldiers in a policing role.[69] In taking the field against insurgents, the Company's troops might suffer a reverse, with all the unpleasant consequences for governmental authority which that would entail, but, even if they remained undefeated, the violent disorder produced by military operations would still damage the Company's interests, disrupting the district's economy, as in this case, through the destruction of property and the displacement of local labour. Quite apart from the harm caused to those interests by its direct impact on the district's revenue stream, 'collateral damage' of this kind would also have generated a certain amount of local ill-will against the Company. While there are other explanations for Ranu Khan's strong reinforcement by the Kukis after he had been driven back for the first time, a general disposition against the Company in the surrounding countryside, exacerbated by the 'pacification' operations of its troops, remains a strong possibility, and the failure of Law's plan to starve out Ranu Khan by punishing any individuals who gave him succour is also open to this interpretation. As Hobsbawm has argued with regard to the suppression of rural banditry in general, the authorities usually deployed troops in affected areas to dissuade local peasants from providing support for outlawed gangs, rather than to accomplish the more difficult task of apprehending highly mobile bandits on their home ground. Peasants, tied to the land they cultivated (at least for a season or two), made an easy target for government forces, but while bullying the peasantry could undermine local support for a 'social bandit',[70] it also risked uniting the peasantry and the bandits against a common oppressor.[71] On the one hand, the beaten Ranu Khan might still have been capable of extorting supplies from isolated communities by force; on the other, there was perhaps sufficient affection for him among some of the local inhabitants, generated by his opposition to the Company or through a sense of tribal loyalty, for him to live off their charity. His successful evasion of the Chittagong authorities for over a decade suggests a certain level of compliance and concealment by the communities of the borderlands; a hated, violent outlaw would surely have been betrayed to the government before very long, if there were not a significant toleration, or even approval, of him in local society. It was in hostile, or, at best, ambivalent, environments such as this that the Company's district officials had to operate, and it goes some way to explaining their often passive or hesitant conduct.

This is not to suggest that early Company officials were significantly more inclined to negotiate the boundaries of governmental authority with indigenous groups than were their later counterparts. Indeed, in many cases, they viewed attempts to engage the government in a dialogue as dangerously subversive. To the early colonial administrator, negotiation with the ruled constituted an admission of weakness on the part of the rulers. Such an attitude is apparent in the conduct of Buller, the acting chief of Chittagong in 1781. Ranu Khan had offered to 'pay his Revenue to government upon Condition the Sepoys . . . were taken off . . . he repented of his sins & he hoped a Pardon for his Crimes'.[72] In essence, he acknowledged his subordinate position within the Company state. Yet, despite the failure of the Chittagong authorities to take him by force (he had been at liberty for four years by that point), Buller hesitated to accept the offer. Promoted temporarily, Buller seems to have been keen to retain his credit by following a risk-averse strategy, rather than solve a nagging local difficulty by a bold stroke, which might alienate his superiors were it unsuccessful.[73] He referred the matter to the Board of Revenue, claiming to doubt his authority to negotiate with a rebel.[74] Apparently preferring to maintain the status quo, he feared that, were the sepoys to be called off, Ranu Khan 'would not sever from his former Course of Outrageous and insolent behaviour'.[75] The Bengali *wadahdar* (revenue officer)[76] through whom Ranu Khan had contacted Buller gave an alternative, and arguably more logical, view, expressing the fervent wish

> on account of having the Revenues of Government paid & for the peace & Quiet of that Part of the Country that the Sepoys detached thither may be Recalled and should He [Ranu Khan] again be guilty of any Disturbances, a Detachment may then be sent to bring him to . . . punishment.[77]

Ranu Khan's activities were still a source of anxiety for the Company's servants in the district, and his plea for pardon presented an opportunity to end this. If it proved to be a *ruse de guerre*, then the sepoys could simply be deployed once more. Yet Buller would not risk such a move and nor, judging by the fact that Ranu Khan continued to cause serious problems for several more years, was it a step which his successors would countenance either.

This reluctance to negotiate with discontented elements arose from the fear of the damaging effects which such a course might have on the Company's authority as an 'Oriental Despot', but, arguably, it was also informed by a desire among district officials to avoid miring themselves in local intrigue and incurring the disapprobation of their superiors. The preferred method of coping with the many threats to local government was to dictate terms with the backing of an overwhelming armed force, or, if that were not possible, to do nothing at all and hope that the threat would evaporate of its own accord. Even if negotiation were an option, as a time-consuming process with an uncertain result it was anathema to the district official, and it was only embarked upon as a last resort.

However, not all attempts at negotiation were as easily dismissed as Ranu Khan's appears to have been. In disputing the level of revenue due on their lands in 1786, the zamindars on the island of Sandwip in the estuary of the Meghna River effectively combined physical resistance to the authority of the Company in Chittagong with political machinations at Fort William. Fearing the consequences of an unfavourable re-evaluation of their estates, the zamindars dispatched an agent, one Pir Mahommed, to Calcutta, where he 'preferred a number of false complaints', thereby getting the diwan of the commissioner overseeing the re-evaluation recalled and effectively stopping the measurement, if only temporarily.[78] The same agent, on his return, also 'behaved insolently' towards the few Company sepoys who were stationed in the vicinity.[79] In response, 'they punished him with a beating' and, again, he was again able to lodge complaints in Calcutta, in the hope of raising questions about the manner in which the commission was operating.[80]

Having delayed the unfavourable re-evaluation for as long as possible, when the balance finally became due, the zamindars raised an armed force, tore down the Company's flag and assaulted a sezawal who had been instructed to collect the outstanding payment, tearing up his parwana in the process. The immediate force available to the Company at Belluah, as the zamindars were certainly aware, was very small. Consequently, in the face of this symbolic disregard for its sovereignty, not to mention an actual loss of revenue, the Company servant on the spot, a Mr Wroughton, forbade any armed reprisal.[81] He could not safely take punitive action with the troops at his disposal (one naik and four sepoys) and so did not wish to be under the 'disagreeable necessity' of opposing the zamindars by force,[82] preferring instead to transfer responsibility for the chaotic situation to the chief at Islamabad.[83]

With the gaze of the Board of Revenue focussed on Sandwip by the petitioning of Pir Mahommed, it is hardly surprising that none of the local officials wished to take any decisions that might exacerbate matters. To respond precipitately with the limited troops on the spot would mean, in the short term at least, almost certain defeat for the Company; to dispatch a punitive expedition and compel the zamindars to obey the dictates of government by brute force could cause instability within the district, provoking fear and anger against the Company from sympathetic local groups. The Sandwip zamindars were not contesting the right of the government to tax them per se, merely protesting about an increase in the amount of tax demanded of them, and, while non-payment of this additional revenue was an affront to the Company, it was by no means the worst possible scenario. Any escalation in the unrest, provoked by too weak or too heavy-handed a response on the part of the Chittagong authorities, could seriously disrupt the collections for an indefinite period, perhaps bringing about a total, if temporary, cessation in the flow of the revenue stream, and possibly affecting collections outside Sandwip. Such a mishandling of the situation, striking at the district administration's core function of revenue extraction, would swiftly bring down Fort William's censure on the heads of the hapless local officials. Therefore, the Company servants at Chittagong passed responsibility back and forth among themselves, each desperately trying not to be the one who had to take action.

In this way, the zamindars appear to have avoided any significant reprisal following their assault on the sezawal. By lodging their appeals through an official framework at Calcutta, they had, to an extent, legitimised their protest, even if some doubt was cast on the veracity of their claims. This approach transformed the Sandwip re-evaluation from a municipal matter into a political issue at the highest level of government, and, whether the zamindars realised it or not, the attention of Fort William having been drawn to Sandwip, the Chittagong officials hesitated to tackle a problem which had the potential to damage their reputation within the Company's service.

Such canny, high-level political manoeuvring on the part of discontented groups, while by no means unique, was not common in this period. In response to the more usual threats, which were of a purely local character, the preferred option of district officials was to use armed force to impose the government's will, but only if the armed forces involved were of a quantity and quality which significantly weighted the outcome of any contest in the Company's favour. As a decisive force of this kind was not often available to collectors, the working solution usually attempted to skirt between negotiation with belligerent groups, which might prove time-consuming, ineffective and, worse still, imply timidity, and the deployment of an inadequate force, which could have even more damaging consequences for the Company's local authority were it to suffer a reverse. The middle way, to ignore local problems which could not be countered in the hope that they would resolve themselves, was one to which collectors seem to have frequently resorted. Such behaviour only becomes visible in those cases where an official's inactivity allowed disruption within the district to escalate hugely, rendering external communication unavoidable, as with Ranu Khan in 1777. Even then it is necessary to read such correspondence 'against the grain' in order to determine the likely course of events which the district official was trying to conceal in order to present himself in a more favourable light.

External threats: the Arakanese refugee crisis, 1775–1800

Chittagong's officials, however, were not troubled just by discontented rural magnates and their adherents: significant disruption was also caused by the activities of groups external to the district. In common with much of the Company's frontier territory in the north and east of Bengal during this period (particularly in the 1770s), Chittagong was disturbed by large bands of Hindu sannyasis as they travelled through the province exacting alms from rural communities. The raiyats lived in 'great Terror' of these armed mendicants, and, fearing robbery or physical violence at their hands, the peasantry began to desert the affected areas. In this way, cultivation was disrupted, prompting a corresponding decline in the territorial revenues which could be realised by the local authorities.[84] Such was the scale of the problem that a response had to be co-ordinated by the central government, rather than leaving operations to the discretion of the individual district administrations. In January 1773, Charles Bentley, the chief at Chittagong, received instructions from Fort William that, on account of the 'frequent and distressing' incursions of the sannyasis, he was to set up a network of police posts across his district to disarm any groups of travellers. Public notice was to be given that 'all Persons or Bodys of men travelling armed thro' the Country will be regarded as Enemies of the Government & pursued accordingly'.[85] Given the embryonic nature of the Company state at this time and the limited resources available to the local authorities, any attempt by the chief to impose a monopoly on the use of violence in his district was certain to be fraught with difficulties, and, unsurprisingly, within two months these orders had been rescinded.[86] Charles Bentley's attitude towards the preservation of Tripura from the sannyasis gives some indication of the problems encountered in providing an adequate defensive force. The Company's military officer in Tripura, Lieutenant Foster Bentley, had been advised by the local raja that 1,000 barqandazes 'would be but barely Sufficient to Guard the Borders of this wild & extensive Country'.[87] As he had only a single company of pargana battalion sepoys under his command (in all likelihood rather fewer than 100 men), and as the raja undertook to pay a large subsidy towards the cost of raising a force of barqandazes, the mercenaries were duly enrolled. Chittagong's chief was infuriated by his namesake's conduct, and raised 'many Objections', considering it an 'Extraordinary Large' expense for Islamabad to bear. Even though, as the lieutenant pleaded, 'the Publick Enemy was . . . nigh at our Doors', the Chittagong authorities could not countenance the expenditure of even 3,000 rupees 'to insure the receipt of a Revenue of nearly 1 ½ Lacks [150,000 rupees]'.[88]

Considerable though the disruption caused by these sannyasi incursions was, the activities of local powers, principally Burma, had as great, if not greater, implications for the district's security. The Burmese threat was ostensibly that of a rival state directly menacing the Company's territory with its armed forces. However, in addition to this external dimension, Burma's assimilation of neighbouring Arakan generated vast numbers of refugees who streamed into Chittagong, presenting the district authorities with a far more complex problem to solve than one of straightforward Burmese aggression and expansion at the Company's expense.

The first major influx of refugees occurred in 1775, when roughly 2,000 Arakanese, fleeing from the political upheavals of their country, spilled into Chittagong.[89] Although the cause of this mass emigration was not explicitly stated by Chittagong's chief, Burmese depredations in Arakan from the late 1760s onwards almost certainly played a significant part.[90] In 1777, the raja of Arakan wrote to the chief demanding the return of several of these refugees, who were presumably his political opponents.[91] No action appears to have been taken in this regard by the Chittagong authorities, and the issue of Arakanese immigration remained in the background until the Burmese invasion of that country in 1785. This triggered a huge exodus, with thousands of people flooding into Chittagong.[92] By the end of the century, it was estimated that at least 25,000 Arakanese immigrants had come to the district, many of them in the period immediately after the 1785 invasion.[93] This influx of large numbers of destitute individuals presented the Chittagong authorities with a tremendous opportunity to develop the district's agrarian economy, but it also generated grave problems. It was not until the early years of the 19th century, after the establishment of a base for them at Cox's Bazar, near Ramu in the south of the district, that the Company's attempts at settlement met with even partial success.[94] The fraught history of the settlement of these refugees in Chittagong reveals much about the nature of the Company's early administration and about the priorities of the local officials.

A prime example of the way in which the post-1785 wave of immigration was to trouble the Chittagong authorities came with the robbery and murder in 1787 of a British subject, one James Raby, at the mouth of the Naaf River.[95] The area where the murder took place was 'an entire Jungle, occasionally inhabited by Muggs (Maghs)'.[96] However, this was not a straightforward case of robbery and murder being carried out by bandits; a closer investigation of the events surrounding Raby's death, commissioned by Shearman Bird, the collector of Chittagong, revealed a more complex process at work. The information which Bird received from the two peons deputed to make enquiries regarding the local Maghs indicated that they had not 'committed such Depredations formerly as have been evinced of late' and suggested by way of explanation for this change 'the peculiar situation of the Inhabitants since the arracan Country was Invaded by the Burmas from Pegue [Pegu: a port city and district in southern Burma]'.[97] The implication was that the Arakan refugees, who formed a sizeable part of the immediate population, were directly linked to the increase in local unrest. How was it that these refugees, far from being utilised by the Company to settle the district's borders and increase the revenue, were actually allowed seriously to disrupt local society and act against the government's interests? The answer to this lies in the context of Raby's murder in early 1787: it occurred in the midst of several incursions into Chittagong by Burmese armies. The first series of raids, commencing in January 1786, were led by Wankechah, the general who had conquered Arakan in the previous year,[98] and in June 1787, a single incursion was made into Chittagong by a large force under Waza, the 'Pegu Raja' (the governor of Pegu).[99]

Wankechah's raids were carried out with the aim of capturing several high-ranking Arakanese who had fled to a village situated on the Naaf River, inside Company territory.[100] Among these political refugees was one Kewooty, Wankechah's principal target, together with the son and son-in-law of Lowardung, the late raja of Arakan. After seeking asylum they had been installed by Chittagong's collector, Charles Croftes, in the house of Joao de Barros,[101] a zamindar of Portuguese descent.[102] Wankechah, wrote to Croftes threatening to attack if Kewooty and the other Arakanese were not immediately surrendered.[103] Clearly unsatisfied with the collector's dilatory reply, he crossed the border in pursuit of the fugitives, killing a number of the Company's Bengali subjects in the process.[104] Kewooty and his followers fled to the hills of the borderlands after being attacked by this Burmese force, but their hiding place was soon betrayed, upon which Wankechah made a further incursion into Company territory and killed Kewooty.[105]

The raid carried out by Waza in June 1787 was essentially a continuation of the task begun by Wankechah in the previous year: Kewooty had been eliminated and now Waza moved to secure the remaining dissidents.[106] The pacification of Arakan had apparently reached a stage where large numbers of troops could be released for the invasion of Chittagong, and this second Burmese army numbered 3,000 to 4,000 musketeers,[107] a large body of swordsmen-pioneers, and an artillery train of 50 light cannon.[108] It was a force at least five times as large as that which the collector could put into the field to oppose it. On 2 June, Waza's soldiers arrived at the village of Barrapallung in the Company's territory, putting the inhabitants to flight, before moving on to nearby Ramu where they imprisoned the Indian *gomasta* (commercial agent), the sole representative of the Company there, and named several high-ranking Arakanese fugitives whom they demanded be given up. There also seems to have been a secondary motive to the raid. Waza was not there simply to eliminate political dissidents: in addition, his men seized a large number of raiyats, whom, the gomasta asserted, were to accompany the Burmese force back to Arakan where they would presumably be put to work in the fields.[109]

An explanation both for Raby's murder and, more broadly, for the failure of the Chittagong authorities to settle the Arakanese immigrants during a period of nearly 20 years may be found in a comment made by Kewooty to the Company officials with whom he had sought refuge. He claimed, 'Those who had fled for Safety into this Province [Chittagong] . . . had not experienced that Security and safety they expected to meet with from the English'.[110] This was the case for him in 1786, it remained so for the refugees during the remainder of the century, and it is equally applicable to the Company's Bengali subjects who were ill-treated by the Burmese troops. Before they could become a productive labour force and act as a bulwark against gradual Burmese encroachment on the frontier, the refugees had to be encouraged to engage in settled cultivation. Naturally, they would not settle where they did not feel safe, and the military resources available to the collector were not sufficient to allow him to protect the refugees against the Burmese raids. Upon receipt of Wankechah's preliminary threats regarding the surrender of Kewooty in 1786, Croftes had ordered part of Chittagong's battalion to march to the mouth of the Naaf and take up a defensive position there.[111] However, Wankechah's force had not yet arrived in those parts, and such a large proportion of the district's troops could not be kept indefinitely at 'the Extremities of the Province',[112] far from the administrative centre of Islamabad. Therefore, the battalion was swiftly recalled, and replaced by a company of sepoys stationed under an NCO at Ramu for the protection of the refugees. Yet again, such was the strain on the district's resources that even so small a body could not be allowed to remain idle, and the 'detachment was recalled soon after when tranquillity appeared to be Re-established'.[113] It was at this point that Wankechah attacked. Likewise, in the following year, the absence of Company troops in the vicinity meant that Waza was able to occupy Ramu, molest its inhabitants, apprise the collector of his presence and then withdraw in good order, apparently without there being even the contemplation of a military reprisal against him.[114] Indeed, given the relative sizes of the local Company and Burmese forces, it is arguable that this is another case of a collector ignoring a threat which it was too dangerous to tackle. Even though the security of the Company's territory had been violated and both its subjects and the Arakanese refugees had suffered terribly, this was less damaging to the standing of the district's chief with his employers than a probable military reverse at the hands of Waza's army.

The inability of the Chittagong authorities to protect the refugees as a whole was the central factor which hindered their settlement. A small number of the Arakanese immigrants, resenting the occupation of their country by the Burmese, determined to prosecute a cross-border guerrilla campaign against their conquerors.[115] Their actions provoked a correspondingly aggressive response from the Burmese, who hoped to eliminate this seat of resistance in the Company's territory and to compel the return of as many refugees as possible in order to bolster their own agrarian economy.[116] For the vast majority of these refugees, fear of the unchecked Burmese raids militated against permanent settlement in Chittagong and investment in regular, or even *jhum*, cultivation.[117] Yet, clearly, they needed to find a means of survival and subsistence. Shearman Bird reported to the Board of Revenue that it was the Arakanese whose leaders had formerly taken refuge at the house of Joao de Barros who were responsible for James Raby's death. Observing the fate of Kewooty, they had despaired of the Company's protection and gone into hiding in the borderlands between Chittagong and Arakan, and it was from here that 'still suspicious and apprehensive of having any settled or fixed habitation within this District or in their own' they 'occasionally resort hither for the purpose of robbing and murdering such of the Chittagong people as they may eventually meet with: an instance of which your Honorable Board has already been informed of in the murder of Mr Raby'.[118] The guilt of these individuals seems to have been so widely credited that Waza, writing to the collector in the aftermath of his raid, cited the murder as part of his rationale in invading.

> Doomeon, Chukma, Keeopa, Leeo, Murrung and other Inhabitants of Arracan have now absconded and taken refuge near the

> Mountains within your Border and exercise Depredations on the people belonging to both countries and they moreover murdered an Englishman at the Mouth of Nauf and stole everything he had with him. Hearing this I came to your boundaries with an Army in order to seize them because they have deserted their own country, are disobedient to my king and exercise the Profession of Robbers. It is not proper that you should give an Asylum to them or the other Mugs who have absconded from Arracan and you will do right to drive them from your Country that a Friendship may remain perfect and that the Road of Travellers and Merchants may be rendered secured. If you do not drive them from your Country and give them up I shall be under the Necessity of seeking them out with an Army in whatever part of your Territories they may be.[119]

For two consecutive years Chittagong had been invaded, and its inhabitants, both sovereign subjects and foreign refugees seeking asylum, had been molested and killed. The local economy had been damaged by these incursions. Existing cultivators had been driven from their lands in terror or kidnapped to serve new masters, and the potential cultivators among the Arakanese immigrants had been prevented from settling through fear of the Burmese raiding parties. Yet Chittagong's collectors had not made any effective military response to these depredations. Now, so disengaged were the authorities at Islamabad from local society away from the urban centre, that a neighbouring power was able to justify an invasion of the Company's territory on the grounds of imposing law and order. In this early period, Chittagong's authorities lacked the military resources to penetrate local society to any great extent, and, whatever the rhetoric in Calcutta, the collector had no notion of imposing a 'rule of law' across his entire district, or of safeguarding every one of the Company's subjects from the violence of neighbouring powers. He was content to accrue as much revenue as possible while ignoring all disruptions within local society other than those which significantly hindered this limited aim. The sacking of a village or two on the frontier did not represent enough of a financial inconvenience to warrant a hazardous military operation against vastly superior numbers of Burmese. In corresponding with Fort William, accounts of the raids could be toned down, their scale subtly reduced; it would be much harder for the collector to spin a military defeat in which the district's troops had been routed in their own territory.

Although the Company claimed to be governing Chittagong, its effective occupation was not district-wide. By keeping the bulk of his forces garrisoned at Islamabad, the chief controlled the district's administrative hub and the immediate surrounding area. Usually, this was all that was necessary for revenue to be accumulated from the mofussil and remitted to Calcutta in amounts sufficient to satisfy the central government's demands. Also, it was often not possible to bring a substantial portion of the district's armed forces to bear on one threat without dangerously weakening the local authorities' grip on another part of the district, perhaps even its administrative headquarters. Although a significant part of the Islamabad garrison was occasionally deployed piecemeal across the district on various duties this was more typical of the 1760s and 1770s;[120] later, Fort William began to threaten district officials with severe punishment if they failed to keep their military strength concentrated.[121] By the 1780s, the permanent stationing of significant bodies of troops anywhere other than Islamabad was much less common; partly because of Fort William's extreme disapproval of the practice, but mainly, one suspects, because a succession of district officials had realised the futility of deploying small parties of sepoys to counter a multitude of simultaneous threats to the public peace. Had those officials created permanent outposts across the district, this would have meant using most of their limited military resources in a futile attempt to impose a 'rule of law' about which they cared very little. At the same time, it would have weakened the seat of power at Islamabad and undermined the wider process of revenue extraction, thereby exposing the district's chief to Fort William's wrath.[122]

With the limited military resources at their disposal, local officials struggled to counter violence within their district, or to protect its inhabitants from external powers. They only took action when the revenue stream was significantly disrupted and the attention of their superiors therefore drawn to the district. This being the case, it is unsurprising that no robust action was taken against the Burmese invaders in 1786 and 1787. These were more formidable opponents by far than the Company's discontented subjects in Chittagong, even those as troublesome as the band led by Ranu Khan, and using the Islamabad garrison to oppose the Burmese on the frontier was fraught with appalling risks. Furthermore, the two collectors, Croftes and Bird, could afford to remain passive, since these were raids with a limited scope. Wankechah and Waza were in Chittagong primarily to eradicate their political opponents and perhaps also to seize some raiyats for the use of Burma's new client kingdom; there was no question of them occupying the Company's territory permanently, at least not yet. It was altogether preferable for the collectors to allow this short-term disruption to the Company's subjects on the periphery than to request military aid from Fort William and risk being blamed for drawing the Company into a costly war with Burma. Although the conversion of the refugees into an economic asset was desirable, the potential benefits of such development were outweighed by the fear that protecting them would actually jeopardise the collectors' professional credit, since it was likely to lead to an escalation in Anglo-Burmese hostilities. Occasional raids might damage the local economy by disrupting the cultivators in the far south of the district, yet, even with these incursions, Chittagong still yielded a considerable amount of revenue for the Company. The stationing of a larger military force in the district, not to say open conflict with Burma, had the potential to render the Company's occupation of Chittagong significantly less profitable for years to come. This was not a state of affairs likely to please Fort William, and it would have had a most detrimental effect on the career of a district official if he were considered responsible for bringing it about.

It was quite natural that the collectors would attempt to conceal events when it lay beyond their power to intervene without considerable risk to their professional standing, and it is notable that the Burmese incursions of 1786 and 1787 appear to have generated very little in the way of correspondence. Other than Croftes's response to Wankechah's threats against Kewooty, a copy of which was forwarded to the Board of Revenue in January 1786, the main document on these raids is the letter of 26 March 1787 from Shearman Bird to the Board, and that itself was prompted by the murder of James Raby which, indirectly, elevated the incursions from a district matter (which could be concealed from Fort William by the collector) to an issue of wider importance.[123] The killing of a Briton in the Company's territory focussed Fort William's attention on Chittagong and raised questions about the security of the revenues in such a lawless environment. Having fixed the blame for the murders squarely on the refugees, Bird was at pains to emphasise that their crimes were not attributable to the shortcomings of the local government, nor was their loss as an economic force something to be mourned.

> I do not conceive that these Freebooters will ever render this Country any essential service. They dare not venture to fix their Habitations on either side of the Naaf, for fear of being Destroyed by the Peguers – and by this means they are driven to the necessity of Plundering the neighbourhood for a subsistence. This induces me to Recommend to your Honorable Board to order a Party of

> Sepoys to be stationed in the Purgunnah of Rammoo for the Purpose of protecting these Districts from any Depredations they may in future attempt.[124]

Bird's denigration of these refugees as 'freebooters' seems rather disingenuous. It ignores the fact that their 'freebooting' had its roots in his unwillingness and that of his predecessor Croftes, to run the risks inherent in providing a secure environment for them. This had turned potential cultivators into hopeless itinerants or, worse still, predatory bands of dakaits, and Bird attempted to conceal this failure through the implicit denial that the Company had any responsibility to intervene. Even though these events were taking place in Company territory, Bird described them in terms of a conflict solely between the Burmese and the Arakanese immigrants; the Company was presented as lacking agency even within its own territory.

Finding itself too weak to keep the peace between the opposing parties, Islamabad had to choose between fighting the Burmese military and fighting the 'freebooters'. This goes some way to explaining why Bird was requesting a garrison of sepoys to keep the refugees in check, rather than one which could defend them against the Burmese raids. It was proportionately less expensive to maintain a small police force capable of suppressing the refugees than an army which could defend the district against thousands of Burmese soldiers supported by artillery. While it had become apparent to Bird that, the attention of Fort William having been drawn to his district, it was now necessary for him to be seen to act, it was also apparent that the cheaper the proposed action, the less likely it was to rile his profit-sensitive superiors. This token company of sepoys was duly authorised by Fort William to protect the southern frontier communities from molestation, and, although this served Bird's immediate purpose of making him appear thrifty yet effective, from a military standpoint it was an unsuccessful measure. It was too small a force to circumscribe the activities of the desperate refugees who continued to flee Arakan throughout the 1790s[125] or to prevent large bodies of Burmese troops from repeatedly invading Chittagong and laying waste to the country in pursuit of them.[126]

The fundamental aim of Chittagong's collectors from 1786 until the turn of the century was to deal quietly with a situation from which they could gain no credit and thereby avoid the censure of Fort William. This was best achieved by appeasing Burma, despite its negative implications for the development of the district's economy and for local society's opinion of the Company's rule. Francis Buchanan, writing in 1798, observed that 'both Rakain and Bengalese are persuaded, that, in the late dispute with the Burmas (1794) the refugees were given up by our Government from fear'[127] and upon speaking to Puran Bisungri, the *thanadar* (police chief) in charge of Ramu, Buchanan discovered that he was 'terribly afraid that the Government of Bengal will be forced to give up to the Burmas all the refugees from Arakan'.[128] Arriving in the district in ever increasing numbers and lacking the security to establish themselves, the refugees were an irritation for a succession of Chittagong's collectors, and, consequently, those Company servants made little attempt to protect a commodity whose value could not be realised.

Local self-interest and the limits of Fort William's authority

In case this suggests that a high degree of collusion took place between district officials in concealing information from Calcutta, engendered by their shared experience of the difficulties of local government, it must be emphasised that these reactions were prompted by individual self-interest, rather than by any sense of professional kinship. As has been seen with the case of the Sandwip zamindars in 1786, the Company's district administrators felt little loyalty to each other, and desperately passed responsibility for failure back and forth among themselves whenever the attention of their superiors was drawn towards them. Indeed, they were not above insuring themselves against future blame or even clearing the field of professional rivals, by informing on their colleagues to Fort William. For example, in November 1771 a dispute arose between Walter Wilkins, the chief at Chittagong, and Thomas Sheeles, the head of the Company's Kulinda textile factory. Finding that the cloth 'pikars' (petty agents) at Kulinda were being subjected to 'undue and oppressive exactions' by two Indian officials, the chief made arrangements to have the perpetrators tried before his court.[129] In so doing, he incurred the enmity of Sheeles, who was responsible for the operation of the factory. Their quarrel over jurisdiction escalated, until Sheeles finally wrote a highly offensive open letter to Wilkins, complaining of the 'pernicious & deplorable Consequen[ce]s' of the chief's behaviour for the Company's interests at Kulinda.[130] It was at this point that Wilkins felt the need to defend himself in the eyes of his employers and to rid himself of a disagreeable colleague. He wrote to Fort William, decrying Sheeles's laxity (although still in the district, he had been absent without leave from his post at Kulinda for 15 months) and acidly observing that the factor's newfound zeal for the Company's interests 'is, at least on this Occasion a mi[s]taken one, if not altogether dictated by Sentiments far less laudable'.[131] Wilkins felt that his 'public character' had been damaged by Sheeles's accusations, which had been 'calculate[d] [m]ost grosly to misrepresent' the chief, and he had responded in kind.[132] A personal attack was employed to counter a personal attack; it was a drama played out for Fort William's benefit since it was the approval of his superiors which each man was aiming to secure. Ultimately, the escalation of the conflict backfired dramatically for Wilkins: the response from Fort William to his letter was that 'both [you] and Mr Sheeles have acted improperly and [you] [h]ave not been free from Blame'.[133] Sheeles was condemned for having been absent from his post, but Wilkins was also castigated for having permitted that state of affairs to continue for so long. Neither man was in place when, 15 months later, tensions between Islamabad and the outlying stations flared up once more. In February 1773, William Barton, the resident at Lakshmipur, wrote to the Controlling Committee of Accounts, complaining bitterly about the conduct of Chittagong's new chief, Charles Bentley. Barton had been pressured to sign off a set of accounts which contained a serious error so that the blame for the discrepancy in funds when it was discovered by their superiors would fall on the resident Barton, rather than the chief Bentley.[134] Barton had angrily refused to comply with the chief's repeated orders, and he appended his response to Bentley and his assistants for the information of the committee:

> You are at entire liberty to make what plea you Choose in excuse for this delay in the transmittal of the Subsidiary Books; but beware, Gentlemen, how you cast any reflections upon me, to save yourselves; as then you will drive me to the '*disagreeable necessity*' of representing the affair in its true colours to the Committee of Accompts; & I flatter myself the result of our recriminations would be to your disparagement not mine . . . I do not think it consistent to avow publick errors with the sanction of my name.[135]

The tone of this letter is characteristic of the personal animosity which frequently developed between local officials as they competed for lucrative posts in the Company's service. It gives a sense of the environment in which district officers operated during this period; not only were they struggling with the threats posed by the local population, they also had to be extremely wary of the machinations of their colleagues. Following hard on this controversy, by the end of the month, Bentley found himself being censured by Warren Hastings for treating the Committee of Revenue's orders with 'little respect' and trying to expand his personal fiefdom by establishing a kachari in neighbouring Tripura.[136] It is tempting to speculate that the attention which Barton had brought to bear on Bentley earlier in the month had resulted in the closer inspection of his affairs by Fort William, and contributed to this reprimand.

Between the 1760s and the 1780s, the relative fluidity and novelty of the Company's territorial administration rendered posts insecure but also provided enormous opportunities for aggrandisement if officials could seize them. Although these public quarrels with their strong element of personal interest are much more apparent during the earlier decades, they did not entirely die out by the end of the period under investigation. Indeed, a prime example of local self-interest, and the powerlessness of the central government to counter it effectively, can be seen in the events following the appointment of Captain Hiram Cox of the Bengal Army as special commissioner for the Arakanese refugees in March 1799.[137] The experience of Cox neatly illustrates the culture of personal interest which existed among district officials in the early Company state. It also gives some indication of their power to curb the encroachments of central government on what they considered to be their preserve.

Over the quarter of a century since the arrival of the initial 2,000 Arakanese in 1775,[138] the number of refugees in the immediate vicinity of Ramu had soared to at least 25,000, and they were suffering great hardship from want of food.[139] Clearly, a crisis on such a scale could not fail to attract the attention of Fort William, and this threatened to force action upon those local officials who had been quietly ignoring the growing refugee problem for a number of years.

The decision to appoint a commissioner was taken by Sir Alured Clarke, the commander-in-chief of British military forces in India, who was made acting governor-general following the departure of Sir John Shore in 1797. To fund the establishment of a settlement and granaries for the Arakanese immigrants, Cox was authorised by Clarke to draw on the Islamabad treasury for whatever sums he required.[140] The sudden arrival in Chittagong of a mere captain of sepoy infantry, however experienced he may have been in Burmese affairs,[141] vested with proconsular powers over the local authorities and demanding, rather brusquely, staggering amounts of ready currency (he requested 80,000 rupees for his use in April 1799), was not calculated to inspire a spirit of cooperation on the part of the district officials, even if it was within their means to supply what he desired.[142] Thomas Powney, the acting collector of Chittagong, baulked at paying 80,000 rupees out of his reserves and even refused the sum of 20,000 rupees demanded by Cox for March. He requested that the collector of Dhaka send him a large quantity of silver to cover the prospective expenditure and refused to release any funds whatsoever until he had received the Board's explicit written authorisation to do so.[143] He did not deem the council's resolution that Cox was 'authorized . . . to draw on the Collector of Chittagong for such advances as may be immediately necessary' to be sufficient authority for him to throw open his treasury.[144]

Cox's response to Powney's concerns was hardly conciliatory, writing as he did that 'if you do not answer my draft *all my operations* must be suspended and the responsibility of the consequences, whatever they may be *must rest with you*'.[145] Cox also scorned Powney's claim that Chittagong's zamindars could not produce the 69,000 maunds of rice and paddy which he had requested for the immediate relief of the Arakanese, observing that it was 'assuredly by no means equal to what this fertile country is capable of supplying'.[146] He went on to instruct Chittagong's acting collector in how he should best carry out his duties.

> I am so well convinced of the abundance of grain in this Country, that if I had power I would be bound to form Granaries of a hundred times the extent of what I have required . . . It is not the representations of a Dewan or the Zemindars to which one should listen, but the population, annual produce, and actual expenditure should be referred to, if we wish to ascertain the truth.[147]

Again, a junior military officer adopting such a tone towards a district collector (albeit an acting one) would hardly foster willing cooperation. Nor indeed did his appeal to the magistrate at Chittagong to bring pressure to bear on Powney have any very happy effect.[148] Chittagong having failed to supply anything approaching the requested amount of money or grain for the settlement at Ramu, Cox began to cast his net wider, to Dhaka and Tripura.[149] This simply caused officials in the two districts to request currency and grain from each other.[150] By the end of April, the eastern districts had still failed to provide for the immigrants, causing Cox to exclaim that the Arakanese were 'from every Quarter disappointed'.[151] Even when, by mid-May, supplies of grain had been collected, it was discovered that the local authorities lacked the means to transport them to Ramu, suitable boats not being procurable in any of the districts.[152] By January 1800 a mere 16,000 maunds had reached the settlement, which was less than a quarter of the amount which Cox had originally requested, and even then, due to the corruption of the settlement officials charged with its distribution, the refugees did not receive all of this paltry supply.[153]

At the end of April 1799, in the midst of this chaos, with huge numbers of Arakanese 'dying daily for want of subsistence' and masses of indignant correspondence circulating between Cox and the officials of the three districts, Clarke decided to recall his commissioner.[154] This was, he said, not only on the grounds of the 'heavy Expense' which was being incurred to very little effect, but also because of 'the embarrassments which . . . are likely to arise from the interference of the authority vested in the Commissioner with the regular and established authority of the Country'.[155] Authority over the Arakanese settlement was transferred to the collector of Chittagong and Cox was relieved of his duties at Ramu, where, shortly afterwards, he fell gravely ill and died.[156]

Chittagong's collector, Francis Pierard, having recovered his health by this time, took over from his assistant Powney, and began to put the settlement's affairs in order. It was decided that the immigrants would have to pay their way if they wanted to receive the support of the district authorities. The first flush of Burmese interest in reclaiming them had died down, and it appeared that a substantial portion of the refugees could now be settled. However, this was not a task which Pierard undertook very willingly, anxious as he was that

> my own Time and attention (which the ordinary duties of my office most urgently called for the whole of) might not be misemployed in the duties of providing food for and portioning out lands for Cultivation to Persons who were averse to Settling themselves for a permanency.[157]

The supply of rice would be discontinued to refugees who had failed to clear their allocated plot of land by a given date,[158] and there was no disguising the fact that the humanitarian element of the scheme was very much subordinate to its profitability; the settlement would have to 'materially contribute to the Increase of the Company's Land Revenues'.[159] By May 1800, the refugees had cleared an estimated 5,000 *bighas* (approximately 1,700 acres) of woodland for cultivation.[160] This was part of a broader initiative on the part of Fort William to put land in the east and south of the district in a state of cultivation, with attempts also being made around this time to encourage the sepoys of the Chittagong invalid thanah to bring wasteland under the plough.[161]

The failure of Cox's efforts to settle the Arakanese at Ramu in 1799 could, at first glance, be ascribed simply to a scarcity of food supplies in eastern Bengal coupled with the weakness of the provincial transport infrastructure. Certainly, Chittagong was famously fertile, but, as Cox himself suggested, shrewd zamindars may have been able to conceal large supplies of rice and paddy from district collectors, and the difficulty of transporting bulky masses of grain without it being spoiled by damp was doubtless considerable.[162] Yet, even if it were that simple, this would seem to provide ample evidence of the failure of the local officials to engage thoroughly with district society. It would have meant that they had allowed themselves, as collectors in an agriculturally based territorial revenue system, to remain unaware of vast hidden stores of grain, and the total inadequacy of the transport infrastructure is testimony to the failure of their attempts at economic development. If anything, this would support the argument that district collectors were content to achieve those limited aims which would satisfy the immediate demands of their superiors, rather than to risk any damaging reverses which might arise from attempting to impose the Company's authority in every corner of their district.

Yet, arguably, it was not that simple, and Cox's efforts seem to have been thwarted, at least in part, by the self-interest of those district officials with whom he had to deal. The recall of Cox after barely a month in the post of commissioner and authority over the settlement subsequently being vested in the district collector strongly suggests a more complex process at work. If it had been that Cox, as an individual, was incapable of solving these supply and transportation problems, then another commissioner would have been appointed, but the post itself was abolished after only a very brief trial.

It seems that it was the imposition of an outsider, a proconsular figure from Fort William, which caused ill-feeling and hampered the necessary cooperation between Cox and the district officials. Much as the collector of Chittagong resented the additional workload, once the refugee crisis had intensified to the point where the acting governor-general was taking an interest in events, he had to be seen to be dealing with the situation himself. There was a strong element of criticism implicit in Fort William's employment of an external commissioner, and this attention from the upper echelons of government demanded swift and visible action in response. To remain on the sidelines while a junior Company officer, appointed behind his back, took charge of civil affairs within his district would have been damaging to the collector's professional reputation, and this may well have been instrumental in prompting Pierard's return from his sickbed.[163]

In addition to the curious abolition of the post of commissioner, the seemingly deliberate obstructionism of Powney, coupled with the uniform inability of officials in Dhaka and Tripura to provide help, allows an interpretation of local administrative resistance to be placed on events. Powney justified his non-cooperation as the necessity of adhering rigidly to established procedure, even though the appointment of a special commissioner was an extraordinary measure and Fort William clearly expected Cox to operate in a flexible way, unconstrained by that procedure, in order to accomplish a difficult task. In addition to the resentment which he may have felt towards Cox as an outsider meddling none too delicately in district affairs, Powney was also in a tenuous professional position. His superior, Pierard, was on long-term sick leave, and Powney had been elevated accordingly. While this temporary promotion provided him with a platform from which to advertise his good qualities to Fort William, the newfound scrutiny of his superiors would also reveal any mistakes which he might make. Cox's demands for huge sums of money on the basis of his ad hoc authority were met with unwavering resistance and this defensive posture was almost certainly influenced by Powney's belief that, if he threw open the doors of his treasury to the commissioner now, he might find that he had insufficient cash reserves when a future crisis beckoned. Under these circumstances, Powney's superiors in Calcutta, and Pierard, might not be entirely sympathetic to the fact that he had allowed the Chittagong administration to fall into such a parlous state, whatever his excuse. His only chance of defending himself in that event was to have everything confirmed in triplicate by the Board of Revenue before funds were released to Cox.

The other collectors and assistants involved in this fiasco – Massie and Moore at Dhaka, and Crommelin and Dandrige at Tripura – had, ostensibly at least, less reason to be deliberately obstructive.[164] Being external to Chittagong, they had no professional responsibility for the refugees in that district, particularly as the Arakanese were gathered in the south, far from the borders of their own territories. However, quite apart from the interest which the collectors would have had in protecting their reserves of grain and currency to help them through future crises in their own districts, all of these officials would have been motivated by the same defensive sentiment which influenced Powney. They wanted to keep Calcutta's commissioners out of local affairs and thereby conceal knowledge of the shortcomings of their district administrations from their superiors. The precedent of a successful commissioner in Chittagong might lead to their increased use elsewhere as Fort William's 'trouble-shooters'. Realisation of the strength of feeling against his interference with the 'regular and established authority of the Country' prompted Clarke's abolition of the post of commissioner for the refugees and the transfer of authority to the district collector. This can be seen as a tacit admission on his part of the surprising power of local officials, on occasion, to resist the edicts of Fort William. They rarely attempted overt resistance, because their strategy was centred on conciliating their employers. A programme of 'everyday resistance', of foot-dragging and dissimulation, was practised by local officials because it achieved their ends without exposing them to the most serious chastisement, whereas open defiance of their superiors' authority would lead to instant dismissal.[165] The episode of Hiram Cox and the Arakanese refugees perfectly illustrates that the resistance of district officials to their superiors was not limited to concealment and passive omission in their correspondence; it also encompassed a policy of active non-cooperation with the agents of the central government.

The preceding chapters have outlined the causes and consequences of the fraught relationship which existed between the local and central authorities of the early Company state. The final chapter of this book will look broadly at changes which occurred in Anglo-Indian attitudes towards the government of that state by the 1820s and how they had been informed by the experience of Anglo-Indians in the precarious military-political environment of the earlier period.

Notes

1 W. W. Hunter, *Imperial Gazetteer of India, Vol. III, Birbhum to Coconada*, 2nd ed., London: Trubner & Co., 1885, p. 433.

2 The senior district official at Chittagong was styled the 'chief of the Chittagong factory' from 1760 until 1787.

3 H. Vansittart to H. Verelst, 1 December 1760, W. K. Firminger (ed.), *Bengal District Records: Chittagong, 1760–1773, Letters Received and Issued*, Vol. 1, Calcutta: Bengal Secretariat, 1923, p. 1.

4 H. Vansittart to H. Verelst, 16 December 1760, *ibid.*, p. 1.

5 The name 'Magh' was often applied indiscriminately by Bengalis and Europeans alike to several peoples living to the east of the district. See Francis Buchanan's remark: 'I find, that, the appellation of Mug is given by the people of this province to all the Tribes, and nations, east from Bengal, who as differing from the Hindoos, and Mussulmans, are considered as having no Cast, and as therefore being highly contemptible', 'An account of a Journey undertaken by Order of the Board of Trade through the Provinces of Chittagong and Tiperah, in order to look out for places most proper for the cultivation of Spices, by Francis Buchanan, M. D. (1798)', BL Add MSS 19, 286, pp. 28, 56, cit. W. van Schendel, 'The Invention of the "Jummas"': State Formation and Ethnicity in Southeastern Bangladesh', *Modern Asian Studies*, 1992, 26 (1): 100. More properly, the Maghs were one of the two largest Arakanese tribes, the other being the Chakmas. See S. Islam, 'Tribal Resistance in the Chittagong Hill Tracts (1776–87)', in N. R. Ray et al. (eds.), *Challenge: A Saga of India's Struggle for Freedom*, New Delhi: PPH, 1984, p. 122.

6 R. Forster, 'Magh Marauders, Portuguese Pirates, White Elephants and Persian Poets: Arakan and Its Bay-of-Bengal Connectivities in the Early Modern Era', *Explorations: A Graduate Student Journal of Southeast Asian Studies*, 2011, 11 (1): 70–71.
7 J. Stewart to C. Bentley, 23 January 1773, Firminger, *BDR: Chittagong*, I, pp. 70–71.
8 W. Wroughton to C. Croftes, 29 July 1786, Islam, *BDR: Chittagong*, pp. 182–183.
9 W. van Schendel (ed.), *Francis Buchanan in Southeast Bengal (1798): His Journey to Chittagong, the Chittagong Hill Tracts, Noakhali and Comilla*, Dhaka: University Press, 1992, p. 2.
10 *Ibid.*, p. xii.
11 W. W. Hunter, *Annals of Rural Bengal*, London: Smith, Elder & Co., 1868, pp. 20–48.
12 H. Vansittart to H. Verelst, 1 December 1760, Firminger, *BDR: Chittagong*, I, p. 1.
13 van Schendel, *Francis Buchanan*, p. xvi.
14 Chief at Chittagong to governor-general and council, 31 May 1777, Islam, *BDR: Chittagong*, p. 82.
15 A phase of Burmese expansion had begun in the middle of the 18th century, firstly with the subjugation of the neighbouring state of Pegu, then Tennaserrim in 1759, and the Arakan peninsula in 1785. This continued well into the 19th century, with the extension of Burmese influence into Manipur and Cachar in 1812, peaking in the period between 1817 and 1822, when the Burmese occupied Assam. See Peers, *Between Mars and Mammon*, p. 148.
16 van Schendel, *Francis Buchanan*, p. 36.
17 H. Verelst to H. Vansittart, 16 February1761, *ibid.*, pp. 148–53.
18 Chief at Chittagong to governor-general and council, 28 December 1778, Islam, *BDR: Chittagong*, p. 80; J. Reed to T. Sheeles, 7 December 1769, Firminger, *BDR: Chittagong*, I, p. 243. Also van Schendel, *Francis Buchanan*, p. 40.
19 F. Bentley to C. Bentley, 8 July 1773, Firminger, *BDR: Chittagong*, I, p. 103.
20 van Schendel, *Francis Buchanan*, p. 123.
21 *Ibid.*, p. 123.
22 'A Monthly Return of Ordnance Standing Ordnance Stores and Ammunition in the Garrison of Islamabad under the Command of Captain [. . .] kens for the Month of May 1771', Firminger, *BDR: Chittagong*, I, p. 50.
23 Chief at Chittagong to governor-general and council, 19 December 1776, Islam, *BDR: Chittagong*, p. 75.
24 Chief at Chittagong to governor-general and council, 15 December 1776, *ibid.*, p. 75.
25 J. Alexander to J. Reed, 8 March 1769, Firminger, *BDR: Chittagong*, I, p. 31.
26 Lacking the resources themselves, the Chittagong authorities had previously sought to procure them from other districts: 'I am informed that some light Boats fit for persuing the Arrakanners have been built by Mr Smith at Sootaloory under your directions. If you can spare ten or twelve such for the use of this Factory & will please to dispatch them hither with all possible expedition, they may at this time be of signal

service; they should be well mann'd with good Rowers and a guard of Seapoys'. J. Reed to T. Kelsall (Chief at Dhaka), 13 January 1769, Firminger, *BDR: Chittagong*, I, p. 211.

27 Chief at Chittagong to governor-general and council, 19 December 1776, Islam, *BDR: Chittagong*, p. 76.

28 Although Magh piracy lessened in intensity after the 1770s, there were still occasional outbreaks in the following decades. At the end of 1787, officials on Sandwip Island had to request reinforcement from Chittagong's collector to protect them from 'the continual Incursions and Depredations of the Dekoyts who at present infest in great numbers those parts of the sea which separate this Island from the Main'. J. Rawlins to S. Bird, 29 December 1787, NAB, Chittagong District Records, December 1787–April 1788 (Letters Received), A2.3/486, p. 42.

29 Although Magh piracy lessened in intensity after the 1770s, there were still occasional outbreaks in the following decades. At the end of 1787, officials on Sandwip Island had to request reinforcement from Chittagong's collector to protect them from 'the continual Incursions and Depredations of the Dekoyts who at present infest in great numbers those parts of the sea which separate this Island from the Main'. J. Rawlins to S. Bird, 29 December 1787, NAB, Chittagong District Records, December 1787–April 1788 (Letters Received), A2.3/486, p. 42.

30 J. Buller to D. Anderson, 12 August 1781, NAB, Islam, *BDR: Chittagong*, p. 86.

31 M. Serajuddin, *The Revenue Administration of the East India Company in Chittagong, 1761–1785*, Chittagong: University of Chittagong Press, 1971, p. 198.

32 Law refers to him as 'a Moutaineer named Runnoo Cawn, who pays the Company a small Revenue on their Cotton Farm'. Chief at Chittagong to governor-general and council, 10 April 1777, Islam, *BDR: Chittagong*, p. 238.

33 R. C. K. Roy, *Land Rights of the Indigenous Peoples of the Chittagong Hill Tracts, Bangladesh*, Copenhagen: IWGIA, 2003, p. 38.

34 Chief at Chittagong to governor-general and council, 10 April 1777, Islam, *BDR: Chittagong*, p. 238.

35 *Ibid.*

36 Serajuddin, *Revenue Administration*, p. 198.

37 Islam, 'Tribal Resistance', p. 23.

38 *Ibid.*, p. 123.

39 'Two thirds of the best of the cultivated Lands in this Province are held by Charity Sunnuds [*sanads* in this context are land grants] and when it is considered the major part is possessed by a set of Drones who wallow in wealth and Luxury, it is Vexatious to think they should not in some small degree contribute to the good of the Community by a Trifling tax'. Chief at Chittagong to the Collector General [. . .]1770, Islam, *BDR: Chittagong*, p. 213.

40 Islam, 'Tribal Resistance', p. 123.

41 *Ibid.*, p. 124.

42 The 22nd battalion of the Bengal Native Infantry, under the command of Captain Edward Ellerker was based at Islamabad at this time. Bengal Military Consultations, IOR, P/18/44, 22 January to 31 December 1777, p. 162.

43 Chief at Chittagong to governor-general and council, 10 April 1777, Islam, *BDR: Chittagong*, p. 238.
44 The Kukis are an ethnic group inhabiting a region which encompasses north-east India, north-west Burma and the Chittagong Hill Tracts. In this period, the Bengali inhabitants of Chittagong used the term to differentiate between those tribes in the east of the district who could not understand the Bengali vernacular and those, denominated *Jummas*, who could. See van Schendel, 'The Invention of the "Jummas"', p. 100.
45 Chief at Chittagong to governor-general and council, 10 April 1777, Islam, *BDR: Chittagong*, pp. 238–240.
46 Islam, 'Tribal Resistance', p. 124.
47 J. Buller to D. Anderson, 12 August 1781, Islam, *BDR: Chittagong*, p. 86.
48 'Derkhaste of Khoosaul Chaund Woddedar', 12 August 1781, *ibid.*, p. 266.
49 J. Buller to D. Anderson, 12 August 1781, *ibid.*, p. 86.
50 J. Buller to E. Ellerker, 11 October 1781, *ibid.*, p. 267.
51 J. Buller to E. Ellerker, 8 April 1782, *ibid.*, p. 272.
52 Chief at Chittagong to E. Ellerker, 4 August 1785, *ibid.*, pp. 298–299.
53 Islam, 'Tribal Resistance', p. 127.
54 *Ibid.*
55 See Board of Revenue Proceedings, 29 March 1787, *ibid.*, p. 128. Also, Roy, *Land Rights*, p. 40.
56 The main sources used for the correspondence between Islamabad and Calcutta during this period have been the two volumes of Chittagong district records edited by Sirajul Islam and W. K. Firminger. Although these published sources are necessarily selective, research undertaken by the author in 2008 at the National Archives of Bangladesh, Dhaka, using the original district letter books, has not revealed any further substantive correspondence on Ranu Khan. His disappearance at this point is confirmed by Islam, 'Tribal Resistance', p. 128.
57 Chief at Chittagong to governor-general and council, 10 April 1777, Islam, *BDR: Chittagong*, p. 238.
58 *Ibid.*
59 *Ibid.*, p. 239.
60 *Ibid.*, pp. 239–240.
61 *Ibid.*, p. 238.
62 The region's cotton supply was much valued by the Company. At the conclusion of the Chakma revolt, Calcutta stipulated that the raja pay his tribute in cotton, and later the Company exacted a 'Cotton Tax' from other groups within the eastern hill tracts. Eventually, the region became such a major source of this material that it acquired the name *Kapas Mahal* ('Cotton Area'). See Roy, *Land Rights*, p. 40; Marshall, *Bengal: The British Bridgehead*, p. 44.
63 Islam, 'Tribal Resistance', p. 123.
64 Law was right to be concerned, but his punishment was not severe. After the outbreak of the Chakma revolt, he was removed from Chittagong almost immediately, but after a brief interval he was employed at the Board of Trade, then as chief of the Lakshmipur factory. He finally returned to Dhaka as commercial chief, where, after a long illness, he died in 1792 at the age of 47.
65 'Juan . . . was lucky to find in Ranu Khan, his naib, an extraordinary leader for such guerrilla resistance', Islam, 'Tribal Resistance', p. 124. The

palwans or 'armies' of Ranu Khan were guerrilla formations drawn from all the hill tract tribes, but especially the Kukis. *Ibid.*, p. 125.

66 Chief at Chittagong to governor-general and council, 10 April 1777, Islam, *BDR: Chittagong*, p. 239.

67 *Ibid.*

68 *Ibid.*

69 *Ibid.*

70 Social bandits may be defined as 'peasant outlaws whom the lord and state regard as criminals, but who remain within peasant society, and are considered by their people as heroes, as champions, avengers, fighters for justice, perhaps even as leaders of liberation', Hobsbawm, *Bandits*, p. 20. While Ranu Khan, as the Chakma raja's *diwan*, was hardly a peasant in the literal sense, he was the member of a socio-ethnic group which considered itself oppressed; he was declared by the Company to be an enemy of the colonial state, and, arguably, he entertained an agenda of political liberation, rather than pure self-enrichment. He also seems to have derived much support from the local population. For these reasons, Ranu Khan may be placed among Hobsbawm's 'social bandits'.

71 'For if the authorities really bring in enough troops (the effect of which is not so much to frighten the bandit but to make the life of the peasants who support him miserable), and if a sufficiently large reward is offered, then his days are counted'. Hobsbawm, *Bandits*, p. 60.

72 Derkhaste of Khoosaul Chaund Woddedar, 12 August 1781, Islam, *BDR: Chittagong*, p. 266.

73 His cautious behaviour on this occasion appears to have done his career no harm, since he went on to become the Company's resident in neighbouring Tripura. S. Bird to J. Buller, 4 December 1787, NAB, Chittagong District Records, December 1787–April 1788 (Letters Received) A2.3/486, p. 1.

74 J. Buller, Acting Chief Chittagong, to D. Anderson, President of the Committee of Revenue at Fort William, 12 August 1781, Islam, *BDR: Chittagong*, p. 86.

75 *Ibid.*

76 The *wadahdar* was the Indian official charged under Warren Hastings's 'Permanent Plan' of 1781 with collecting revenue from the district's zamindars and remitting it to Calcutta. See Serajuddin, *Revenue Administration*, p. 100.

77 Derkhaste of Khoosaul Chaund Woddedar, 12 August 1781, Islam, *BDR: Chittagong*, p. 266.

78 'Translation of the Complaints of the Talookdars of Sundeep with the Remarks of Dyaram on Each article', *ibid.*, p. 191.

79 *Ibid.*, p. 193.

80 *Ibid.*

81 W. Wroughton, Belluah, to C. Croftes, 29 July 1786, *ibid.*, p. 183.

82 *Ibid.*

83 *Ibid.*

84 F. Bentley to C. Bentley, 8 July 1773, Firminger, *BDR: Chittagong*, I, p. 103.

85 J. Stewart to C. Bentley, 23 January 1773, *ibid.*, pp. 70–71.

86 J. Stewart to C. Bentley, 11 March 1773, *ibid.*, p. 80.

87 F. Bentley to C. Bentley, 8 July 1773, *ibid.*, p. 103.

88 *Ibid.*

89 Chief at Chittagong to governor-general and council, 17 November 1775, Islam, *BDR: Chittagong*, pp. 73–74.
90 In 1798, Francis Buchanan's conversation with an Arakanese priest at Manipur revealed that 'thirty years ago the Burmese first invaded their country and for eight years continued to lay it waste'. van Schendel, *Francis Buchanan*, p. 135.
91 Chief at Chittagong to governor-general and council, 31 May 1777, Islam, *BDR: Chittagong*, pp. 81–82.
92 van Schendel, *Francis Buchanan*, p. xvi.
93 H. Cox to F. Pierard or T. Powney, 19 March 1799, Bengal Revenue Consultations: 5 to 26 April 1799, IOR, P/54/2.
94 *Ibid.*
95 S. Bird to the Board of Revenue, 26 March 1787, BRC: 29 March to 30 April 1787, IOR, P/51/6 and 'Letter from the Arakan raja to the collector of Chittagong', 16 June 1787, Islam, *BDR: Chittagong*, p. 116.
96 S. Bird to the Board of Revenue, 26 March 1787, BRC: 29 March to 30 April 1787, IOR, P/51/6, pp. 475–476.
97 *Ibid.*, p. 476.
98 *Ibid.*
99 'Arzee from Muctaram, Gomastah of Sheebchurn', 5 June 1787, Islam, *BDR: Chittagong*, pp. 113–114.
100 S. Bird to the Board of Revenue, 26 March 1787, BRC: 29 March to 30 April 1787, IOR, P/51/6, p. 476.
101 *Ibid.*, pp. 476–477.
102 Serajuddin, *Revenue Administration*, p. 200.
103 S. Bird to the Board of Revenue, 26 March 1787, BRC: 29 March to 30 April 1787, IOR, P/51/6, p. 477.
104 *Ibid.*
105 *Ibid.*, p. 479.
106 A Letter from the Arakan Raja, 16 June 1787, Islam, *BDR: Chittagong*, p. 116.
107 'Arzee from Muctaram, Gomastah of Sheebchurn', 5 June 1787, *ibid.*, pp. 113–114.
108 van Schendel, *Francis Buchanan*, p. 57.
109 'Arzee from Muctaram, Gomastah of Sheebchurn', 5 June 1787, Islam, *BDR: Chittagong*, pp. 113–114.
110 S. Bird to the Board of Revenue, 26 March 1787, BRC: 29 March to 30 April 1787, IOR, P/51/6, p. 477.
111 *Ibid.*
112 *Ibid.*
113 *Ibid.*
114 'Arzee from Muctaram, Gomastah of Sheebchurn', 5 June 1787, Islam, *BDR: Chittagong*, pp. 113–114.
115 A Letter from the Arakan Raja, 16 June 1787, *ibid.*, p. 116.
116 See S. Bird to the Board of Revenue, 26 March 1787, BRC: 29 March to 30 April 1787, IOR, P/51/6 and 'Arzee from Muctaram, Gomastah of Sheebchurn' 5 June 1787, *ibid.*, pp. 113–114.
117 Jhum cultivation is a system of shifting cultivation practiced in north-eastern India and Bangladesh. Its practitioners engage in 'slash and burn' agriculture for short periods, and, having harvested their crops, move on to new areas.

118 S. Bird to the Board of Revenue, 26 March 1787, BRC: 29 March to 30 April 1787, IOR, P/51/6, p. 479.
119 A Letter from the Arakan Raja, 16 June 1787 Islam, *BDR: Chittagong*, p. 116.
120 J. Reed to T. Sheeles, 7 December 1769, Firminger, *BDR: Chittagong*, I, p. 243.
121 Revenue Committee Circular, 25 August 1783, Firminger, *BDR: Rangpur*, III, p. 70.
122 This was also the opinion of Sir William Wilson Hunter, based on an examination of the Company's administration in Birbhum during the same period: 'The English collectors interfered only when crimes of violence reached the point at which they endangered the revenue'. Hunter, *Annals of Rural Bengal*, p. 348.
123 C. Croftes to Board of Revenue, 12 January 1786, encl. S. Bird to the Board of Revenue, 26 March 1787, BRC: 29 March to 30 April 1787, IOR, P/51/6, p. 477.
124 S. Bird to the Board of Revenue, 26 March 1787, *ibid.*, pp. 480–481.
125 J. Witheston to P. Murray, 10 April 1791, BRC: 25 March to 22 April 1791, IOR, P/52/28, pp. 525–528.
126 J. Witheston to P. Murray, 25 April 1791, BRC: 6 to 27 May 1791, IOR, P/52/30, pp. 322–324.
127 van Schendel, *Francis Buchanan*, p. 60.
128 *Ibid.*, p. 82.
129 W. Wilkins to J. Cartier, November 1771, Firminger, *BDR: Chittagong*, I, p. 62.
130 *Ibid.*, p. 63.
131 *Ibid.*
132 *Ibid.*
133 J. Cartier to W. Wilkins, 2 December 1771, Firminger, *BDR: Chittagong*, I, pp. 66–67.
134 W. Barton to Controlling Committee of Accompts, 2 March 1773, *ibid.*, pp. 77–78.
135 W. Barton to C. Bentley, 3 March 1773, *ibid.*, p. 79.
136 W. Hastings to C. Bentley, 23 March 1773, *ibid.*, p. 83.
137 H. Cox to F. Pierard or T. Powney, 19 March 1799, BRC: 5 to 26 April 1799, IOR, P/54/2.
138 Chief at Chittagong to governor-general and council, 17 November 1775, Islam, *BDR: Chittagong*, pp. 73–74.
139 H. Cox to F. Pierard or T. Powney, 19 March 1799, BRC: 5 to 26 April 1799, IOR, P/54/2.
140 *Ibid.*
141 Cox had been the Company's resident at the port of Rangoon from October 1796 until November 1797. H. Cox, *Journal of a Residence in the Burmhan Empire*, London: John Warren, 1821.
142 H. Cox to F. Pierard or T. Powney, 19 March 1799, BRC: 5 to 26 April 1799, IOR, P/54/2.
143 T. Powney to the Board of Revenue, 28 March 1799, *ibid.*, and T. Powney to the Board of Revenue, 30 March 1799, *ibid.*
144 H. Cox to T. Powney, 26 March 1799, *ibid.*
145 *Ibid.*

146 *Ibid.*
147 *Ibid.*
148 H. Hooper to J. Stonehouse, 25 March 1799, BRC: 5 to 26 April 1799, IOR, P/54/2.
149 E. Moore to the Board of Revenue, 3 April 1799, *ibid.*, and G. Dandridge to the Board of Revenue, 8 April 1799, *ibid.*
150 C. Crommelin to S. Middleton, 25 March 1799, *ibid.*
151 H. Cox to E. Moore, 24 April 1799, BRC: 5 to 26 April 1799, IOR, P/54/3.
152 E. Moore to the Board of Revenue, 13 May 1799, *ibid.*
153 Report of W. Berrie (Clerk and Inspector, Grain Office), 2 January 1800, BRC: 2 to 30 January 1800, IOR, P/54/9; and Extract of a Letter to the Board of Revenue from the Collector of Chittagong, 22 March 1800, encl. T. Graham to the Revenue and Judicial Department 9 May 1800, BRC: 3 April to 29 May 1800, IOR, P/54/11. Also, L. Moloney to the Board of Revenue, 19 March 1802, BRC: 4 March to 29 April 1802, IOR, P/54/24.
154 H. Hooper to J. Stonehouse, 25 March 1799, BRC: 5 to 26 April 1799, IOR, P/54/2.
155 Vice President in Council's Resolution (No. 22) 26 April 1799, *ibid.*
156 'In an active performance of the arduous duties of this situation, and in a climate peculiarly noxious to an European constitution, Captain Cox persevered til his own life became a sacrifice to his zeal and sense of public duty', H. C. M Cox's preface to Cox, *Journal of a Residence in the Burmhan Empire*, p. vii.
157 F. Pierard to the Revenue and Judicial Department, 12 May 1800, BRC: 3 April to 29 May 1800, IOR, P/54/11.
158 *Ibid.*
159 *Ibid.*
160 *Ibid.*
161 T. Gerard to L. Hook, 5 January 1801, BRC: 5 March to 30 April 1801, IOR, P/54/17.
162 Islam, *BDR: Chittagong*, p. 313.
163 Order of the vice president in council forwarded to the Board of Revenue by G. H. Barlow 31 May 1799, BRC: 3 May to 28 June 1799, IOR, P/54/3.
164 E. Moore (assistant collector of Dhaka) to Board of Revenue, 3 April 1799, BRC: 5 to 26 April 1799, IOR, P/54/3.; J. Stonehouse to W. Massie (collector of Dhaka), 29 March 1799, *ibid.*; C. Crommelin (commercial resident at Lakshmipur) to S. Middleton, 25 March 1799, *ibid.*; and G. Dandridge (collector of Tripura) to Board of Revenue, 8 April 1799, *ibid.*
165 J. C. Scott has examined the way subordinates respond to superiors in hierarchies of power, arguing that 'everyday resistance' achieves subalterns' aims without exposing them to the dangers which would accrue from open defiance. J. C. Scott, *Weapons of the Weak: Everyday Forms of Peasant Resistance*, New Haven, CT: Yale University Press, 1985, p. 32.

6 The Company state in the 1820s

Hegemony, retrenchment and reform

By 1818, the Company state was the paramount power on the Indian subcontinent. With the destruction of the last vestiges of Maratha resistance in the third Anglo-Maratha (or *Pindari*) war of 1817–18, its military and political dominance were now unchallenged by any European rival or significant Indian power.[1] Indeed, the corner had been turned by as early as 1803 with the British victory at Assaye during the Second Anglo-Maratha War, the third war being essentially a matter of smaller-scale pacification.[2] True, the 1820s were to see both the first Anglo-Burmese war (1823–26) and the collapse of the Persian buffer following the Russo-Persian War (1826–28), but while the former was the Company's most expensive conflict to date, the Burmese military machine was not capable of seriously threatening the British position in India,[3] and, while the latter raised the spectre of unchecked Russian expansion into Central Asia, for the time being, it remained just that, a shadow without substance.[4] What, then, were the implications for the Company's bureaucracy and its armed forces of this rapid ascent to dominance after the early 19th century?

The clear belief of the Court of Directors was that British paramountcy having been established, it was now time for the Company's servants to come off a war-footing and instead to focus on making economies and honing the state's bureaucracy. This period has been identified as one of retrenchment and reform by modern historians, and those qualities are certainly apparent in the directives issuing from the higher echelons of the Company's administration.[5] A succession of governors-general – the Marquess of Hastings (1813–23), William Pitt Amherst (1823–28), and William Bentinck (1828–35) – were each instructed to make economies in government their priority. Even though they all struggled in this regard, the fact that retrenchment was being more forcibly pressed by the Court of Directors is indicative of the spirit of the age. The bloody contest for subcontinental supremacy had ended, the military-political position of the Company state had stabilised, and it was high time that the Indian empire started to pay for itself. The Directors' principal concern now was 'to check burgeoning expenditure' and to 'coax a surplus out of the revenues'.[6]

The pressure exerted by the Directors on the Company's employees to reduce government spending had been increasing steadily from the early years of the 19th century until it finally permeated every aspect of public life. Visiting India for the first time in 1822, the Anglo-Indian travel writer Fanny Parkes was both astonished and amused at the frugal example set by the newly arrived Lord Amherst:

> The new Governor-General is so economical he has discharged a number of servants, quenched a number of lamps; *on dit*, he intends to plant potatoes in the park at Barrackpore; people are so unaccustomed to anything of the sort in India, that all this European economy produces considerable surprise.[7]

Amherst, like his predecessor the Marquess of Hastings, and Bentinck, the man who was to replace him, was charged with making large savings as a matter of urgency. The military expenditure arising from difficult campaigns against the Gurkhas and Marathas had, in combination with the cost of maintaining an immense standing army, made unsustainable inroads into the public purse.

The outbreak of the first Anglo-Burmese war in 1823 further hampered attempts to economise, and this was exacerbated by a number of minor, but still costly, operations undertaken in the same period. Following the fall of the Jat stronghold of Bharatpur in Rajastan to Lord Combermere in January 1826, and the settlement of the war with Burma under treaty later that year, India sank into a state of exhausted tranquillity. Naturally, the cost of this prolonged military activity was enormous; the Burma campaign alone cost £13 million. Amherst's attempts to restrain public spending had been a disastrous failure, and it was made abundantly clear to his successor William Bentinck that he was being offered the post of governor-general on the understanding that he would put an end to the long series of crippling financial deficits: by 1828–29, the government of India was burdened with a rapidly accumulating debt of some £40 million.[8] The pressure to reverse the trend was enormous, and, in the light of the British hegemony, the army was an obvious target for cuts. However, given the fundamentally coercive nature of the Company's rule in India, and the recent memory of military conquest which had carved out its state, demilitarisation was a hugely controversial issue.

Writing in 1828, Bentinck was convinced that 'our military establishments of battle are far higher than a state of peace requires'.[9] It was a position which Bentinck had 'every confidence' would be acknowledged by his colleagues, but opinion in the wider Anglo-Indian community was by no means behind him.[10] Many Anglo-Indians, particularly those with a military interest, such as John Malcolm and Thomas Munro, cautioned against army reductions, as they had been doing for over 20 years. They were joined by a younger and equally vociferous generation of Company officials, exemplified in Mountstuart Elphinstone, governor of Bombay, and Charles Metcalfe, an experienced member of the Anglo-Indian political and diplomatic service, who would later hold the top government posts in Jamaica and Canada. In his minute on the future government of India, Metcalfe argued, 'We retain our dominion only by a large military establishment; and without a considerable force of British troops, the fidelity of our native soldiery could not be relied on'. In consequence of this, he had no doubt that 'we ought to maintain all [the soldiers] we can pay'.[11] The insistence on military retrenchment from the 1810s onwards alarmed these members of the Empire of Opinion school, who feared that its corollary would be a reduction in the military reputation which had so far sustained the colonial state. To do anything which might reduce the operational efficiency of the army would, Malcolm warned, be to 'neglect those collateral means by which the great fabric of our power in India has hitherto been supported'.[12] Malcolm had published the *Political History* in order to argue that British India was never truly at peace, that the army was central to the security of the colonial state, and that nothing should be done which damaged its capacity to overawe dissident elements within Indian society. It was a view which found much support in the Anglo-Indian community. Metcalfe too voiced the opinion, 'Our greatest danger is not from a Russian invasion, but from the fading of the impression of our invincibility from the minds of the native inhabitants of India'.[13] To maintain an army capable of fulfilling this role, he argued, 'We require all the revenue that we can raise'.[14] If savings were needed, they must be made elsewhere.

In contrast, the conviction of the Directors, the Board of Control and senior elements at Fort William was that, with the removal of its immediate rivals, British India was now secure. In 1828, Bentinck expressed the conviction that 'at no period of our history have we had less danger to apprehend than at the present moment'.[15] Nevertheless, the military lobby was strong, and, as has been indicated, a succession of threats could be identified to justify protecting the army's budget. The Directors, however, were determined that cuts would be made, and Bentinck, very much their man, was appointed to force through those economies. Advantage had to be taken of the relative peace to execute reforms and, crucially, to reduce public spending. In keeping with the tone which had been set for his administration, Bentinck wrote to the Directors on military allowances in December 1828, stating,

> In the present posture of our political affairs, no object exists . . . for keeping the army in such a complete state . . . while our financial condition requires that every safe and practicable reduction of expenditure should be enforced.[16]

The army and the Company state after 1800

This book has argued that the Company state in the period between 1765 and the early 19th century was characterised by a failure among local officials to impose the government's authority comprehensively throughout Indian society. They were hampered by a dearth of India-specific governmental knowledge with which to guide their conduct, but also, crucially, by a lack of immediately available military resources to buttress their daily administration. Reacting particularly to this deficiency in their means to impose government by force of arms, the Company's servants in the early period tended to be risk averse in their behaviour. They often stood apart from those events within their district which they decided could only bring them disgrace by exposing their weakness, with the consequences for local government which have been examined in previous chapters.

Before the turn of the 19th century, the role of the army in conquering and defending territory made it central to the Company state's existence, but it was used mainly for regular warfare, and it was only deployed in direct support of district administrations with great reluctance. After the early 1800s, however, with Indian competitor states very much on the wane, the need for so massive (and costly) an instrument of regular warfare became questionable. If demilitarisation was to be prevented, a new role had to be found for the army. The natural alternative to open warfare lay in concerns over the internal security of British India, and the army's transformation into a military police force found many influential and vocal supporters in the Anglo-Indian community just at the time when major rival powers had been subdued.

The army's reinvention was, of course, a gradual process. Victory in the Second Anglo-Maratha War did not herald the sudden redeployment of the army across northern India in support of the district administrations. Quite apart from anything else, sporadic conflicts could still be used to justify a regular operational role (as with Nepal in 1814 or the Burmese in 1823). Even so, the change insinuated itself into Fort William's military strategy. As has been seen, the practice of deploying the Bengal Army more widely throughout the presidency, in many small garrisons, had been growing since the early 1800s. It is indicative of the gradually diminishing scale of the direct military threat posed by Indian powers, which had formerly required the semi-permanent concentration of troops in larger numbers to allow for rapid mobilisation. In 1800, of the 30 regular infantry battalions attached to the Bengal military establishment, one-third was based at just three posts, with the remaining 20 battalions distributed between 18 posts.[17] By 1820, there was double the number of infantry battalions at the presidency, but five of the six largest posts had fewer than four battalions each. More than two-thirds of the Bengal Army's infantry were now deployed in formations of fewer than two battalions, and one-third of its total infantry strength was deployed in sub-battalion units – a distinctly more diffuse pattern of deployment than was seen before the turn of the century.[18] It is these 'small garrisons' of the 1810s and 1820s, which Peers identifies as an indicator of the army's role as 'a gendarmerie of last resort', positioned 'to monitor local society' and to suppress resistance. This was, however, a comparatively new role for the Bengal Army, and one which had only been enabled by the dominance which the Company had begun to enjoy over its indigenous rivals after the turn of the 19th century.

Once the prospect of regular warfare with other Indian states had diminished, it became clear to many Anglo-Indians that the next great threat was a revolt of the population within the Company's own territory. It might be instigated by the clandestine activities of a European power; 'externally induced internal disaffection', to use M. E. Yapp's phrase.[19] This threat was brought more sharply into focus in 1828 by the shift in geo-politics occasioned by the collapse of the Persian buffer, following Russia's decisive victory in the Russo-Persian war. Traditionally, Persia had been the ally with which Britain had defended India, and this relationship had proved satisfactory throughout the Napoleonic wars. However, with Persia's defeat, and the subsequent growth of Russian influence in Central Asia after 1828, it became apparent that Persia could no longer be relied on in that capacity. Britain found itself stripped of an ally and faced with a powerful opponent; consequently, the British home government came to fear that 'whenever Britain opposed Russia in Europe, Russia would threaten to invade India'.[20] Thus the Company's government was put in the unenviable position of having to find a way of securing British India against externally induced unrest, while at the same time making significant military economies.[21] Such was the nature of colonial administration, however, that even without external influences there remained the ever-present danger of civil strife. The population of India was huge and, at best, ambivalent towards British rule; a rule imposed by a handful of representatives of an alien power, whose military regime was supported by an army largely composed of Indian troops. 'Our subjects', wrote Metcalfe, 'are internal enemies, ready at least for change, if not ripe for insurrection'.[22]

With the army's role as an instrument of regular conquest seemingly diminished, it had to be reconfigured to meet this threat of internal unrest which was now the most pressing security issue. The regular army was redeployed so as to make its stabilising presence felt more widely across northern India from the 1810s onwards (a significant boost to the confidence of district authorities). Simultaneously, much attention was also being directed towards the role of the Company's invalid thanahs in securing the mofussil against unrest. These thanahs were the stations where the Company's sepoys and their families were settled after retiring, either through age or infirmity, from the Company's service. Such settlements of military pensioners served a twofold purpose. They were a very public demonstration of the Company's worth as an employer, identifying it closely with the Mughal practice of assigning rent-free land grants to imperial retainers, and thereby lending it legitimacy in the eyes of its Indian subjects.[23] The settlements also represented 'pockets of influence' for the Company and were particularly useful 'for policing Company territory and training its new recruits' in frontier areas and in the recently conquered Maratha domains.[24] However, by the 1810s, problems had begun to arise with these hitherto effective bulwarks of state power which limited their usefulness. Some thanahs, like those of Bihar, which were located on the fringes of settled land, became depopulated because of the difficulty experienced by pensioners' families in subsisting in areas prone to periodic flooding, serious epidemics of disease and attacks by the wild animals which inhabited the forests and hills of these border regions.[25] At the other extreme, thanahs such as those in Awadh and Benares, bolstered by a more stable, cultivated environment, had prospered hugely, but, heady with this new affluence, the pensioners there had become less amenable to the Company's control. There was also the serious problem everywhere of imposters visiting the kacharis from which the invalids were paid their allowance and fraudulently claiming the benefits which were due to genuine pensioners.[26] In the early 1820s, the mechanisms supporting the thanah programme began to be reformed, and from 1825, increased numbers of European officials were employed to oversee its administration. Even in the midst of retrenchment elsewhere, every effort was made shore up this vital component in the internal policing of the Company's more difficult territory.[27] In 1827, the government of India actually increased spending on thanah administration through an expanded establishment of regional paymasters, designed to incorporate the invalids more closely into the fabric of the state.[28] However, while the 1820s saw the strengthening of the invalid thanahs, largely because of their importance as a police force acting in support of district authorities, this was not typical of the Company's regular military establishment during this period, which found its traditional supremacy within the state under threat.

The half-batta order as an indicator of change

The 1820s and 1830s were to see several important measures for the reform of the army, but the first, and most inflammatory, was the reduction in officers' *batta* (field allowance), the great controversy in military spending which Hastings and Amherst had both failed to tackle, and which Bentinck was now charged with bringing under control.[29] Both its implementation at this time and the manner in which the move was received is indicative of the changed priorities of the Anglo-Indian community in the 1820s as compared with their counterparts of previous decades. As a case study of relations between the civil and military spheres in British India, the half-batta order of November 1828 reveals much about the shift which occurred in the priorities of the Company state during the first quarter of the 19th century. The urgent reliance on regular military forces which had been a hallmark of its early period of rapid territorial expansion was by no means so apparent in the more secure military-political context of British India in the 1810s and 1820s.

Batta was an allowance, awarded to both officers and men in the Company's army, to enable them to obtain accommodation when serving in the field or outside Company territory; this stipend was not granted when in cantonments, since those quarters were already furnished at the Company's expense. However, in 1801, Fort William granted full-batta at all times and passed responsibility for finding quarters to the officers themselves. The Court of Directors never sanctioned this change to the established practice. In 1814, the Directors instructed Fort William to revert to the original half-batta system, but the governor-general, the Earl of Moira (later the Marquess of Hastings), realised that this would be deeply unpopular with his officers and refused to comply. It is doubtless that he had in mind the consequences of the recent attempt to curtail officers' perquisites, which had resulted in the 1809 'White Mutiny' in the Madras Army. On that occasion, officers had refused to obey orders and threatened a coup following the ending of an allowance related to the purchase of tents and field equipment.[30]

Bentinck's feelings on the batta reduction seem to have been regret that such a move was necessary; however, with the advent of the Duke of Wellington's Tory administration in January 1828, his capacity for opposing the measure was substantially weakened. It became clear that he could expect little leeway from a ministry led by a man who was 'deeply prejudiced' against him, both politically and personally, and who 'might be glad of a chance to get rid of him'.[31] Despite Bentinck's personal misgivings, and those of his council, that the half-batta reduction was likely to cause immense ill-feeling within the army, the key condition of the Court of Directors' continued support was unambiguous: military retrenchment. Therefore, allowances were cut under the half-batta general order of November 1828, which mulcted many Company army officers of their additional income, but which left the allowances of the rank and file untouched. Contemporary feeling concerning this reduction identified it as an attempt on the part of Bentinck to curry favour with the Directors. This belief is exemplified in the private correspondence of Henry Spry, who at the time of Bentinck's governor-generalship was a junior medical officer in the Bengal Army:

> It is no excuse the Governor General saying that he could not have avoided it . . . The Marquis of Hastings refused three distinct times to carry it into effect and so did Lord Amherst, but they (the Court of Directors) have found in the mongrel House of Bentinck a wretch fit for such dirty work.[32]

In addition to hurting them financially, the half-batta order was believed by many officers to have seriously damaged the army's discipline. Colonel Thomas Seaton of the Bengal Army observed that when the order was issued the sepoys 'could not divest themselves of the idea that a curtailment of their own pay would follow that of their officers'.[33] However, when it became clear that it was only the officers' pay which was to be touched, the sepoys 'twirled their moustaches in pride, strutted about with a lordly, swaggering air, and gave every indication that they had formed an overweening estimation of their own importance'.[34] The commander of a sepoy infantry regiment protested to Bentinck that the cut in his allowances 'degraded' him in the eyes of his sepoys, who would view such a well-publicised loss of perquisites as a pointed chastisement of the officer corps.[35]

The precise amount of money saved by the implementation of half-batta is unclear, although contemporaries were unanimous in condemning it as insufficient to justify the trouble that was taken to obtain it.[36] If the figure of £6,000 cited by the London *Times* is to be believed, then the saving amounted to less than 0.05 percent of a military budget of £10,773,966.[37] However, the greatest significance of the half-batta order was not financial. The fact that such a materially insignificant, but controversial, economy was pressed for by the Court of Directors is indicative not only of a desperate desire to reduce public expenditure but also of a belief that the Company's military-political position in India was now so secure that it was safe to tamper with the army's perquisites without fear of exposing the state to danger. Not only had all major Indian rivals been subdued, but the chances of the Company's officers actually mutinying were, by the late 1820s, substantially reduced. The Europeans and Indians of the Company's army in the 18th century may have been 'mercenaries who could not tolerate anything other than the strictest and most punctual observance of what they considered to be due to them', but this was now much less the case. The Company's army, like its civil bureaucracy, had matured as an institution over that period, and its officers were now less inclined to oppose a well-established central authority through such radical means. In the mid-18th century, mutinous officers rebelling against their conditions of service were not uncommon, and, as has been seen, this continued, with decreasing frequency, until as late as 1809. However, in 1829, no mutiny took place in response to the half-batta order. There was a great deal of angry talk, particularly within the hard-hit Bengal Army (as Seaton described), but whereas previous generations of officers would have ceased to perform their official duties, committed acts 'that bordered on outright mutiny' and thrown the army into chaos, the officer corps of the mature Company state was, by and large, content to resort to the milder measure of boycotting the governor-general's dinners and balls.[38] True, there were isolated instances of suspected sabotage on the part of disaffected individuals, as was widely believed in the case of the destruction of the Allahabad magazine, which Spry reports was 'set fire to intentionally by the people who were discharged from his [Bentinck's] penny half-penny clippings'.[39] Yet, even were Spry correct, in the main, the conduct of the officers was far less dramatic. A more representative act was the dispatching to London in 1831 of two delegates with a petition against the half-batta order, which Wellington rejected in order to preserve the government of India's authority over its military establishment.[40]

This last point touches upon what was perhaps the most important element of the half-batta issue. The 1828 order was not simply geared towards recouping a few thousand pounds in military perquisites; rather, it was a question of establishing whether the army or the civil power was to be paramount in Indian policy-making. In his discussion of Anglo-Indian militarism, Peers has argued that the civil and military authorities in India were 'partners in empire', and that the dividing line between them was highly ambiguous, not least because of the number of army officers employed in civil roles, often in the political service.[41] Certainly, the army, bolstered by its historical position as guarantor of the colonial state's existence, enjoyed considerable influence, and the government struggled to control it. On this occasion, however, the civil power, represented by Bentinck, was certainly not in partnership with the military.

The principle of the Anglo-Indian military remaining subordinate to civilian authority was one which particularly concerned the Whiggish Bentinck (as it would his successor Lord Curzon some 70 years later). Should he fail to challenge the influence of the military lobby he would forfeit the support of the Directors, but, more importantly, he would be 'subordinating his office to the army', who would 'interpret this as proof that their position of dominance was secure'.[42] The fact that the half-batta reduction was successfully carried out against the army's wishes demonstrates that the power of the Anglo-Indian military lobby had actually diminished in the years leading up to the order and that by the end of the 1820s, the army was truly subordinate to the civil power. Traditionally, the Company's army had enjoyed overwhelming political influence arising from its central role in carving out the Indian empire. However, that influence was much reduced following the establishment of a British military hegemony during the first quarter of the 19th century, and the prevailing policy of military retrenchment which became apparent almost simultaneously may be taken as an indicator of this sea-change. In consequence, if it was to protect itself against swingeing government economies, the army had to find a new role, that of directing its stabilising influence inwards onto the Indian population.

The origins of Sir John Malcolm's political thought

As has been mentioned previously, it was during the relative tranquillity of the 1820s that Sir John Malcolm chose to publish his clarion call, the hugely influential *Political History*, in which he urged British India to adopt an aggressive forward policy in its relations with neighbouring states, emphasised the centrality of the army, and cautioned against the replacement of government by Indian norms and through Indian structures with a 'rationalised' British system of rule.[43]

In 1828, Bentinck had asserted that British dominion 'was acknowledged and feared' throughout India; 'Our power', he wrote, 'is irresistible'.[44] It was this apparent complacency regarding the colonial state's security which the Empire of Opinion school found so offensive. In the *Political History*, Malcolm was reacting against such assessments, which he described as the 'rash confidence' of a colonial government resting on its laurels after meeting only the first of many challenges.[45] Rival Indian powers may have been conquered and incorporated into the Company state, but, Malcolm argued, the judicious application of armed force and an understanding of the vast population which they governed would still be required by alert colonial administrators. As such, the *Political History* may be seen as a canonical text for the large number of Anglo-Indians who sought to preserve the army from retrenchment in an age of ostensible peace and security. The stress which they laid on its continued importance as a deterrent against internal unrest may be seen as both a reaction to an earlier, more uncertain period of the Company state's history, as well as an indicator of British India's comparative security from Indian rivals after the early 1800s.

For Malcolm, the integrity of the Company state was maintained by 'the wise and politic exercise of . . . military power'. Therefore, its limited military resources needed to be maximised, and, even then, it was necessary for the Company to cultivate the good opinion of Indian society in order to avoid arousing discontent which might grow into armed resistance and stretch those resources to breaking point. This was to be achieved not only by protecting the 'religious prejudices and civil rights of our Indian subjects' but also by emphasising the honesty and 'good faith' of the colonial government, and, further, by demonstrating the state's willingness to use armed force to crush dissidence and to defend itself against external threats.[46] In the *Political History*, Malcolm sought to make these points through a highly partisan account of the acts of the governors-general from Cornwallis to Lord Hastings, his ultimate aim being to celebrate the forceful, expansionist policy of

Richard Wellesley, which confirmed the pre-eminence of the military in affairs of state. As a corollary of this, Malcolm's attitude towards moderates and cost-cutters was scathing. Following the government's failure to aid their ally the Nizam of Hyderabad against Tipu Sultan under the terms of the treaty of Paungul, Malcolm wrote that Sir John Shore (who replaced Cornwallis as governor-general in 1793) had been 'content to sacrifice . . . part of that high reputation and character which the conduct of his immediate predecessor had obtained for British government in India'.[47] Likewise, Sir George Barlow, who replaced Cornwallis after his brief second administration in 1805, was attacked by Malcolm for his neutral stance and his dissolution of defensive alliances. As Malcolm saw it, this line of policy caused serious problems for Barlow's successor, Lord Minto (1807–13). In particular, the Company's relations with the Sikhs were put under strain, since Ranjit Singh, the ruler of the Punjab, was encouraged to expand his territory after Barlow had withdrawn Company protection from the petty chieftains south of the Sutlej River.[48] 'The government of Lord Minto', Malcolm declared, 'had no result more important than the impression it conveyed to the authorities at home of the utter impracticability of perseverance in that neutral policy they had desired to pursue'.[49] In comparison, the Marquess of Hastings's energetic military response to the Gurkha threat in the Anglo-Nepalese war (1814–16), and his general policy of protecting weaker Indian states against indigenous aggression was lauded by Malcolm as the correct way to maintain the reputation of the colonial government under present conditions.[50] The preservation of a strong Anglo-Indian military establishment was clearly central to Malcolm's political thought.

Given its publication date of 1826, the warnings inherent within the *Political History* may seem somewhat unusual, anachronistic even; the Company was paramount in India and its territory was apparently more secure than it had ever been. One explanation for this seeming anomaly may be found in the argument already posited that, in this new era of relative peace, the Anglo-Indian military had a vested interest in protecting themselves against government cuts and were not afraid to exaggerate possible dangers to the state which only they could counter; 'imaginative or enterprising officers could always detect a potential threat tucked away somewhere in the interior of the subcontinent'.[51] The fact that a precursor to the 1826 *Political History*, Malcolm's *Sketch of the Political History of India*, had appeared as early as 1811, lends weight to it being a reaction against possible demilitarisation arising from the development of the Company's hegemony.

This may in part account for the timing of Malcolm's publications, in the opening phase of military retrenchment (evidenced by the initial attempts to restore half-batta) and at the height of Anglo-Indian militarism in the mid-1820s, when army officers were becoming increasingly alarmist as they perceived their importance within the colonial state becoming less pronounced.[52] Malcolm had a considerable talent for self-promotion and used his writings to position himself for the major governorship which would cap his career.[53] Yet, as well as being a piece of self-interested political manipulation, Malcolm's stern warning not to take the security of British India for granted (echoed by Elphinstone, Metcalfe and Munro, among others) may also be viewed as a deep-seated reaction to his personal experience in the precarious Company state of the earlier period.[54] He had first arrived in India in 1783 at the age of 14, having been awarded a cadetship in the army of the Madras presidency through the good offices of family friends following the bankruptcy of his father in 1780.[55] The service which he joined had, since 1779, suffered several humiliating reverses at the hands of Mysore's ruler Haider Ali, whose highly mobile forces outmatched the under-resourced Madras Army. The most famous of these defeats had been the total destruction of Colonel William Baillie's division at Perambaucum in September 1780, which, as has been seen, was reckoned by Lord Cornwallis to have 'removed some part of that awe' with which Indian society viewed the Company's army.

Malcolm's biographer, Jack Harrington, has argued that his posting to this impoverished presidency at a young age heavily influenced Malcolm's ideas about the British position in India for the rest of his life: his 'world-view changed little from his early days as a cadet in Madras'.[56] The Company's authorities there were heavily reliant on support from both their northern neighbours in Bengal and the local nawab, and the uncertain financial situation severely restricted the size of the military forces which the presidency could afford to put into the field. Consequently, Madras was 'strategically weak and always undermanned'.[57] An early anecdote from Malcolm's military career neatly illustrates conditions at this time: a British officer, returning from a diplomatic mission to Mysore, crossed into Company territory and was met on the border by a boy in the uniform of a Madras ensign (Malcolm). Clearly expecting some large military formation to be guarding this frontier zone, he asked to be taken to its commanding officer. '*I* am the commanding officer', piped the young Malcolm.[58] Barely a teenager, Malcolm found himself part of a woefully inadequate army trying to defend an area with thousands of miles of coastline and unsettled internal borders. As Harrington has remarked, 'The sense of the precariousness of British influence was unavoidable in Madras during the first twenty years of Malcolm's career'.[59]

The origins of Malcolm's political thought lay, then, in these early experiences at Madras, a presidency whose conditions were at least partly analogous with those in Bengal, and, indeed, with the environment of the Company state in the 18th century more generally. While Bengal may have been considered a 'wealthy, self-confident' province in relation to Madras, the authorities in the north still suffered from significant under-resourcing and the onslaught of hostile indigenous groups, which, as has been seen in earlier chapters, had a significant impact on the operation of the Company's government.[60] Of course, these were on a different scale to sustained warfare with Mysore, but the operation of Bengal's district authorities were certainly threatened by Burmese interventions in Chittagong and the activities of Nepalese groups in Rangpur, not to mention the ravages of internal resistance from the likes of Ranu Khan or the sannyasis. Indeed, service at any of the three presidencies in the early 1780s would have convinced Malcolm of the tenuous nature of British rule in India; the fact that he was posted to troubled Madras simply made his anxieties over the security of the colonial state more acute. The careful arguments which Malcolm advanced in the 1810s and 1820s were a reflection of this earlier, uncertain period of British rule, and, quite understandably, the central tenet of his ideology, as expressed in the *Political History*, was that military security could only be guaranteed by the judicious, politically astute application of armed force.

However, the coherent implementation of any political strategy required the consensus of the Anglo-Indian military-political community, and, as has been seen, such a consensus was extremely difficult to achieve in the period before the 1810s. The existence of a widespread 'garrison state mentality', so characteristic of Anglo-Indian thought during the 1820s and 1830s, was only made possible by the development of the colonial state's structures and the forging over more than 50 years of a corporate Anglo-Indian identity. It was the 'cohesiveness and insularity' of this new community which marked it out from earlier Anglo-Indian society.[61]

In the 18th century, the framework of the colonial bureaucracy was still fluid, and there was too little precedent concerning what constituted proper conduct on the part of an Indian administrator to mould the Company's servants into a homogenous, bureaucratic 'type'. Indeed, the wider Anglo-Indian community which Malcolm joined in 1783 was one riven by disunity, corruption and internecine conflict. Warren Hastings had been consistently undermined by a hostile majority in the supreme council for much of the 1770s, and in 1780, he had actually fought a duel with one of his own councillors. He had also been accused of large-scale bribery and extortion, and the Company's government had been all but brought to its knees by the controversy with the Supreme Court at the end of the 1770s. Now, as Malcolm arrived in India, the governor-general left for Britain, where he would soon face impeachment before Parliament. The final quarter of the 18th century was a troubled time for the internal administration of the Company state, with its grasping servants fighting furiously among themselves for power and the wealth it brought. It was a time and a place in which personal interest frequently overrode greater corporate concerns. From Hastings and Francis quarrelling bitterly at the top of government, to the wrangling and squabbles of junior officials on its fringes, the Company's servants lacked a powerful, unifying ethos. This was the environment which convinced Malcolm of the danger posed to the security of the colonial state by discord among Anglo-Indians. As well as professional self-interest in protecting the power of the army, it was Malcolm's direct experience of this unstable environment which prompted him to argue for the continued pre-eminence of the military and for the government to act with 'unshaken firmness' to preserve British India.[62]

Malcolm's political thought was based on two concerns which are central to this book. Firstly, that Malcolm's appraisal of the colonial state was to a great extent the product of his exposure to the unstable military-political environment of Madras, and of India more widely, prior to the 1810s. Secondly, the fact that Malcolm felt the need to warn his countrymen against viewing their Indian empire with self-satisfaction 'in the pride of power' strongly suggests that a change was occurring in military policy during the 1810s and 1820s, as the Company became paramount on the subcontinent.[63] Alongside the 'pressing need to guarantee security', exemplified in the culture of Anglo-Indian militarism, there also existed by the 1810s an increasingly powerful determination among senior Company figures, in both London and Fort William, to reduce military overheads in the light of their newfound subcontinental dominance. This is what Malcolm and his adherents were reacting against, regardless of whether they were motivated by genuine concern over the state's security, by a narrow interest in protecting their professional existence, or, most likely, by a combination of both. The peaking of Anglo-Indian militarism in the 1820s, as officers clamoured to make a case for the army's continued centrality in a 'peacetime' British India, is indicative of a colonial state which had passed through the initial phase of conquest to one of consolidation, in which the need for the army (other than in a police role) was reduced. Further, the reduction in the scale of the armed threat facing the colonial state from the early 1800s enabled administrators to operate with less fear of the consequences of violent unrest in their districts. The great emphasis laid on the reinvention of the army as a tool of military policing was a catalyst in this process, as it led to a more widespread pattern of deployment, helping to stabilise the Company's hinterland, and thereby reassuring the previously under-resourced district administrators.

The Anglo-Indian civil servant in 1820

By 1820, then, the Company state had reached a point of development at which, despite the self-interested alarmism of the military lobby, it could be viewed by many contemporaries as the firmly established subcontinental hegemon; it was a period of respite in which economies could be made, and important questions about the principles which were to underpin imperial rule could be debated. The army, having secured British India from rival powers, was redeployed to monitor the Company's territory for internal unrest. The colonial bureaucracy had matured and grown in 'professionalism' (no longer an anachronistic term). From the opening decade of the 19th century, comparative peace in British India allowed time for reflection on its administration. At the Board of Control George Canning, during his term as president (1816–21), sought to instil a greater degree of regularity into the Anglo-Indian bureaucracy, and larger numbers of specialised committees were convened and dedicated secretaries appointed to analyse and process the huge volume of information being received from the Company's officials in India.[64] Further, the cumulative experience of two generations of Anglo-Indian administrators had fed into the service, which was now staffed by a much more homogenous type of Company bureaucrat than 50 years previously.

Nowhere is the state's development more apparent than in this changed condition of the Anglo-Indian civil servant. In the 1750s, no formal professional training was offered or required by the Company; appointments to the service were not made on merit, and the motives of covenanted servants tended to lie in hopes of rapid self-enrichment rather than honourable employment. Writerships (the most junior civil post) lay largely within the patronage of the Court of Directors. Huge fortunes could be made by those lucky enough to survive the Indian climate, and, consequently, great pressure was brought to bear by well-connected families who wanted the Directors to create more posts for their young men. In Bengal, the number of civil service appointments rose nearly sixfold between the 1750s and early 1780s.[65] The posts were filled by civil servants who, other than their influential connections, often had little more than basic literacy and numeracy to recommend them. However, the shortcomings of these early administrators, which have been examined in previous chapters, soon became a source of concern among senior Company officials, both in India and London. The gradual 'professionalisation' of the service after the late 18th century was a direct response to the rampant culture of personal interest within the Company's bureaucracy at that time. From the end of the 1780s, the effects of Lord Cornwallis's reforms began to be felt. He cut out sinecures and superfluous offices, while at the same time seeking to encourage Company servants to attend more closely to their professional duty than to personal enrichment. This was to be achieved through an increase in the salaries attached to civil posts which, it was hoped, would focus and regularise the conduct of civil servants, who would have adequate recompense for their efforts without needing to abuse their situation for private gain.[66] The aim was to transform the Anglo-Indian civil service from what was regarded by many of its members as simply an opportunity to acquire an illicit fortune at the Company's expense into 'a well rewarded career for gentlemen'.[67]

This process of professionalisation was further aided by efforts at creating training establishments both in England and Bengal for prospective Company servants. In 1800, Lord Wellesley sponsored the creation of a civil service college at Fort William which aimed to promote the better understanding of oriental languages and usages among European officials. Importantly, its curriculum was also intended 'to fix and establish sound and correct principles of religion and government in their minds at an early period of life'.[68] Although the college was abolished in 1802, with only a reduced establishment remaining for the teaching of languages and regulations, it had set the trend for moulding new entrants to the service into a homogenous type. With the closure of Fort William College, the role of providing an approved, centralised course of instruction for those destined to be employed by the Company was taken up by the East India College, which was opened at Hertford in 1806, moving to Haileybury in 1809. It provided a broad curriculum, including European studies and oriental languages and history; like its predecessor, it also sought to inculcate religious belief and high standards of personal morality. The standardisation of the Anglo-Indian civil service was further accelerated by the Charter Act of 1813, which made all appointments to writerships conditional on applicants having spent at least four terms at Haileybury.[69]

As with the civil service in general, the role of the Company collector, in particular, was also changing throughout the period, with the district officer's duties becoming better defined. From the post's inception, the Company collector's remit was far broader that of his immediate predecessor, the Mughal *amil* (revenue officer), and it encompassed a bewildering array of duties. As has been seen, the role was an amalgam of various judicial and police functions in addition to those of revenue assessment, but the powers granted by the central authorities to aid the collector in performing these duties were subject to frequent revision in the early period. It was only over the course of several decades that the collector 'came to represent the might of Government and exercise a measure of executive authority'.[70] This is exemplified in the history of the collector's judicial power. In 1772, the collector was granted the authority to hear all civil suits in his district, but in 1780, his remit was limited to cases relating to revenue, with civil suits relating to property being tried by judges. In 1787, full authority to hear all civil cases was restored to the collector, only for that authority to be removed entirely six years later. The extent of the collector's judicial remit was not firmly settled until 1822 when the power to hear civil cases related to revenue was once again vested in him.[71] Likewise, the civil police force which supported the collector in his judicial capacity underwent much disruption between the 1770s and the 1810s. The faujdari-zamindari system was gradually phased out in the 1770s and 1780s, and replaced by Cornwallis's daroga-based police network in the 1790s. The abortive experiment with police *amins* (commissioners) between 1807 and 1810 was complemented by an equally ill-fated urban *chaukidari* police establishment which was inaugurated in 1812. It was not until as late as 1817 that the duties and powers of the civil police were defined comprehensively.[72]

At the same time, compared with the 1770s and 1780s, by the 1810s, the necessity for the collector to use significant armed force against groups within his district had declined noticeably. With the gradual pacification of the mofussil, the growth and widespread deployment of the army, and the development of the civil police force, the district collector was not likely to find himself forced to undertake military operations against local groups. From the closing years of the 18th century, the Bengal district records reveal a sharp decline in the open resistance being experienced by the Company's collectors, even though low-level dakaiti remained a perennial problem until well after 1810.[73] If one looks, for example, at the Bengal Revenue Consultations dealing with Chittagong and Rangpur in this later period, the comparison with the earlier collectors' correspondence is marked. Whereas 30 or

40 years previously the Chittagong authorities had been challenged by violent groups of various descriptions, by the 1810s, the collectors' correspondence almost without exception relates to the awarding of pensions to cooperative Indians, to the extension of the invalid thanah in the district, and to the cultivation of fallow land.[74] Likewise, in the Rangpur correspondence, collectors, whose predecessors had desperately struggled to cope with armed threats in their midst, now concerned themselves with enhancing the district's opium cultivation and regulating the internal government of Koch Bihar, confident that adequate military resources were available for any emergency which might arise; an emergency which, in any case, would now be placed firmly within the military sphere, rather than the civil.[75] The development of a modern, specialised bureaucratic structure is evident in the fact that by the 1810s collectors were no longer called upon to exercise any great degree of military judgement; there was no need for them to fret about the internal deployment of revenue troops as George Bogle and his contemporaries had done, or to ride out at the head of a band of hastily raised mercenaries, in the manner of D. H. McDowall.

Consequently, the need for a collector to conceal unrest in his district from Fort William was much reduced. This was due in large part to the reaction at the top of the colonial bureaucracy against the excessive and habitual personal interest which had been the guiding principle of those below. The armed forces which supported the collector's authority had improved in size and quality, and the elimination of Indian rivals had allowed the army to be redeployed. Its officers, keen to justify their continued professional existence under the threat of military retrenchment, embraced the notion that the army should be used to overawe local society. The widely dispersed garrisons now discouraged violent disturbances by their presence, and the collector had less reason to fear unrest. Further, the Company's civil service was beginning to offer him a stable and comfortable career. While the potential for amassing a fortune was diminished, so too was the highly politicised (and personalised) *cursus honorum* of the 18th century. In short, much of the Company's territory in India, and Bengal, in particular, was rapidly becoming both politically and administratively stable. The contrast between the character of government in the early Company state and that which developed after the 1810s is neatly encapsulated by the observation of John Beames, a member of the Indian Civil Service during the second half of the 19th century. Writing on his early experiences in Purnea during 1858, he described it as 'an old possession . . . where rules had had time to take root and harden into a settled system of procedure, in which there was no room for the exercise of individual character on the part of officials'.[76] It is this transformation, from a system of colonial governance dictated by 'individual character' to an institutional 'settled system of procedure', which this book has sought to explain.

Notes

1 The *Pindaris* were irregular horsemen, large numbers of which were employed by Maratha chiefs at this time. In addition to acting in a light cavalry role, they also fulfilled commissariat functions in the Maratha armies. B. K. Sinha, *The Pindaris, 1798–1818*, Ann Arbor: University of Michigan Press, 1971.

2 J. Pemble, 'Resources and Techniques in the Second Maratha War', *Historical Journal*, 1976, 19 (2): 275.

3 Peers, *Between Mars and Mammon*, p. 144.

4 E. Ingram, 'The Rules of the Game: A Commentary on the Defence of British India, 1798–1829', *Journal of Imperial and Commonwealth History*, 1975, 3 (2): 274.

5 Peers, *Between Mars and Mammon*, p. 211.

6 *Ibid.*, p. 219.

7 W. Dalrymple (ed.), *Begums, Thugs and White Mughals: The Journals of Fanny Parkes*, London: Eland, 2002, p. 24.

8 Misra, *Central Administration*, p. 55.

9 Bentinck to W. Astell, 21 July 1828, C. H. Philips (ed.), *The Correspondence of Lord William Cavendish Bentinck*, Vol. 1, Oxford: Oxford University Press, 1977, p. 53.

10 Bengal government to the Court of Directors, 10 December 1828, *ibid.*, p. 116.

11 Minute by Sir Charles Metcalfe on the future government of India, 11 October 1829, Philips, *Correspondence of Lord William Cavendish Bentinck*, I, p. 314.

12 Malcolm, *Political History*, I, p. 7.

13 Minute by Sir Charles Metcalfe on the future government of India, 11 October 1829, Philips, *Correspondence of Lord William Cavendish Bentinck*, I, p. 311.

14 *Ibid.*, p. 314.

15 Bengal government to the Court of Directors, 10 December 1828, Philips, *ibid.*, p. 116.

16 *Ibid.*

17 Bengal Military and Civil Statement, 1799–1800, IOR, L/MIL/8/10, pp. 2–6.

18 Bengal Military Establishment Annual Statement 1819–20, IOR, L/MIL/8/29.

19 M. E. Yapp, *Strategies of British India: Britain, Iran and Afghanistan, 1798–1850*, Oxford: Oxford University Press, 1980, p. 591.

20 Ingram, 'The Rules of the Game', p. 258.

21 The notion of the 'Great Game' was already well established in Anglo-Indian society at this time. In April 1828, the diarist Fanny Parkes, who was the wife of a junior Company official in Allahabad, wrote, 'Our politicians are all on the *qui vive* at the *mêlée* between the Russians and Persians, and the old story of an invasion of India is again agitated – we are not alarmed'. Dalrymple, *Begums, Thugs and White Mughals*, p. 56.

22 Minute by Sir Charles Metcalfe on the future government of India, 11 October 1829, Philips, *Correspondence of Lord William Cavendish Bentinck*, I, p. 314.
23 Alavi, 'The Company Army and Rural Society', pp. 154–156.
24 *Ibid*., p. 157.
25 *Ibid*., p. 167.
26 *Ibid*., p. 168.
27 Alavi, *The Sepoys and the Company*, pp. 135–143.
28 Alavi, 'The Company Army and Rural Society', p. 75.
29 Other than half-batta, the two most contentious reforms were Bentinck's army reorganisation programme of 1834–35, and the abolition of corporal punishment for the native army in 1835. The former was geared towards effecting 'a considerable, immediate, and a large prospective reduction in our military expenditure', principally by reducing the number of Europeans serving in the artillery and by reducing the number of staff posts. Minute of the governor-general, 9 August 1834, IOR, L/MIL/5/401/196, p. 54. The abolition of corporal punishment, however, was not an economic measure, but rather an expression of Bentinck's liberal beliefs. See D. M. Peers, 'Sepoys, Soldiers and the Lash: Race, Caste and Army Discipline in India, 1820–1850', *Journal of Imperial and Commonwealth History*, 1995, 23 (2): 211–247.
30 S .P. Cohen, *The Indian Army*, Berkeley: University of California Press, 1971, p. 19.
31 Wellington had never forgiven his former subordinate for his conduct during the Peninsula War (1807–14), when Bentinck had neglected the operations against the French in Catalonia in order to indulge his passion for interfering in Italian politics. J. Rosselli, *Lord William Bentinck: The Making of a Liberal Imperialist*, Los Angeles: University of California Press, 1974, p. 304.
32 H. Spry to E. Spry, 20 January 1831, IOR, Photo Eur 308/4.
33 T. Seaton, *From Cadet to Colonel: The Record of a Life of Active Service*, Vol. 1, London: Savill and Edwards, 1866, p. 85.
34 *Ibid*., p. 86.
35 W. Bentinck to Col. Craigie, 9 November 1833, BP/Pwjf/2696, cit. Rosselli, *Lord William Bentinck*, p. 312.
36 Writing of a temporary encampment constructed for a state visit by Bentinck to Allahabad in October 1829, Fanny Parkes acidly observed, 'These new tents, the elephants, camels, horses, and thousands of servants, will the cost the Company more than half *batta* saves in the course of a year'. Dalrymple, *Begums, Thugs and White Mughals*, p. 74.
37 The *Times*, 5 November 1829, cit. Peers, *Between Mars and Mammon*, p. 223.
38 Peers, 'The East India Company and Efforts to Reform Its Army', p. 385.
39 H. Spry to E. Spry, 20 January 1831, IOR, Photo Eur 308/4.
40 *Ibid*.
41 Peers, 'The East India Company and Efforts to Reform Its Army', p. 386.
42 Peers, *Between Mars and Mammon*, p. 221.
43 For a detailed discussion of Malcolm's influence on imperial policy, see Harrington, *Sir John Malcolm*, pp. 129–157.
44 Bengal government to the Court of Directors, 10 December 1828, Philips, *Correspondence of Lord William Cavendish Bentinck*, p. xix.

45 Malcolm, *Political History*, I, p. 7.
46 *Ibid.*, p. 8.
47 *Ibid.*, p. 141.
48 *Ibid.*, pp. 410–411.
49 *Ibid.*, p. 440.
50 *Ibid.*, p. 458.
51 Peers, *Between Mars and Mammon*, p. 1.
52 Peers, 'The East India Company and Efforts to Reform Its Army', p. 387.
53 Harrington, *Sir John Malcolm*, p. 12.
54 The *Sketch of the Political History of India*, which foreshadowed many of the themes of the later work, first appeared in print in 1811.
55 Harrington, *Sir John Malcolm*, p. 16.
56 *Ibid.*, p. 37.
57 *Ibid.*, p. 40.
58 J. W. Kaye, *The Life and Correspondence of Major-General Sir John Malcolm*, Vol. 1, London: Smith, Elder & Co., 1856, pp. 10–11.
59 Harrington, *Sir John Malcolm*, p. 18.
60 *Ibid.*, p. 19.
61 Peers, *Between Mars and Mammon*, p. 54.
62 Malcolm, *Political History*, I, p. 8.
63 *Ibid.*, p. 60.
64 L. Zastoupil, *John Stuart Mill and India*, Stanford CA: Stanford University Press, 1994, p. 546.
65 Marshall, *East Indian Fortunes*, p. 15.
66 Under Cornwallis's reforms of 1786, district collectors were to receive an increased salary of 1,500 rupees per month. Misra, *Central Administration*, p. 157.
67 P. J. Marshall, 'British Society in India under the East India Company', *Modern Asian Studies*, 1997, 31: 99.
68 Wellesley's minute, 10 July 1800, Martin, *Wellesley's Despatches*, Vol. 2, p. 346, cit. Misra, *Central Administration*, p. 389.
69 *Ibid.*, p. 402.
70 *Ibid.*, p. 154.
71 *Ibid.*, p. 155.
72 *Ibid.*, p. 367.
73 That is, robbery with violence, rather than the large-scale depredations of the kind orchestrated by Ranu Khan and Gungaram Thapa in the 1770s and 1780s, or indeed the sannyasi activity which continued up until the 1790s.
74 IOR, BRC Indexes, 1810–1819, Z/P/697–Z/P/706.
75 *Ibid.* In particular, BRC Index 1813, IOR, Z/P/700 and BRC Index 1817, Z/P/704.
76 J. Beames, *Memoirs of a Bengal Civilian*, London: Eland, 2003, p. 129.

Conclusion

This book has argued that, until the early 19th century, the character of the Company's district government was profoundly shaped by local officials' anxieties over their personal prestige. They were particularly concerned about their standing with senior Company servants at Fort William, who could easily find replacements for unsatisfactory administrators in the ultra-competitive early civil service. Concern among collectors was heightened by the widespread presence of hostile local groups and the limited armed forces which district authorities were allocated to counter them. This combination threatened the security of the district's revenue stream, the profitability of which was the prime criterion of a collector's success or failure in the debt-ridden Company administration of the 18th century.

Consequently, local officials were forced to be risk averse in their approach to government, caught as they were between violent unrest in their district and the machinations of their colleagues. The effect of this administrative culture was to limit the Company's bureaucratic penetration of Indian society. Since they so often lacked the resources to counter serious armed threats with confidence, the Company's collectors frequently remained passive in the face of unrest, as with the 'tranquil spectator' Francis Law and the 'patient witness' Richard Goodlad. They sought to conceal unpalatable events, or to misrepresent them to their superiors. To do otherwise would be to advertise their apparent ineptitude to Fort William and so invite dismissal from their post.

At the higher levels of the Company's service, discontent with this defensive attitude was a key driving force behind the gradual professionalisation of the colonial state's mechanisms and procedures from the late 1780s onwards. In a reaction against the primacy of personal interest which prevailed throughout service, the authorities in Fort William and London sought to regulate the Company's bureaucracy through better training, salaries and working conditions for its civil servants, together with much improved military resources to bolster their authority. This, combined with the accretion over time of governmental practices, produced a comparatively self-assured colonial bureaucracy by the 1810s, which was staffed by a more homogenous type of civil servant. It was the development of this cohesive community, with its shared assumptions and distinctly Anglo-Indian identity, which enabled the widespread dissemination of Anglo-Indian militarist sentiment throughout the 1820s, championed by the Empire of Opinion school of Anglo-Indians.

Competition and personal interest in the Company's service

During the opening decades of British rule in India, even at the higher reaches of the Company's administration in Calcutta, the key concern of officials lay with their personal prestige, rather than with that of a greater corporate whole. Warren Hastings, for example, believed that his power to govern was sustained far more by his public reputation as an individual than by the status attached to the office of governor-general. Until the colonial state's structures became more developed during the first quarter of the 19th century, Indian interlocutors tended to view Company servants as personalities, rather than as the organs of an Anglo-Indian bureaucracy; they were monitored closely, and the personal information thus gained was used to estimate the Company's capacity to impose its rule. Indians treated the government accordingly, tailoring their responses to the perceived strengths or weaknesses of key figures, as is shown in the case of Hastings by Chait Singh's refusal to provide his subsidy in 1780 following reports of the governor-general's fresh troubles with his councillors.

Perhaps most importantly, Company servants also monitored each other's public standing and used that knowledge to advance themselves at their colleagues' expense. Before the early 19th century, the Company's administration was characterised by this culture of self-interest: Hastings was relentlessly (and personally) attacked by his own councillors over a period of several years, every effort was made to discredit him through charges of fraud and misgovernment and, finally, his very person was threatened when he fought his duel with Philip Francis. Only as the Company's governmental mechanisms began to solidify after the late 1780s did governors-general enjoy relative security from the machinations of cliques among their subordinates, protected to an extent by their powers as office-holders rather than reliant on their personal authority as individuals. The resolution of grievances through official mechanisms, rather than by force or personal influence, was a hallmark of the later Company state, after the 1810s, as the contrast between the army officers' mutinies of the 18th century and the comparatively staid, formal protests surrounding the half-batta order in the late 1820s demonstrates. Even so, while authority at the top of government became more institutionalised, factionalism remained rife at the lower levels of the administration until at least the turn of the 19th century. Junior Company servants (including those in the districts, far removed from Fort William) attached themselves to the parties of more senior men, hoping to gain advancement in a highly competitive service through some fortunate connection. In turn, those senior servants actively cultivated a personal following, since they drew both prestige and practical influence from this support base (witness, for instance, George Bogle's attempt to enlist Richard Goodlad on behalf of Warren Hastings).

As has been seen, throughout the 1770s and 1780s, notwithstanding the shocking mortality rate of Europeans in India, the Company's service was becoming so overmanned that the odds were stacked against continued employment, let alone promotion. In such a competitive environment, corporate values of cooperation were inevitably sacrificed to ensure that an individual's position remained secure. Colleagues were first and foremost rivals, and conflict between individuals was personal as well as professional. This is neatly illustrated not only by the Hastings-Francis duel but also by several examples in the district case studies from the clashes between the Company's servants at Lakshmipur and Kulinda with the Chittagong collector in the early 1770s to the increasingly desperate efforts of Hiram Cox to obtain assistance from his intransigent colleagues three decades later. As such, to gain advancement, or even simply to remain employed, required that great attention be paid by Company servants to their personal reputation. With so many potential rivals jockeying for position, Fort William would not hesitate to replace an individual who was perceived as having failed in his duty.

The military resources available to district officials

For a collector to govern a district to his superiors' satisfaction, its inhabitants had to be given enough protection from harm to guarantee the regular collection and remittance of territorial revenue. This, in turn, was dependent to a great extent on the armed forces which Fort William was willing to provide for the collector's use. As the case studies of Chittagong and Rangpur have shown, there was no shortage of violent groups in Bengal, ready and eager to cause disruption. These included elements from within Indian society (including dakaits, sannyasis and recalcitrant zamindars) and cross-border raiders, such as Gungaram Thapa's band in Baikanthapur, and those from Arakan and Burma in Chittagong.

The armed forces at the collector's disposal were often insufficient to impose the government's authority on these disruptive groups, or even to draw limits to their activities. From the 1770s to the early 1800s, the bulk of the Bengal Army was concentrated in the west and south of the province, if not beyond its territorial boundaries in Awadh, Benares and the former Maratha territories; there was comparatively little regular army presence in the northern and eastern areas of Bengal. Furthermore, even when regular military units were comparatively close at hand, there was a marked reluctance on the part of Fort William to allow them to be used for 'provincial duties' in support of district administrations. Instead, as has been outlined, various paramilitary corps were more usually detailed for this service, each sharing the common attribute that, as well as being as small an establishment as possible, they often lacked discipline and an adequate executive infrastructure. In both districts examined in the case studies, these forces frequently struggled to counter local threats.

This book has argued that reasons of economy alone are insufficient to explain the general military under-resourcing of district administrations by the central government; it was also prompted by the desire to extend a system of checks and balances throughout the service, although this had the side effect of limiting the Company's local authority, and its revenues, as outlined earlier. The metropolis-periphery relationship of London and Calcutta was reproduced in miniature by that of Calcutta and the district headquarters. Just as London sought to regulate the powers of governors-general through their councils, so too did Fort William seek to limit the power of local officials by denying them military forces. The limiting of what troops they were permitted, and the insistence that they were not to be deployed piecemeal, was intended to reduce the number of individuals in the Company's hierarchy who enjoyed the capacity for undertaking significant, independent, violent action. The risk inherent in delegating military authority within a comparatively undeveloped state structure is brought into sharp focus by McDowall's unauthorised invasion of Nepal in 1786, following his reinforcement by a regular battalion. Yet while Fort William sought to curb the power of collectors, at the same time, it expected that the district revenues would be realised, meaning that, at the very least, the more threatening instances of armed resistance had to be countered, and this often demanded the dispatching of troops to several sectors of the district simultaneously, thereby forcing the collector to juggle the conflicting directives of his superiors.

The conduct of district officials and its implications

District officials measured their responses to armed threats according to the quantity and quality of their own armed forces. However, perhaps more surprisingly, the case studies have also shown that the level of armed force available to those officials had a significant impact on how they represented such threats in their correspondence with the central government. A common pattern of behaviour was exhibited by officials in both Rangpur and Chittagong, in which they sought to conceal the extent of serious unrest within their districts because they lacked the armed forces to intervene with confidence, preferring instead to remain inactive, hoping that any turbulent individuals would either move on or fall victim to the volatile environment of 18th-century Bengal. These people were often based on the fringes of the district, and the collector usually had little intelligence about them (see, for example, Francis Law's initial uncertainty over the scope of Ranu Khan's activities). The danger inherent in confronting such groups with the district's limited forces frequently outweighed what little credit might be gained by a victory. If they were put down successfully, then the collector was simply doing his job; if, on the other hand, his forces suffered a reverse (by no means unlikely), then, together with defeat, the collector faced the unwelcome scrutiny of his superiors. This increased the chances of his being reprimanded, or even replaced, thereby damaging his prospects for professional advancement and accompanying personal enrichment.

The Company's urgent need to increase Bengal's revenue yield throughout the closing decades of the 18th century underlies many of the issues detailed in the case studies. It strongly informed the conduct of the collectors, both by revealing the priorities of their employers, with whom they wished to curry favour, and, conversely, by making it harder for them to do so by fomenting indigenous resistance against them. In Chittagong, the Company imposed a tax farmer on the Chakma raja's lands, which had been held rent-free under the Mughals, and so provoked the Chakmas to rebel. Similarly, in Rangpur Devi Singh's attempts to wring a profit from the district resulted in the most serious peasant uprising yet experienced by the Company. In both cases, the collectors must have been aware, if only dimly, of what the tax farmers were doing and the effect it was having on local society, but they did not act, even though Law, at least, admitted to hearing bad reports of his farmer. Both collectors knew that their employers were interested in maximising revenues almost to the exclusion of everything else and that any complaints about the unsavoury methods used by the tax farmers would not be welcomed by Fort William. While the revenues were paid promptly and in sufficient quantity, a great deal else would be forgiven; the notion of a duty of care between ruler and ruled was quite alien in this environment, regardless of the impassioned, humanitarian tone of Burke's declamations against 'the tyranny of Debi Sing' over the 'poor unfortunate husbandmen'.[1]

Even if the collector felt some sense of responsibility for the well-being of his district's inhabitants, he frequently lacked the means to put it into practice, as is made clear by several examples from the case studies, particularly the Baikanthapur raids and the Burmese incursions into Chittagong. In this early period, little attempt was made to impose the government's authority comprehensively throughout a district and a threat to the safety of its inhabitants was rarely of pressing importance unless it compromised the district's profitability. The few troops available were used to secure the wider process of revenue extraction, rather than to safeguard the district's population for its own sake. In particular, those inhabiting remoter areas could expect little protection from the local authorities. The collector's influence became weaker the further removed events were from his kachari, since, given the limited armed forces at his disposal, often only the key area immediately around the district headquarters could be deemed secure. A collector who dispersed his forces in an attempt to counter all the simultaneous threats to the public peace would not only be defying Fort William, who had demanded that revenue troops be kept concentrated; he would also be inviting military defeat in detail and with it serious damage to his capacity to protect the revenue stream. By confining his troops to a very few areas in the district, the collector effectively abandoned control over great expanses of what was nominally Company territory, but in this way, he could at least aim to protect some key parganas. The regular remittance of a certain amount of revenue, even if it was not the maximum yield, was better than risking losing all by trying to gain all.

Collectors, then, were often powerless to defend the Company's subjects, particularly on the fringes of its territory, and an example of this may be seen in the conduct of William Amherst, the acting collector of Rangpur in 1786. To oppose the concentration of various hostile groups in Baikanthapur, numbering more than 1,000 Nepalese raiders, sannyasis and political malcontents, Amherst could muster just 17 sebundy sepoys and 20 barqandazes. His accompanying public 'letter of encouragement' to the local raiyats was a gesture which merely served to underline the Rangpur collectorate's utter inability to protect them, or, indeed, to influence, far less control, events in large sections of the district.

The relationship between the Company's local and central authorities in the half century after 1765 was characterised by what might be termed a 'culture of concealment'. Isolated collectors were able to hide much of what went on locally from their distant superiors, and they were encouraged in this by the weakness of their military resources, which made it difficult to do other than remain passive in the face of a multitude of dimly realised threats. However, as soon as violent disruptions seriously reduced the amount of revenue being remitted from the district, concealment became impossible. As is shown in the cases of Goodlad and Law, it was only at this point, when they would inevitably be betrayed by the next set of monthly accounts, that the collectors were finally compelled to make a military response as a last throw of the dice, together with a long justification of their previous conduct to Fort William.

The immediate availability of military resources was crucial in shaping the behaviour of district officials, and the argument that a collector's representation of a threat to his superiors was heavily informed by the force available to counter it is equally applicable to those, much rarer, occasions when a strong armed force was on hand. This is demonstrated by the example of D. H. McDowall in 1786. Provided with a battalion, he represented Gungaram Thapa's raids as deserving of a campaign which encompassed the invasion of a sovereign state, whereas his predecessors, backed by little or no armed force, had portrayed them as minor border disturbances. However, McDowall's rationale was arguably the same as his less fortunate predecessors: the maintenance of his personal prestige with his employers. While Charles Purling and George Bogle found that they had too few troops to intervene in any meaningful way, and subsequently seem to have played down a situation from which they could not emerge with credit, McDowall saw an opportunity for personal distinction because he had the means to act offensively. Consequently, far from being a 'tranquil spectator', within a week of arriving in Rangpur, he had invaded Nepal.

The nature of the Company's service began to change from the late 1790s, quickening in pace during the first quarter of the 19th century. The professionalisation of the state's bureaucratic structures, the accumulation of a body of Anglo-Indian governmental knowledge and the gradual improvement in their military resources, brought some degree of confidence to local officials by stabilising their position and prospects within the Company's hierarchy. Hiram Cox's encounter with the local authorities of east Bengal in 1799 is illustrative of the bridging stage between the bureaucracies of the 18th and 19th centuries. The commissioner for the refugees at Ramu found his best efforts frustrated by the self-interested behaviour of several Bengal collectors; their uniform unwillingness to help him was prompted, at least in part, by their resentment at this proconsular agent of the central government meddling in local affairs. However, the adroit way in which they handled him and, indeed, the swift abolition of the post of commissioner, suggests that it was not merely the experience of the administrative side of Anglo-Indian governance which had been accumulated by district collectors. Unlike the clumsy, semi-successful attempts to discredit that other commissioner, John Paterson, in the 1780s, the thwarting of Cox was achieved not by personal influence in the upper echelons of government, so characteristic of the 18th-century Company state, but by pressure from below, exerted by the secure local officials of a rapidly modernising professional bureaucracy.

There has been vigorous debate in the historiography of British India concerning whether the Company state can best be understood as an aggressively military-fiscalist entity, determined to maximise profit, or as a reactive, minimalist 'nightwatchman' state, seeking to balance profit again the dangers of over-involvement in Indian society. The argument presented in this book is that these characterisations are not mutually exclusive, that they can be applied to the Company state simultaneously and that the extent to which one dominated the other is dependent on the immediate time and place under examination.

From the 1760s onwards, the edicts which issued from the centre of power at Fort William indicated a marked military-fiscalist bent; while, in the districts, the Company's officials often displayed a nightwatchmanly disengagement in their professional conduct. In the latter half of the 18th century (and earlier), one can see the predominance of nightwatchmanism within the nascent Company state; whereas by the 1820s, with the redeployment of the army and the professionalisation of the district bureaucracy, military-fiscalism is paramount. Were one to attempt a general characterisation of the Company state across the whole of the period covered by this book, it would be that the colonial edifice was military-fiscalist in the upper echelons of its government and nightwatchmanly on its peripheries. The more remote the periphery – and the earlier the date – the more minimal the intrusion of government.

Until the early 19th century, then, the isolated position of the Company's collectors, together with the slender resources allocated to them, and the highly competitive, volatile and underdeveloped professional environment in which they operated, combined to encourage a risk-averse culture among the district administrations. These subaltern officials were perpetually conscious of the need to conciliate their superiors; their governmental practice was shaped by the desire to conceal problems so as to preserve their professional standing and perquisites.

The key flaw in the relationship between the agents of central and local government was that whereas Fort William sought to maximise income for the state, district collectors were concerned with minimising risk to their careers. Local officials sought to draw limits to encroachment from above, employing subaltern tactics of feigned ignorance, false compliance and dissimulation in their relations with their superiors.[2] Such behaviour illustrates how the primacy of personal interest within the Company's service of the 18th century limited its administrative grip on rural Bengal. That limitation was only eased after the early 19th century by the gradual development of a professional colonial bureaucracy with better-structured career progression and guaranteed, if moderate, rewards for its civil servants.

This book has examined the experience of local officials and questioned the Company's effective occupation of its territory for much of the first 50 years of the state's existence. Its broad themes, however, are not just applicable to the period before the 1810s. The isolated collector of the 18th century, struggling to govern his district with limited armed forces and imperfect knowledge of its inhabitants, provides an example in miniature of the difficulties which would continue to test the colonial establishment until Indian independence. Although on a different scale, issues surrounding the control of military resources and the army's relationship with the civil power remained contentious until well into the 20th century. The focus on personality became less pronounced, but the standing which the government enjoyed in Indian society continued to be perceived as a crucial instrument of rule, helping to offset its shortcomings in terms of manpower and material.

These were perennial concerns for the colonial state, as may be seen in the lasting influence of the Empire of Opinion school and that of John Malcolm in particular. Deeply affected by the military insecurity of the 18th century, Malcolm reminded his Anglo-Indian audience of their ever-present vulnerability in the 1820s and continued to be a major influence on government policy and Anglo-Indian service culture long after his death in 1833. Ultimately, considerations of armed force and prestige were to remain of first importance for the duration of British rule in India.

Notes

1 Marshall, *Writings and Speeches of Edmund Burke*, VI, pp. 415, 418.
2 These are classic tactics of subaltern resistance. See Scott, *Weapons of the Weak*, p. 29.

Bibliography

Unpublished sources

British Library: India Office Records

Eur MSS D75: Account of the District of Ronggepur by F. Buchanan.
Eur MSS D506: Rangpur Commission Papers.
Eur MSS E226: George Bogle Papers.
Eur MSS E424/2: William Bentinck Papers, 1828 to 1830.
F/4/8/709–F/4/173/3076: Board of Control's Collections, 1783 to 1805.
H/734–36: John Malcolm Papers.
L/MIL/5/ 361–418: Military Department, Compilations and Miscellaneous.
L/MIL/8/ 1–29: Bengal Annual Military Statements, 1784/5 to 1819/20.
L/MIL/10/ 130–139: Bengal Army Muster Rolls and Casualty Returns, 1716 to 1813.
P/18/41–44: Bengal Military Consultations, 29 March 1771 to 31 December 1777.
P/51/6–P/54/24: Bengal Revenue Consultations 29 March 1787 to 29 April 1802.
Photo Eur 308/4: Spry Correspondence, 1827 to 1835.
Z/P/407–Z/P/426: Bengal Military Consultations Indexes, 1808 to 1819.
Z/P/697–Z/P/706: Bengal Revenue Consultations Indexes, 1810 to 1819.

British Library: manuscript collections

Add MSS 13,592: Richard Wellesley Papers.
Add MSS 29,117: Warren Hastings Papers.
Add MSS 45,421; Add MS 45,427; Add MSS 45,436: David Anderson Papers.

Gloucestershire Archives: Ducarel family collection

D2091/F14/5–20: G. G. Ducarel's correspondence with Richard Goodlad.

National Archives of Bangladesh, Dhaka: district records

A2.2/456–479: Chittagong, August 1768 to August 1797 (Letters received and issued).

A12.1/20–A12.2/306.13: Rangpur, April 1786 to March 1811 (Letters received and issued).

University of London: Institute of Historical Research

'Ninth Report of the Secret Committee of 1773', *Reports from Committees of the House of Commons*, 12 vols., 1803–1806.

The Royal Kalendar and Court and City Register for England, Scotland, Ireland, and the Colonies, London: J. Almon, 1819.

Published sources

Beames, J., *Memoirs of a Bengal Civilian*, London: Eland, 2003.

Benjamin, L. S. (ed.), *The Wellesley Papers: The Life and Correspondence of Richard Colley Wellesley, Marquess Wellesley, 1760–1842*, 2 vols., London: H. Jenkins, 1914.

Burn, R., Cotton, J. S., Meyer, W. W. and Risley, H. H. (eds.), *The Imperial Gazetteer of India, XIX, Náyakanhathi to Parbhani*, Oxford: Clarendon Press, 1908.

Cox, H., *Journal of a Residence in the Burmhan Empire*, London: John Warren, 1821.

Dalrymple, W. (ed.), *Begums, Thugs and White Mughals: The Journals of Fanny Parkes*, London: Eland, 2002.

Dodwell, H. H. (ed.), *Warren Hastings' Letters to Sir John Macpherson*, London: Faber & Gwyer, 1927.

Firminger, W. K. (ed.), *Bengal District Records: Chittagong, 1760–1773, Letters Received and Issued*, Calcutta: Bengal Secretariat, 1923.

——— (ed.), *Bengal District Records: Rangpur, Letters Received and Issued*, 6 vols., Calcutta: Bengal Secretariat, 1914–1928.

Forrest, G. W. (ed.), *Selections from the State Papers of the Governors General of India: Lord Cornwallis*, 2 vols., Oxford: Blackwell, 1926.

——— (ed.), *Selections from the State Papers of the Governors General of India: Warren Hastings*, 2 vols., Oxford: Blackwell, 1910.

Furber, H. (ed.), *The Correspondence of Edmund Burke, Vol. V, July 1782 to June 1789*, Cambridge: Cambridge University Press, 1965.

Gibbon, E., *The History of the Decline and Fall of the Roman Empire*, London: Westley and Davis, 1837.

Gleig, G. R. (ed.), *Memoirs of the Life of the Right Hon. Warren Hastings, First Governor-General of Bengal*, 3 vols., London: Richard Bentley, 1841.

Goldman, L. (ed.), *Oxford Dictionary of National Biography*, Oxford: Oxford University Press, 2004.

Hodges, W., *Travels in India, During the Years 1780, 1781, 1782, and 1783*, 2nd ed., London: J. Edwards, 1794.

Hunter, W. W., *Annals of Rural Bengal*, London: Smith, Elder & Co., 1868.

———, *The Imperial Gazetteer of India, III, Birbhum to Coconada*, 2nd ed., London: Trubner & Co., 1885.

———, *The Imperial Gazetteer of India, XI, Páli to Ratiá*, 2nd ed., London: Trubner & Co., 1886.

Islam, S. (ed.), *Bangladesh District Records: Chittagong, 1760–1787*, Dhaka: University Press, 1978.

——— (ed.), *Bangladesh District Records: Dacca District (1784–1787)*, Dhaka: University Press, 1981.

Kaye, J. W. *The Life and Correspondence of Major-General Sir John Malcolm*, 2 vols., London: Smith, Elder & Co., 1856.

———, *Lives of Indian Officers: Lord Cornwallis; Sir John Malcolm; Mountstuart Elphinstone; Henry Martyn; Sir Charles Metcalfe*, London: W. H. Allen, 1869.

Lunt, J. (ed.), *From Sepoy to Subedar: Being the life and adventures of Subedar Sita Ram, a Native officer of the Bengal Army Written and Related by Himself*, London: Routledge, 1970.

Macaulay, T. B., *Lays of Ancient Rome with Selections from the Essays*, London: Ward Lock, 1884.

Malcolm, J., *The Political History of India from 1784 to 1823*, 2 vols., London: John Murray, 1826.

Marshall, P. J. (ed.), *The Writings and Speeches of Edmund Burke, Vol. V, India: Madras and Bengal, 1774–1785*, Oxford: Oxford University Press, 1981.

——— (ed.), *The Writings and Speeches of Edmund Burke, Vol. VI, India: The Launching of the Hastings Impeachment, 1786–1788*, Oxford: Oxford University Press, 1991.

Mathison, J. (ed.), *East India Company Register and Directory, 1810*, 2nd ed., London: Cox, Son and Baylis, 1810.

Mill, J., *The History of British India*, 6 vols., 3rd ed., London: Baldwin, Cradock and Joy, 1826.

Minto, N. (ed.), *Lord Minto in India*, London: Longmans, Green and Co., 1880.

Philips, C. H. (ed.), *The Correspondence of Lord William Cavendish Bentinck*, 2 vols., Oxford: Oxford University Press, 1977.

Ross, C. (ed.), *Correspondence of Charles, First Marquis Cornwallis*, 3 vols., London: John Murray, 1859.

Schendel, W. van (ed.), *Francis Buchanan in Southeast Bengal (1798): His Journey to Chittagong, the Chittagong Hill Tracts, Noakhali and Comilla*, Dhaka: University Press, 1992.

Seaton, T., *From Cadet to Colonel: The Record of a Life of Active Service*, 2 vols., London: Savill and Edwards, 1866.

The Times (London ed.), London: R. Nutkins, 1788 present.

Williams, J., *An Historical Account of the Rise and Progress of the Bengal Native Infantry from Its First Formation in 1757 to 1796*, London: John Murray, 1817.

Yule, H. and Burnell, A. C., *Hobson-Jobson: The Definitive Glossary of British India*, K. Teltscher (ed.), Oxford: Oxford University Press, 2013.

Secondary literature: journal articles and book chapters

Alavi, S., 'The Company Army and Rural Society: The Invalid Thanah, 1770 to 1830', *Modern Asian Studies*, 1993, 27(1): 147–78.

Amussen, S. D., 'Punishment, Discipline, and Power: The Social Meanings of Violence in Early Modern England', *Journal of British Studies*, 1995, 34(1): 1–34.

Barua, P., 'Military Developments in India, 1780–1850', *Journal of Military History*, 1994, 58(4): 599–616.

Bayly, C. A., 'The British Military-Fiscal State and Indigenous Resistance in India 1750–1820', in *An Imperial State at War: Britain from 1689 to 1815*, L. Stone (ed.), London: Routledge, 1993, pp. 322–355.

Benton, L. 'Colonial Law and Cultural Difference: Jurisdictional Politics and the Formation of the Colonial State', *Comparative Studies in Society and History*, 1999, 41(3): 563–588.

Bowyer, T. H., 'The Appointment of Philip Francis to the Bengal Supreme Council', *Historical Journal*, 1995, 38: 145–149.

Boyce, D. G., 'From Assaye to the *Assaye*: Reflections on British Government, Force, and Moral Authority in India', *Journal of Military History*, 1999, 63(3): 643–668.

Bruce-Watson, I., 'Fortifications and the "Idea" of Force in Early East India Company Relations with India', *Past & Present*, 1980, 88: 70–87.

Bryant, G. J., 'Asymmetric Warfare: The British Experience in Eighteenth-Century India', *Journal of Military History*, 2004, 68(2): 431–469.

———, 'Pacification in the Early British Raj', *Journal of Imperial and Commonwealth History*, 1985, 14(1): 3–19.

Callahan, R. 'The Company's Army, 1757–1798', in *The East India Company: 1600–1858, V, Warfare, Expansion, and Resistance*, P. Tuck (ed.), London: Routledge, 1998, pp. 21–31.

Caplan, L., '"The Bravest of the Brave": Representations of "The Gurkha" in British Military Writings', *Modern Asian Studies*, 1991, 25(3): 571–597.

Chakraborty, R. L., 'Chakma Resistance to Early British Rule', *Bangladesh Historical Studies*, 1977, 2: 136–147.

Chatterji, B., 'The Darogah and the Countryside: The Imposition of Police Control in Bengal and Its Impact (1793–1837)', *Indian Economic and Social History Review*, 1981, 28(1): 19–42.

Cobban, A. B. C., 'Edmund Burke and the Origins of the Theory of Nationality', *Cambridge Historical Journal*, 1926, 2(1): 36–47.

Cohn, B. S., 'The Initial British Impact on India: A Case Study of the Benares Region', *Journal of Asian Studies*, 1960, 19(4): 418–431.

———, 'Political Systems in Eighteenth Century India: The Banaras Region', *Journal of the American Oriental Society*, 1962, 82(3): 312–320.

Cooper, R. G. S., 'Wellington and the Marathas in 1803', in *Warfare and Empires: Contact and Conflict between European and non-European Military and Maritime Forces and Cultures*, D. M. Peers (ed.), Aldershot: Ashgate, 1997, pp. 305–312.

Elias, N., 'On Transformations of Aggressiveness', *Theory and Society*, 1978, 5(2): 229–242.

Forster, R., 'Magh Marauders, Portuguese Pirates, White Elephants and Persian Poets: Arakan and its Bay-of-Bengal Connectivities in the Early Modern Era', *Explorations: A Graduate Student Journal of Southeast Asian Studies*, 2011, 11(1): 63–80.

Gilbert, A. N., 'Law and Honour among Eighteenth-Century British Army Officers', *Historical Journal*, 1976, 19(1): 75–87.

———, 'Recruitment and Reform in the East India Company's Army, 1760–1800', *Journal of British Studies*, 1975, 15(1): 89–111.

Harling, P. and Mandler, P., 'From "Fiscal-Military" State to Laissez-Faire State, 1760–1850', *Journal of British Studies*, 1993, 32(1): 44–70.

Huttenback, R. A., 'The French Threat to India and British Relations with Sind, 1799–1809', *English Historical Review*, 1961, 76(301): 590–599.

Ingram, E., 'The Rules of the Game: A Commentary on the Defence of British India, 1798–1829', *Journal of Imperial and Commonwealth History*, 1975, 3(2): 257–279.

Islam, S., 'Tribal Resistance in the Chittagong Hill Tracts (1776–87)', in *Challenge: A Saga of India's Struggle for Freedom*, N. R. Ray et al. (eds.), New Delhi: PPH, 1984, pp. 122–140.

Lees, J., '"A Character to Lose": Richard Goodlad, the Rangpur *Dhing*, and the Priorities of the East India Company's Early Colonial Administrators', *Journal of the Royal Asiatic Society of Great Britain & Ireland*, 2015, 25(2): 301–315.

———, 'A "Tranquil Spectator": The District Official and the Practice of Local Government in Late Eighteenth-Century Bengal', *Journal of Imperial and Commonwealth History*, 2010, 38(1): 1–19.

———, 'Sepoys and Sebundies: The Role of Regular and Paramilitary Forces in the Construction of Colonialism in Bengal, c. 1765–c. 1820', in *Culture, Conflict and the Military in Colonial South Asia*, K. Roy and G. Rand (eds.), Abingdon: Routledge, 2018, pp. 45–63.

Lorenzen, D., 'Warrior Ascetics in Indian History', *Journal of the American Oriental Society*, 1978, 98(1): 61–75.

Marshall, P. J., 'Britain and the World in the Eighteenth Century, IV: The Turning Outwards of Britain', *Transactions of the Royal Historical Society*, 2001, 6(11): 9.

———, 'British-Indian Connections c. 1780 to c. 1830', in *Romantic Representations of British India*, M. J. Franklin (ed.), London: Routledge, 2006, pp. 45–64.

———, 'British Society in India under the East India Company', *Modern Asian Studies*, 1997, 31: 89–108.

———, 'Early British Imperialism in India', *Past & Present*, 1985, 106: 164–169.

———, 'The Personal Fortune of Warren Hastings', *Economic History Review*, 1964, 17(2): 284–300.

———, 'Western Arms in Maritime Asia in the Early Phases of Expansion', *Modern Asian Studies*, 1980, 14(1): 13–28.

Miles, G. B., 'Roman and Modern Imperialism: A Reassessment', *Comparative Studies in Society and History*, 1990, 32(4): 629–659.

Mukherjee, R., 'Early British Imperialism in India: A Rejoinder', *Past & Present*, 1985, 106: 169–173.

Peers, D. M., 'Between Mars and Mammon: The East India Company and Efforts to Reform Its Army, 1796–1832', *Historical Journal*, 1990, 33(2): 385–401.

———, 'Colonial Knowledge and the Military in India, 1780–1860', *Journal of Imperial and Commonwealth History*, 2005, 33(2): 157–180.

———, '"The Habitual Nobility of Being": British Officers and the Social Construction of the Bengal Army in the Early Nineteenth Century', *Modern Asian Studies*, 1991, 25(3): 545–569.

———, 'Sepoys, Soldiers and the Lash: Race, Caste and Army Discipline in India, 1820–1850', *Journal of Imperial and Commonwealth History*, 1995, 23(2): 211–247.

Pemble, J., 'Resources and Techniques in the Second Maratha War', *Historical Journal*, 1976, 19(2): 375–404.

Perlin, F., 'Proto-Industrialisation and Pre-Colonial South Asia', *Past & Present*, 1983, 98: 30–95.

———, 'State Formation Reconsidered: Part Two', *Modern Asian Studies*, 1985, 19(3): 415–480.

Phillips, J., 'Parliament and Southern India, 1781–83: The Secret Committee of Enquiry and the Prosecution of Sir Thomas Rumbold', *Parliamentary History*, 1988, 7(1): 81–97.

Preston, A., 'Sir Charles MacGregor and the Defence of India, 1857–1887', *Historical Journal*, 1969, 12(1): 58–77.

Schendel, W. van, '"The Invention of the 'Jummas'": State Formation and Ethnicity in Southeastern Bangladesh', *Modern Asian Studies*, 1992, 26(1): 95–128.

Scott, J. C., 'Prestige as the Public Discourse of Domination', *Cultural Critique*, 1989, 12: 145–166.

Stein, B., 'State Formation Reconsidered: Part One', *Modern Asian Studies*, 1985, 19(3): 387–413.

Stokes, E., 'The First Century of British Colonial Rule in India: Social Revolution or Social Stagnation?' *Past & Present*, 1973, 58: 136–160.

Washbrook, D. A., 'India 1818–1860: The Two Faces of Colonialism', in *Oxford History of the British Empire*, Vol. 3, A. N. Porter (ed.), Oxford: Oxford University Press, 1999, pp. 395–422.

———, 'Law, State and Agrarian Society in Colonial South India', *Modern Asian Studies*, 1981, 15(3): 649–721.

———, 'Progress and Problems: South Asian Economic and Social History c.1720–1860', *Modern Asian Studies*, 1988, 22(1): 57–96.

Wegener, B., 'Concepts and Measurement of Prestige', *Annual Review of Sociology*, 1992, 18: 253–280.

Wenger, R., 'George Bogle, Part 3: Into Bhutan and Tibet', *Journal of the Families in British India Society*, 2006, 16: 14–25.

Wilson, J. E., '"A Thousand Countries to go to": Peasants and Rulers in Late Eighteenth-Century Bengal', *Past & Present*, 2005, 189: 81–109.

Secondary literature: books

Alam, M. and Subrahmanyam, S. (eds.), *The Mughal State, 1526–1750*, 3rd ed., Delhi: Oxford University Press, 2003.

Alavi, S., *The Sepoys and the Company*, Delhi: Oxford University Press, 1995.

Bayly, C. A., *The Birth of the Modern World, 1780–1914*, Oxford: Oxford University Press, 2004.

———, *Empire and Information: Intelligence Gathering and Social Communication in India, 1780–1870*, Cambridge: Cambridge University Press, 1996.

———, *Imperial Meridian: Britain and the World, 1780–1830*, London: Routledge, 1989.

———, *Indian Society and the Making of the British Empire*, Cambridge: Cambridge University Press, 1988.

———, *Origins of Nationality in South Asia: Patriotism and Ethical Government in the Making of Modern India*, Delhi: Oxford University Press, 1998.

———, *Rulers, Townsmen, and Bazaars: North Indian Society in the Age of British Expansion 1770–1870*, Cambridge: Cambridge University Press, 1983.

Brewer, J., *The Sinews of Power: War, Money and the English State, 1688–1783*, Cambridge, MA: Harvard University Press, 1990.

Callahan, R., *The East India Company and Army Reform, 1783–98*, Cambridge, MA: Harvard University Press, 1972.

Choksey, R. D., *Mountstuart Elphinstone: The Indian Years, 1796–1827*, Bombay: Popular Prakashan, 1971.

Cohen, S. P., *The Indian Army*, Berkeley: University of California Press, 1971.

Cohn, B. S., *Colonialism and Its Forms of Knowledge: The British in India*, Princeton, NJ: Princeton University Press, 1996.

Colley, L., *Britons: Forging the Nation, 1707–1837*, New Haven, CT: Yale University Press, 1992.

Cooper, R. G. S., *The Anglo-Maratha Campaigns and the Contest for India: The Struggle for Control of the South Asian Military Economy*, Cambridge: Cambridge University Press, 2003.

Datta, R., *Society, Economy and the Market: Commercialization in Rural Bengal, c. 1760–1800*, New Delhi: Manohar, 2000.

Duffy, C., *Frederick the Great: A Military Life*, London: Routledge & Kegan Paul, 1985.

Fisher, M. H., *Indirect Rule in India; Residents and the Residency System, 1764–1854*, Delhi: Oxford University Press, 1991.

——— (ed.), *The Politics of the British Annexation of India, 1757–1857*, Delhi: Oxford University Press, 1993.

Frykenberg, R. E., *Guntur District, 1788–1848: A History of Local Influence and Central Authority in South India*, Oxford: Clarendon Press, 1965.

Furber, H., *John Company at Work: A Study of European Expansion in India in the Late Eighteenth Century*, Cambridge, MA: Harvard University Press, 1951.

Guha, R., *Elementary Aspects of Peasant Insurgency in Colonial India*, Durham, NC: Duke University Press, 1999.

Harrington, J. H. L., *Sir John Malcolm and the Creation of British India*, Basingstoke: Palgrave Macmillan, 2011.

Hobsbawm, E., *Bandits*, 2nd ed., London: Abacus, 2007.

Husain, A., *British India's Relations with the Kingdom of Nepal, 1857–1947: A Diplomatic History of Nepal*, London: Allen and Unwin, 1970.

Hussain, N., *The Jurisprudence of Emergency: Colonialism and the Rule of Law*, Ann Arbor: University of Michigan Press, 2003.

Ingram, E., *In Defence of British India: Great Britain in the Middle East, 1775–1842*, London: Frank Cass and Co., 1984.

Kolff, D. H. A., *Naukar, Rajput, and Sepoy: The Ethnohistory of the Military Labour Market of Hindustan, 1450–1850*, Cambridge: Cambridge University Press, 1990.

Kumar, K., *The Making of English National Identity*, Cambridge: Cambridge University Press, 2003.

Mandler, P., *The English National Character: The History of an Idea from Edmund Burke to Tony Blair*, New Haven: Yale University Press, 2006.

Marshall, P. J., *Bengal: The British Bridgehead: Eastern India 1740–1828*, Cambridge: Cambridge University Press, 1987

———, *East Indian Fortunes: The British in Bengal in the Eighteenth Century*, Oxford: Clarendon Press, 1976.

——— (ed.), *The Eighteenth Century in Indian History: Evolution or Revolution?*, New Delhi: Oxford University Press, 2005.

———, *The Impeachment of Warren Hastings*, Oxford: Oxford University Press, 1965.

———, *The Making and Unmaking of Empires: Britain, India and America, c.1750–1783*, Oxford: Oxford University Press, 2005.

——— and Williams, G., *The Great Map of Mankind: Perceptions of New Worlds in the Age of Enlightenment*, Cambridge, MA: Harvard University Press, 1982.

McLane, J. R., *Land and Local Kingship in Eighteenth-Century Bengal*, Cambridge: Cambridge University Press, 1993.

Metcalf, T., *Ideologies of the Raj*, Cambridge: Cambridge University Press, 1994.

Misra, B. B., *The Central Administration of the East India Company, 1773–1834*, Manchester: Manchester University Press, 1959.

Peers, D. M., *Between Mars and Mammon: Colonial Armies and the Garrison State in Early Nineteenth Century India, 1819–1835*, London: I. B. Tauris, 1995.

Philips, C. H., *The East India Company, 1784–1834*, Manchester: Manchester University Press, 1961.

Porter, R., *English Society in the Eighteenth Century*, London: Penguin, 1982.
Ray, S., *Transformations on the Bengal Frontier: Jalpaiguri, 1765–1948*, London: Routledge, 2002.
Rosselli, J., *Lord William Bentinck: The Making of a Liberal Imperialist*, Los Angeles: University of California Press, 1974.
Roy, K., *War, Culture and Society in Early Modern South Asia, 1740–1849*, Abingdon: Routledge, 2011.
Roy, R. C. K., *Land Rights of the Indigenous Peoples of the Chittagong Hill Tracts, Bangladesh*, Copenhagen: IWGIA, 2003.
Scott, J. C., *Domination and the Arts of Resistance: Hidden Transcripts*, New Haven, CT: Yale University Press, 1990.
———, *Weapons of the Weak: Everyday Forms of Peasant Resistance*, New Haven, CT: Yale University Press, 1985.
Serajuddin, M., *The Revenue Administration of the East India Company in Chittagong, 1761–1785*, Chittagong: University of Chittagong Press, 1971.
Singha, R., *A Despotism of Law: Crime and Justice in Early Colonial India*, Delhi: Oxford University Press, 1998.
Sinha, B. K., *The Pindaris, 1798–1818*, Ann Arbor: University of Michigan Press, 1971.
Sneyd Hutchinson, R. H., *An Account of the Chittagong Hill Tracts*, Calcutta: Bengal Secretariat, 1906.
Stern, P. J., *The Company-State: Corporate Sovereignty and the Early Modern Foundations of the British Empire in India*, Oxford: Oxford University Press, 2011.
Stokes, E., *The English Utilitarians and India*, Delhi: Oxford University Press, 1959.
Travers, R., *Ideology and Empire in Eighteenth Century India: the British in Bengal*, Cambridge: Cambridge University Press, 2007.
Wagner, K. A., *Thuggee: Banditry and the British in Early Nineteenth-Century India*, Basingstoke: Palgrave Macmillan, 2007.
Wilson, J. E., *The Domination of Strangers: Modern Governance in Eastern India*, Basingstoke: Palgrave Macmillan, 2008.
Yang, A. A., *The Limited Raj: Agrarian Relations in Colonial India, Saran District, 1793–1920*, Berkeley: University of California Press, 1989.
Yapp, M. E., *Strategies of British India: Britain, Iran and Afghanistan, 1798–1850*, Oxford: Oxford University Press, 1980.
Zastoupil, L., *John Stuart Mill and India*, Stanford, CA: Stanford University Press, 1994.

Unpublished theses

Bourne, J. M., 'The Civil and Military Patronage of the East India Company, 1784–1858', unpublished PhD thesis, University of Leicester, 1977.
Harrington, J. H. L., '"No Longer Merchants but Sovereigns of a Vast Empire": The Writings of Sir John Malcolm and British India, 1810 to 1833', unpublished PhD thesis, University of Edinburgh, 2009.

Index

For Product Safety Concerns and Information please contact our EU representative GPSR@taylorandfrancis.com
Taylor & Francis Verlag GmbH, Kaufingerstraße 24, 80331 München, Germany

www.ingramcontent.com/pod-product-compliance
Ingram Content Group UK Ltd.
Pitfield, Milton Keynes, MK11 3LW, UK
UKHW022110190926
475702UK00013B/1358

* 9 7 8 0 3 6 7 7 8 5 9 3 2 *